PENGUIN BOOKS

AMERICAN INDIANS AND THE LAW

N. Bruce Duthu is an internationally recognized scholar on Native American issues, including tribal sovereignty and federal recognition of Indian tribes. He is professor of Native American studies at Dartmouth College, and he is a United Houma Indian Nation tribal member.

Colin G. Calloway is a professor of history and of Native American studies at Dartmouth College. He is the series editor of The Penguin Library of American Indian History. He lives in Norwich, Vermont.

THE PENGUIN LIBRARY
OF AMERICAN INDIAN HISTORY

The Cherokee Nation and the Trail of Tears
Theda Perdue and Michael D. Green

The Shawnees and the War for America
Colin G. Calloway

Iroquois Diplomacy on the Early American Frontier
Timothy J. Shannon

Cahokia: Ancient America's Great City on the Mississippi
Timothy Pauketat

The Lakotas and the Black Hills
Jeff Ostler

Ojibwe Women and the Survival of Indian Community
Brenda J. Child

GENERAL EDITOR: COLIN G. CALLOWAY
Advisory Board: Brenda J. Child, Philip J. Deloria, Frederick E. Hoxie

AMERICAN INDIANS

AND

THE LAW

N. BRUCE DUTHU

THE PENGUIN LIBRARY
OF AMERICAN INDIAN HISTORY

PENGUIN BOOKS

PENGUIN BOOKS

Published by the Penguin Group
Penguin Group (USA) Inc., 375 Hudson Street, New York, New York 10014, U.S.A.
Penguin Group (Canada), 90 Eglinton Avenue East, Suite 700, Toronto,
Ontario, Canada M4P 2Y3 (a division of Pearson Penguin Canada Inc.)
Penguin Books Ltd, 80 Strand, London WC2R 0RL, England
Penguin Ireland, 25 St Stephen's Green, Dublin 2, Ireland (a division of Penguin Books Ltd)
Penguin Group (Australia), 250 Camberwell Road, Camberwell,
Victoria 3124, Australia (a division of Pearson Australia Group Pty Ltd)
Penguin Books India Pvt Ltd, 11 Community Centre, Panchsheel Park, New Delhi – 110 017, India
Penguin Group (NZ), 67 Apollo Drive, Rosedale, North Shore 0632,
New Zealand (a division of Pearson New Zealand Ltd)
Penguin Books (South Africa) (Pty) Ltd, 24 Sturdee Avenue,
Rosebank, Johannesburg 2196, South Africa

Penguin Books Ltd, Registered Offices:
80 Strand, London WC2R 0RL, England

First published in the United States of America by Viking Penguin,
a member of Penguin Group (USA) Inc. 2008
Published in Penguin Books 2009

1   3   5   7   9   10   8   6   4   2

THE LIBRARY OF CONGRESS HAS CATALOGED
THE HARDCOVER EDITION AS FOLLOWS:
Duthu, N. Bruce.
American Indians and the law / N. Bruce Duthu.
p. cm.
ISBN 978-0-670-01857-4 (hc.)
ISBN 978-0-14-311478-9 (pbk.)
1. Federally recognized Indian tribes.   2. Indians of North America—Law and legislation.
3. Indians of North America—Politics and government.   I. Title.
KF8210.R32D88 2008
342.7308'72—dc22   2007018930

Printed in the United States of America
Set in Granjon
Designed by Katy Riegel

For Hilde, Lisa, Joe and Alanna

CONTENTS

PREFACE
AND ACKNOWLEDGMENTS

AT THEIR CORE, most legal disputes involve conflicts over power, money or respect, or some combination of those elements. The legal battles involving American Indian tribes are particularly volatile since they often involve challenges relating to all three elements. This book uses the lens of federal law relating to Indian tribes to tell the story of this nation's historic struggles to respond to a fundamental question: What is the proper place of Indian tribes within America's constitutional framework? Most Americans who think of it regard Indian tribes as distinct racial groups who surface in the national consciousness around Thanksgiving or in connection with controversies over sporting team mascots or in debates surrounding casino gambling. Few Americans know that Indian tribes have a legal status unique among America's distinct racial or ethnic groups: They are also sovereign governments who engage in governmental relations with the Congress. The United States Constitution expressly provides that Congress has power to "regulate Commerce with foreign Nations, and among the several States, and with the Indian Tribes." Trying to make sense of this single constitutional provision is a central purpose of this book.

In order to do that, we'll have to canvas a fair bit of this nation's legal and political history as it relates to Indian tribes and try to uncover many of the underlying assumptions and values that informed the various policies, acts or decisions that make up the field known as federal Indian law. Perspective is critical in this field and it will be important to consider the range of expectations from all sides of the controversies that spilled into the courtrooms or the halls of Congress over time. On that note, it is critical to give voice to the expectations of Indian tribes and their members. The history books and the law often silenced the tribal voices, or treated them as marginal or inconsequential in relation to the interests of the dominant society. The tide shifted dramatically in favor of Indian tribes in the early 1970s with the adoption of Congress's policy of Indian Self-Determination where Congress declared "its commitment to the maintenance of the Federal Government's unique and continuing relationship with, and responsibility to, individual Indian tribes and to the Indian people as a whole through the establishment of a meaningful Indian self-determination policy."[1] Determining whether that relationship is "meaningful" requires a clear understanding of tribal perspectives and aspirations. Of course, with over 560 federally recognized Indian tribes in the United States today, one can expect a fair amount of diversity in tribal perspectives and aspirations. In general, however, Indian tribes have asked, and continue to ask, that their lifeways and traditions be respected, that their ancestral homelands be protected and that they be allowed to exercise those inherent powers of self-governance that have persisted since time immemorial.

A number of people and institutions provided invaluable assistance to me in writing this book. First and foremost, I thank my colleague at Dartmouth College, Colin Calloway, for asking me to contribute this book as part of the Viking/Penguin series. I am indebted to him for his support on this particular project and for his friendship and collegiality over these many years. My colleagues at Vermont Law School, particularly President and Dean Jeff Shields and Vice Dean for Academic Affairs Stephanie Willbanks, provided significant institutional support that helped make this book possible. Laura Gillen and Judy Hilts also provided important support in the production of the manuscript and Lynn Hodgens dedicated hours of her valuable student time to help me with research materials.

Most of this book was written at the University of Wollongong in New South Wales, Australia, where I was fortunate to have an appointment as Visiting Faculty Fellow. I am grateful for the support and encouragement provided by Dean Luke McNamara, Professors Damien Considine and Rick Mohr and the entire faculty and administrative staff at UOW. In addition to the UOW family, I had the support and encouragement of several Wollongong families who took me into their homes and into their lives. I'm particularly grateful to "Auntie" Barbara Nicholson, a respected scholar, activist and traditional elder of the Wadi Wadi Aboriginal people in New South Wales, for her inspiration, encouragement and vital support throughout my time in Australia.

Law professors Philip P. Frickey and John Greabe read the entire draft manuscript and offered valuable advice and encouragement for which I am most thankful. Carolyn Carlson and Ellen Garrison of the Penguin Group also provided helpful guidance and suggestions on the manuscript. I owe a particular debt of gratitude to all the scholars who contributed to the 2005 edition of *Cohen's Handbook of Federal Indian Law*. The *Cohen Handbook* is the leading treatise in the field and served as an invaluable resource to me in writing this book. Nell Jessup Newton served as editor-in-chief of the *Handbook* with Robert Anderson, Carole Goldberg, John LaVelle, Judith Royster, Joseph Singer and Rennard Strickland serving as executive editors.

Finally, I thank my entire family for their love, support and encouragement—Hilde, Joe and Alanna in Vermont, our daughter Lisa and her family in New Jersey and all our relatives in other parts of the country. They are the ones who give meaning to my life.

GENERAL OVERVIEW OF FEDERAL INDIAN POLICY: MAJOR POLICIES, STATUTES AND CASES

TREATY FEDERALISM (1780s–1870s)

Trade & Intercourse Act (1790)

(Requires congressional approval of transactions relating to Indian lands)

Johnson v. *McIntosh* (1823)

(Recognized "Indian title" as right of occupancy within ancestral homelands subject to extinguishment by sovereign)

Indian Removal Act (1830)

(Authorized president to exchange lands west of the Mississippi River for eastern tribal lands)

Cherokee Nation v. *Georgia* (1831)

(Tribes recognized as "domestic dependent nations")

Worcester v. *Georgia* (1832)

(States prohibited from acting unilaterally to disrupt federal-tribal political and legal arrangements)

ALLOTMENT ERA (1870s–1930s)

End of Treaty Making (1871)

Major Crimes Act (1885)

(Established federal jurisdiction for Indian Country crimes committed by Indians)

General Allotment (or Dawes) Act (1887)

(Authorized division of reservation lands into parcels allotted to individual tribal members with "surplus" lands opened for homesteading by non-Indians)

U.S. v. Kagama (1886)

(Upheld legality of Major Crimes Act under powers derived from Congress's protectorate relationship with tribes)

Talton v. Mayes (1896)

(Inherent tribal sovereign powers not constrained by provisions of Constitution though subject to Congress's general authority over tribes)

Lone Wolf v. Hitchcock (1903)

(Congress has power unilaterally to abrogate tribal treaty rights)

Winters v. U.S. (1908)

(Recognized implied reserved rights to enough water to fulfill purposes of reservation)

Indian Citizenship Act (1924)

(Conferred U.S. citizenship on noncitizen Indians)

INDIAN REORGANIZATION (1930s–1950s)

Indian Reorganization Act (1934)

(Ended allotment policies and authorized tribes to organize for political and economic purposes)

TERMINATION (1950s–1960s)

House Concurrent Resolution 108 (1953)

(Announced Congress's purpose to end tribal wardship status and sever federal obligations to tribes)

Public Law 280 (1953)

(Provided for state civil and criminal jurisdiction in Indian Country)

Urban Relocation Program

(Federal program to move Indian reservation residents to selected urban centers)

Termination Acts

(Federal legislation ending formal political relationship with select tribes)

Tee-Hit-Ton v. *U.S.* (1955)

(Extinguishment of "Indian title" does not trigger legal obligation to make compensation)

Williams v. *Lee* (1959)

(Absent federal authority, state courts have no jurisdiction to hear reservation-based civil suit)

SELF-DETERMINATION (1960s–present)

Indian Civil Rights Act (1968)

Indian Self-Determination and Education Assistance Act (1975)

Indian Child Welfare Act (1978)

American Indian Religious Freedom Act (1978)

Indian Gaming Regulatory Act (1988)

Native American Graves Protection and Repatriation Act (1990)

McClanahan v. *Arizona State Tax Commission* (1973)

(State may not impose income tax on Indian reservation resident)

Morton v. *Mancari* (1974)

(Federal "Indian preference" system within the Indian service creates political, not racial, classifications that are constitutional if rationally related to federal obligations toward recognized tribes and their members)

Oliphant v. *Suquamish Indian Tribe* (1978)

(Tribes lack inherent sovereign power to prosecute non-Indians)

U.S. v. *Wheeler* (1978)

(Tribal member may be subject to successive prosecution by federal and tribal governments since each entity exercises its own sovereign authority)

Santa Clara Pueblo v. *Martinez* (1978)

(Indian civil rights claims not involving challenges to one's detention may only be raised in tribal court)

U.S. v. *Sioux Nation* (1980)

(Taking of "recognized title" is compensable under Fifth Amendment)

Montana v. *U.S.* (1981)

(Except in limited circumstances, inherent tribal sovereignty will not support the exercise of civil jurisdiction over nonmembers on reservation fee lands)

Merrion v. *Jicarilla Apache Tribe* (1982)

(Upheld tribal power to tax non-Indian corporate entities operating on reservation trust lands)

National Farmers Union Ins. Co. v. *Crow Tribe* (1985)

(Parties objecting to tribe's jurisdiction in civil cases must first exhaust tribal court remedies before seeking federal court review of such questions)

California v. *Cabazon Band of Mission Indians* (1987)

(State not authorized to regulate tribal gambling activities that do not violate state policy)

Lyng v. *Northwest Indian Cemetery Protective Association* (1988)

(Tribes have no First Amendment religious freedom right to halt federal land management practices on public lands that contain sacred tribal spaces)

Mississippi Band of Choctaw Indians v. *Holyfield* (1989)

(Tribe has exclusive jurisdiction in adoption matters involving Indian children born to Indian parents who are domiciled on reservation)

Employment Division v. *Smith* (1990)

(State may deny unemployment benefits to tribal member fired for use of peyote)

Duro v. *Reina* (1990)

>(Tribes lack inherent sovereign power to prosecute non-member Indians)

Nevada v. *Hicks* (2001)

>(Tribal inherent sovereign authority does not extend to state official alleged to have committed unlawful acts on reservation trust lands)

Atkinson Trading Co. v. *Shirley* (2001)

>(Tribal taxing authority does not typically reach non-Indians operating on reservation fee lands)

U.S. v. *Lara* (2004)

>(Congress may relax federal restrictions on inherent tribal sovereign powers)

INTRODUCTION

IN JUNE 1855, a Yakama head chief named Kamiakin joined leaders from neighboring tribes in central Washington to attend a treaty council at the behest of Isaac Stevens, Washington's new territorial governor. The tribal leaders were well aware that Stevens's mission was to buy as much land as he could from the tribes to make way for the rush of white settlers and to clear a legal pathway for the railroads that would connect the western territories to the rest of a growing nation. They also understood that encroaching white settlements in other Indian communities contributed to the spread of disease among Indian people and led to recurring battles over territory and the forced removal of tribal populations by federal military forces. These western tribal leaders had long heard from other Indian tribes about how the "Great Father" in the East forced the southeastern tribes to give up their treaty-protected homelands for new lands west of the Mississippi River. They had every reason to be suspicious about the federal government's intentions regarding the northwestern tribes.[1]

In an effort to avoid a similar fate, Kamiakin and the leaders of the Walla Walla and Nez Perce tribes organized a major tribal council in 1854 that convened in the Grand Ronde valley in eastern Oregon. Over the course of five days, the leaders hammered out a strategy for defending their homelands. By the following summer, however, the momentum for an allied resistance had dissipated, in large part due to threats of armed conflict communicated by Stevens's advance agents. With great reluctance and bitterness, Kamiakin joined his fellow tribal leaders to negotiate terms for land cessions. The treaty text, prepared by United States treaty commissioners, displayed remarkable ignorance or disregard of tribal political structures in that it lumped fourteen distinct tribes into "one nation" under the name "Yakama" and declared Kamiakin its head chief.[2] Notwithstanding these flaws, on June 9, 1855, Kamiakin rose last among his fellow tribal leaders, made his mark on the treaty and returned to his seat with his lips "covered with blood, having bitten them with suppressed rage."[3]

This episode contains elements of the conventional tale most Americans know about the early history of Indian-white relations in America. In that story, Indian tribes appear as the noble defenders of vast but underused aboriginal homelands, adhering to a way of life that Euro-Americans considered intriguing and savage but ultimately incompatible with the superior, civilized Christian societies engulfing them. There is no Indian future in the winner's version of American history. From the earliest days of the nation, Americans showed a fascination with portraying Indian people as members of a dying race. James Fenimore Cooper's *The Last of the Mohicans,* published in 1826 and regarded as an American literary classic, celebrated the enterprising spirit and individualism of colonial settlers and, in the process, etched the view of Indians as a dying race into the national consciousness. That perspective quickly gained momentum among some of the most influential people in American society. In 1828, Justice Joseph Story of the United States Supreme Court echoed those sentiments in a talk before the Essex Historical Society. "What can be more melancholy than their history?" wrote Justice Story. "By a law of their nature, they seem destined to a slow, but sure extinction. Everywhere, at the approach of the white man, they fade away. We hear the rustling of their footsteps, like that of the withered leaves of autumn, and they are gone forever. They pass mournfully by us, and they return no more."⁴ Justice Story's contemporary, the celebrated Chief Justice John Marshall, received a copy of Justice Story's address and sent this reply: "I often think with indignation on our disreputable conduct (as I think it) in the affair of the Creeks of Georgia; and I look with some alarm on the course now pursuing in the North west. Your observations on this subject are eloquent, and are in perfect accordance with my feelings."⁵

This fascination with proclaiming the Indians' imminent demise reached a bizarre climax in 1913 when President William Howard Taft presided over a ground-breaking ceremony on Staten Island, New York, where a monument to the "departed race" would be constructed on land Congress had set aside for that very purpose. The monument would depict a gigantic figure of a young Indian with hand raised in peace. Had the structure been built as planned, it would have eclipsed the Statue of Liberty in height by fifteen feet. President Taft told the audience, which included a number of "aging chiefs," that the statue "tells the story of the march of empire and the progress of Christian civilization to the uttermost limits."⁶ The tradition of "honoring" dead Indians continues even today in the form of sporting team symbols and mascots—the Braves, Fighting Sioux, Fighting Illini, Redskins and Chiefs—all justified as a means of honoring a once proud people now believed to have vanished from the modern landscape.

From a different perspective, however, the Yakama treaty encounter tells a very different story. This perspective focuses on the treaty itself as the critical point of contact between two different societies. Through the formal exchange of promises, the treaty signers effectively redistributed political power over certain territories and shifted control over particular natural resources, but otherwise agreed that their respective communities would coexist as distinct cultures with different views and ways of living. In meeting with the United States commissioners in formal treaty negotiations,

Kamiakin and his fellow tribal leaders were continuing a tradition of diplomatic governmental relations between Indian tribes and other governments dating back to colonial times. This recognition of the tribes' legal status as the first sovereigns, possessing inherent powers of self-government, survives today as the cardinal principle of federal Indian law and serves to distinguish Indian tribes from all other distinct cultural groups in the United States. In contrast to the winner's version of American history, these legal narratives establish tribes as enduring political bodies with a past, present and future. They recognize and validate the tribes' deep and abiding relationship with their ancestral lands, and the obligations of stewardship that flow from that relationship.

Bringing these little-known encounters to the surface or seeing them from another perspective necessarily complicates the conventional national story. From the vantage point of tribes, the national story is a story of contradictions, where the ugly side of the nation's colonial past surfaces from the shadows and stands side by side with the preferred American story of freedom, liberty and the pursuit of happiness for all. The creation stories of other nations bear qualities similar to our national mythology, with stories that mix elements of truth with a dose of denial, fantasy and reinvention in service of a national story that purports to unite and bind a people to a common past and a shared future. We perpetuate such mythologies at our peril, however, because inevitably the national structure built on those false foundations gives way, causing nations to fracture, dissolve or suffer periodic spasms of violence or civil war. An alternative to perpetuating the national mythologies is to attempt to reconstruct the actual and more complete national stories, however complicated or disturbing they may be. As historian Howard Zinn notes, "If history is to be creative, to anticipate a possible future without denying the past, it should, I believe, emphasize new possibilities by disclosing those hidden episodes of the past when, even if in brief flashes, people showed their ability to resist, to join together, occasionally to win. I am supposing, or perhaps only hoping, that our future may be found in the past's fugitive moments of compassion rather than in its solid centuries of warfare."[7]

In providing an overview of the major legal principles governing relations among Indian tribes, the United States government and the states, this book will show how federal Indian law reflects the paradoxes and tensions of our past but also contains the critical elements that could be useful in developing a more respectful and mutually beneficial framework for political relations. As we'll see, the course of federal Indian law and policy has flowed like many of our ancient rivers, steady and predictable in some seasons, violent and destructive in others. This fact has made it difficult over the years for tribal leaders to govern effectively in their local communities. It is within these ancestral homelands that the heart of tribal sovereignty resides, and where it is given expression on the ground by tribal people in their exercise of self-government. Our story will move to and from Indian Country in trying to capture how legal developments in the nation's capital affected life in the tribal communities. In recounting those developments, I will endeavor to include much of the language used by federal lawmakers from all three branches to give readers a better sense of the underlying values and assumptions that informed and influenced the resulting legal principles.

In Part One, we focus attention on the legal status of Indian tribes as governments, the first sovereigns to exercise political authority in the lands that now make up the United States. As noted above, the United States Constitution specifically recognizes Indian tribes as among the sovereign bodies with which Congress may exercise its powers under the "Commerce Clause."[8] In the early 1830s, the United States Supreme Court, notwithstanding the private musings of the justices noted above, affirmed the legal status of Indian tribes as political bodies with inherent governmental powers that are subordinate only to the national power.[9] The Supreme Court under Chief Justice John Marshall characterized the legal status of Indian tribes as "domestic dependent nations,"[10] and later drew upon well-established norms of international law to acknowledge that a "weaker power" does not forsake its legal claims to self-government by aligning itself with and seeking the protection of a stronger government.[11] Indeed, the very structure of the political relationship between Indian tribes and the federal government, according to the Court, gave rise to a trust obligation on the part of the federal government to protect the tribes' political integrity and territorial possessions.[12] Even today, the Court acknowledges the longstanding legal status of tribes as "self-governing sovereign political communities" that continue to exercise "inherent powers of a limited sovereignty which has never been extinguished."[13] As we will see, however, federal Indian law has not been constant in its treatment of or respect for tribal sovereignty. Like the waters of an ancient river, the law has shaped and altered the nature of inherent tribal sovereignty in response to changing conditions and needs of the dominant society.

In Part Two, we turn our attention to the tribes' ancestral homelands or, at least, the residual portions of those homelands that exist in the form of Indian reservations and other Indian lands. These lands are the legal spaces within which tribal sovereignty operates on the ground to address the needs of the tribal community. In Chapter Four, we will examine how the Supreme Court developed the legal framework and justification for making Indian tribes guests in their own homelands. The subsequent treaties with tribes purported to secure the tribes' homelands "for as long as water flows or grass grows," but as a practical and legal matter, tribes continued to lose significant quantities of their ancestral homelands over the years as a result of government policies that reclaimed—or simply took—tribal lands to satisfy the insatiable demands of white settlers eager to move westward in pursuit of their own American dream. The federal government's allotment policies in the late nineteenth century decimated Indian land holdings as reservation lands were carved up and allotted to individual Indian families, with the remainder or "surplus lands" opened up to white homesteaders, who typically received titles in fee simple. "Fee simple" ownership is the highest and most complete form of property right recognized by law. On the lands that remain part of the tribes' territorial base, tribal governments continue to work actively to fulfill their obligations of stewardship over the lands and the natural resources they contain. In addition, tribal ancestral lands serve as the principal resource to help support or revitalize local tribal economies, the subject of Chapter Six.

Part Three gives a brief overview of two very significant areas of law that pose challenges to efforts to accommodate tribes as the nation's first sovereigns. Our legal tradition of respect for individual civil rights complicates the task of reconciling the rights of tribes, which are often conceived as a form of group rights. At the heart of these tensions lies a clash of fundamental values between traditional tribal interests and those of the dominant society. Beyond these ideological and philosophical tensions, we continue to see broader institutional pressure points that make it difficult to "fit" Indian tribes within the nation's constitutional democracy. The Constitution provides one express means by which the federal government is empowered to conduct relations with foreign nations and Indian tribes—through the use of formally approved treaties. In 1871, however, Congress unilaterally ended the practice of treaty-making with Indian tribes. This gave rise to one of the many paradoxes that still plague federal Indian law, in that the retained sovereignty of Indian tribes is recognized as predating the formation of the United States but is considered to be subsumed within and subordinate to the national power.

Finally, in Part Four, we retrace foundational principles of intergovernmental relations from both Indian philosophy and practice and early federal Indian law to identify those strands of diplomatic practice that might help to create a more secure place for Indian tribes within the nation's constitutional framework. This examination will bring us back full circle to Kamiakin and his fellow tribal leaders in urging a return to the practice of treaty-making or, more specifically, negotiated conventions on tribal sovereignty.

In using the lens of federal Indian law to explore these hidden episodes in the history of Indian-white relations, it becomes clear that Indian people did not remain passive as their worlds were turned upside down around them. At every point where their rights to maintain their political systems or their ancestral homelands were threatened, Indian people responded, at times through armed resistance, but most often by relying on the rule of law. Their principal legal struggle was to combat the federal government's resort to unilateralism as the national policy for Indian affairs, a doctrine totally at odds with the language and history of the Constitution. The tribes' objective, then and now, is to return to a more respectful course of bilateralism, in which relations between the differing cultures are negotiated through arm's length and principled agreements.

In the final analysis, the stories I am about to share will show that despite a history of legal relations that predates the founding of this nation, the status of Indian tribes within the framework of our democratic system is still not fully resolved or clarified. For starters, one should look at the structural location of the Bureau of Indian Affairs (BIA)—the largest (but not the only) federal bureaucracy dedicated to managing federal relations with tribes and individual Indian citizens.[14] The BIA is lodged within the Department of the Interior, where it joins the U.S. Fish & Wildlife Service, the Bureau of Land Management, the Bureau of Reclamation, National Park Service, and the Office of Surface Mining and the Minerals Management Service—all branches dedicated to the management of the nation's natural resources. During the Clinton administration, a tribal leader suggested moving Indian affairs from the Interior to the State Department: "The Department of the Interior deals with wildlife, and State deals with governments."[15] Before being moved to the Interior Department in 1849, Indian Affairs was managed through the Department of War.[16] Neither the Clinton nor the Bush administrations gave serious thought to shifting Indian affairs to a more prominent position in the executive branch hierarchy, although at least one presidential candidate for the 2008 election—New Mexico governor Bill Richardson—has pledged to elevate Indian affairs to its own cabinet-level position.[17]

Beyond this structural indignity, there are larger questions of institutional "fit" when it comes to Indian tribes as governments. The notion of sovereignty that pervades this area refers to an inherently relational system and process by which governmental bodies engage with each other and their constituent members. What exactly is the nature and scope of the tribes' sovereign authority in relation to that of the federal and state governments? How do we mediate claims of citizens who belong to some or all of these various governmental bodies? To the extent that there are differences among the respective sovereign powers—and there are plenty—what underlies those differences? Some scholars argue that the unsettled or ambiguous state of affairs relating to tribal legal status and powers stems from entrenched bias and even racist tendencies contained in the law that simply cannot or will not support tribal authority, especially over non-Indians.[18] Tribal sovereignty, by this account, represents the devolution of political power "to a racial or ethnic group; it is multiculturalism with political power."[19] A variation on these observations is the view that law relating to indigenous peoples is too deeply stained with the legacy of colonialism and that even modern laws designed to advance the legal position of indigenous peoples retain a "deep colonizing" effect that prevents any true expression of indigenous sovereign authority.[20] Others maintain that nation-states like the United States resist fully embracing tribal claims to sovereignty out of self-interest, to preserve their political dominance and their control of the mythology about nation building.[21] Fully addressing the claims of tribes, by this account, would entail making "the state different, and not merely to grant [tribes] some autonomy within limited bounds, restricted by the existence of a state which, in being unchanged for the majority, denies to a people a large part of a country once owned and now lost."[22] Still others find it problematic for tribes to even embrace "sovereignty" as their model for tribal self-governance, finding the concept incompatible with traditional Indian conceptions of legitimate governance and justice.[23] Those conceptions proceed from an "imperative of respectful, balanced coexistence among all human, animal, and spirit beings, together with the earth. Justice is seen as a perpetual process of maintaining that crucial balance and demonstrating true respect for the power and dignity of each part of the circle of interdependency."[24]

In telling the story of Indian-white relations through the lens of law and policy, we will, of necessity, venture deeply into the waters of history—back to the formative years of this nation (and sometimes earlier)—to understand the broader context for addressing contemporary disputes arising in Indian Country. The various currents and tensions noted above will be revealed along the way and should prove instructive. As noted by the authors of the leading legal treatise in the field, *Cohen's Handbook of Federal Indian Law* (2005), "Only against such a background is it possible to distinguish between those cases that mark the norms and patterns of our national policy and those that illustrate the deviations and pathologies resulting from misunderstandings and corruption."[25]

This journey into the experiences of Indian people and tribes as reflected in law will show the tenacity of Indian people in claiming for themselves and their communities the fundamental right to remain Indian on their own terms, to maintain and strengthen their ties to ancestral homelands and to preserve a significant measure of political control over their territories. Federal law has often aided these efforts, but it has also thwarted them, a fact plainly acknowledged by the federal BIA.[26] Ultimately, as I've noted, our journey will bring us back full circle to Kamiakin and to the treaty-making process. It is there that we may yet find the seeds for more fruitful, respectful relations on the ground in American Indian homelands.

AMERICAN INDIANS
AND THE LAW

PART ONE

INDIAN TRIBES
AS GOVERNMENTS

1

THE DIGNITY OF TRIBAL GOVERNMENTS

Tribal sovereignty today finds at least as much meaningful definition in the growth, development and day-to-day functioning of effective tribal governments as it finds in the volumes of the law library. Far from being relics of a bygone era, Indian tribal powers bear the fine burnish of everyday use.
—Bruce S. Jenkins, U.S. senior district judge,
MacArthur v. San Juan County
Greenberg, 391 F. Supp. 2d 895, 940 (D. Utah 2005)

IN THE EARLY 1990s, the Pueblo of Isleta in New Mexico encountered stiff resistance from the City of Albuquerque when the Pueblo chose to take into account tribal ceremonial practices, among many other interests, in establishing water quality standards for the Rio Grande, which passes through the Pueblo's lands. Their regulations, made enforceable outside the reservation through force of federal law (the Clean Water Act), required substantial changes by the City of Albuquerque in managing its municipal discharges into that river.[1] Among the arguments made by the city, and rejected by the federal courts, was that enforcing the Pueblo's water quality standards through federal law would violate the Constitution's prohibition against an established religion because of the link to Pueblo ceremonial and religious life. This episode illustrates that tribal governments often face unique challenges in ensuring that tribal values are integrated into their governance rules and practices, especially when the practical effects of government operations may affect people who are not members of the tribe or reach activities outside tribal lands.

The Isleta are among the over 560 federally recognized Indian tribes in the United States today exercising governmental authority over tribal territories that vary tremendously in terms of geographical size, demographic makeup, nature and quality of natural resources and proximity to major population centers—all factors that contribute to the quality of life in each tribal community.[2] The source of that governmental authority most often stems from the tribe's exercise of inherent sovereign powers, but it may also derive from powers acknowledged or delegated by the federal government through treaties or statutes, respectively.[3] In some tribal homelands, tribal members constitute the vast majority of permanent residents (e.g., the Navajo Nation, Jicarilla Apache Nation); in others, they are a distinct minority of the population (e.g., Confederated Salish and Kootenai tribes). According to the 2000 census, there are nearly 2.5 million people identified as American Indian or Alaska Native, with about one-third of that population living in "American Indian areas."[4] These areas include about 310 reservations and the Indian lands in Oklahoma.[5]

In their day-to-day operations, tribal governments grapple with issues common to all local political bodies, as noted by U.S. senior district judge Bruce S. Jenkins:

> Today . . . modern tribal governments routinely exercise civil governmental authority over a range of day-to-day activities, much like comparable state and local government entities. Tribal codes and ordinances govern subject matter ranging from agriculture to zoning, and tribal departments and agencies administer and deliver an expanding array of community services—from police, fire, and other emergency services to education, health, housing, justice, employment assistance, environmental protection, cultural preservation, land use planning, natural resource conservation and management, road maintenance, water

and public utilities. Indian tribes fit squarely within the ranks of modern American civic bodies, sharing the common duty and responsibility to provide essential services to the people of the communities they serve.[6]

As modern tribal governments embrace an increasingly broad and complex array of social and economic activities, they encounter growing resistance from various quarters—state or local governments, private citizens or corporations, the federal government and, on occasion, even their own tribal members. The legal question underlying this resistance is often a challenge to the tribe's jurisdiction—or in other words, its basic legal authority to pronounce and enforce the law. There is rich irony in the fact that "jurisdiction" derives from the Latin "*juris dictio*" (the act of saying or pronouncing law), when one considers that so much of federal Indian policy was characterized by government efforts to stamp out the tribes' distinctive cultural and political voices. Many of these jurisdictional disputes begin in the local tribal courts, of which there are more than 275 in operation today. At other times, the parties seek access to either state or federal courts to resolve a reservation-based dispute. Even there, the parties may have to grapple with jurisdictional questions. As we'll see shortly, the contours of tribal sovereignty and jurisdiction are often determined as the by-product of cases in which another sovereign—usually a state—is asserting authority in Indian Country. Beyond the question of jurisdiction, the courts must also determine which substantive laws govern the dispute (tribal, state or federal law) and must consider the range of appropriate remedies or enforcement mechanisms that will bring the matter to a close. The resolution of these questions involves consideration of a number of interrelated legal, political, social and economic considerations, all with the potential to affect—positively or negatively—the "dignity of the tribal government."[7]

Few areas of federal Indian law rival the controversy surrounding the nature and scope of tribal sovereignty and jurisdiction. These disputes are controversial because they are, fundamentally, contests about political power and, in particular, about whether Indian tribes are proper holders of that power in a given circumstance. Given our national ambivalence about the place of Indian tribes in American history, coupled with the gravitational pull still exerted by the "dying race" thesis, it is perhaps unsurprising that the dramatic rise in the volume and intensity of these jurisdictional challenges has coincided with the rise of tribalism in the modern era of self-determination.

A small sampling of the contemporary jurisdictional challenges presented to tribal courts in recent years illustrates this point.

LUMMI NATION, WASHINGTON

The survivors of a reservation-resident tribal member who allegedly died of side effects caused by prescription drug medication sued the off-reservation drug manufacturer in tribal court for wrongful death damages. The uncontested evidence showed that the drug maker's sales representatives regularly visited the tribe's health clinic in person, and that these contacts led to sales of prescription drugs to the clinic, which were then used to fill the deceased tribal member's prescription.[8]

NORTHERN CHEYENNE TRIBE, MONTANA

A reservation-resident tribal member (a minor) was injured when the vehicle he was driving struck a horse that had wandered onto the roadway. The minor's representatives brought a lawsuit in tribal court for money damages alleging negligence against the horse's owner. The horse was owned by another permanent reservation resident who happened to be an enrolled member of the Oglala Sioux tribe living on lands he owned in fee simple. The accident happened on a Bureau of Indian Affairs road running through the reservation over which the tribe exercised significant management responsibilities.[9]

Navajo Nation, Arizona

A reservation-resident tribal member, working as an on-duty law enforcement officer for the Navajo Nation, was killed when the Ford Expedition patrol vehicle she was driving rolled over on a reservation road maintained by the tribe. In a wrongful death product liability action brought in tribal court, the parties disputed the cause of the accident with the deceased tribal member's survivors alleging product defect and the vehicle manufacturer, Ford, claiming driver error. The patrol vehicle was part of a fleet of vehicles acquired by the tribe through a lease-purchase arrangement with a wholly owned Ford subsidiary. The agreement contained a provision stating, "All actions which arise out of this Lease or out of the transaction it represents shall be brought in the courts of the Navajo Nation." Furthermore, evidence showed that Ford conducted advertising targeting reservation residents.[10]

Navajo Nation, Arizona

The Navajo Nation prosecuted an enrolled member of the Oglala Sioux tribe for criminal assault on another tribal member alleged to have been committed on reservation lands. The defendant, Indian activist Russell Means, was formerly married to a Navajo woman and lived on the Navajo reservation for a decade before returning to the Sioux reservation. The events in question allegedly occurred while Means was on a return visit to the Navajo reservation.[11]

BEFORE COURTS REACH the merits of controversies like these, they must first determine that they possess proper jurisdiction over the parties and the subject matter of the case. Unfortunately, in federal Indian law, that analysis alone can occupy the courts' attention for years. Since the scope of tribal powers has not remained static over the years, contemporary actors must play the role of legal archaeologists, slowly peeling back the layers of legal history to find the answers. The work of the United States Congress and the United States Supreme Court over the years has added immeasurably to the confusion and incoherence that plague this area of law. We will return to the four factual scenarios a bit later to see how each court or courts addressed the jurisdictional questions before them. But first, we will journey across the legal landscape that contains the story of tribal sovereign power to better appreciate the challenges facing today's tribal governments.

AT AN EARLIER point in our national history, the nature and scope of tribal authority within tribal lands was fairly clearly marked out, at least as a matter of law. Chief Justice John Marshall, architect of the "domestic dependent nations" concept used to describe the legal status of Indian tribes, wrote in the landmark case of *Worcester* v. *Georgia* (1832) that federal laws "manifestly consider the several Indian nations as distinct political communities, having territorial boundaries, *within which their authority is exclusive,* and having a right to all the lands within those boundaries, which is not only acknowledged, but guarantied by the United States" (emphasis added).[12] As a result, Georgia's unilateral effort to extend its laws within Cherokee lands was struck down as unconstitutional. In so holding, the Court affirmed both the territorial integrity of tribal homelands and the primacy of tribal authority within those lands.

However well founded as a matter of law, the *Worcester* decision respecting tribal rights was starkly at odds with the political climate then prevailing in the other branches of the federal government. Two years before the Court's ruling, Congress had passed the Removal Bill, legislation that would eventually lead to the forced relocation of thousands of Indian families from the Southeast to what is now Oklahoma. Buttressed by the twin pillars of greed and racism,[13] the removal policy would clear the way for white southerners to claim the tribes' fertile agricultural lands and gold resources. As historians Theda Perdue and Michael Green note, "These two phenomena—a sharply intensified demand for Indian land fed by burgeoning populations and the development of the idea that the Indians were racially rather than culturally inferior and therefore unchangeable—came together in the 1820's to create an atmosphere of extreme tension."[14]

The atmosphere was even more toxic over in the executive branch. President Andrew Jackson, a firm believer in the "dying race" thesis,[15] staunchly maintained that the tribes could not expect to sustain their claims to lands and their traditional ways in the midst of ever-encroaching white settlement. Lewis Cass, Jackson's secretary of war (the federal department that then managed Indian affairs), voiced the commonly held view that Indians were inherently inferior to whites. Despite the persistence of agricultural traditions among the southeastern "civilized" tribes, organized systems of governance and, in the case of the Cherokee, a written syllabary of their indigenous language, Cass could still proclaim the following: "A principle of progressive improvement seems almost inherent in human nature. . . . We are all striving in the career of life to acquire riches in honor, or power, or some other object, whose possession is to realize the day dreams of our imaginations; and the aggregate of these efforts constitutes the advance of society. But there is little of this in the constitution of our savages."[16]

The Indians' choices were either to assimilate and be governed under state law or to move; white Georgians would accept nothing else. Historian and Jackson biographer H. W. Brands notes, "Given the racist realities of the time, Jackson was almost certainly correct in contending that for the Cherokees to remain in Georgia risked their extinction. To preserve the Cherokees as a tribe—to enforce [Chief Justice] Marshall's decision—would have required raising and sending federal troops to Georgia, stationing them there indefinitely, and ordering them to shoot white Georgians who threatened the Indians. Jackson realized that American democracy simply wouldn't sustain such a policy. It was one thing to threaten to use force to preserve the Union; in such an endeavor he could expect broad support from the people who would actually do the fighting. It was another thing to ask white citizens to risk death protecting Indians. They wouldn't do it."[17]

Chief Justice Marshall likely understood these political realities as well as President Jackson but remained firm in his support for the tribal claims. In private writings, he condemned the federal removal legislation as equally offensive as the state's action. To Marshall, the legislation represented "parts of the same system . . . [of] coercive measures begun by the states," and he expressed the "greatest astonishment, that, after hearing the arguments in both houses, Congress could pass this bill."[18] He also observed that the removal of the Indians from their ancestral homelands was a subject that "affects deeply the honor, the faith and the character of our country."[19] Notwithstanding his earlier endorsement of the "dying race" thesis, Marshall's statements regarding the removal legislation suggested that he (and perhaps others on the Court) considered the federal power in Indian affairs to be limited or constrained by the structural guarantees enshrined in both the Constitution and the treaties. In other words, to Marshall, the promise of a secure tribal homeland was the necessary result of negotiated political arrangements reached between sovereign bodies that demanded the respect and honor of the new nation, its citizens and its constituent states. A significant percentage of the general American population agreed with Marshall's view, as over 1 million people out of America's general population of about 12 million publicly voiced their opposition to Congress's Removal Bill in letters and petitions to that body.[20]

Not surprisingly, *Worcester*'s bright-line rule supporting a territorially based vision of tribal power eventually gave way to greater accommodations of state interests and, over time, to the interests of non-Indians within Indian territories. In *Williams* v. *Lee* (1959), for example, the Court shut the doors of the state courthouse to a reservation-based contract dispute between a non-Indian creditor and Indian debtor, but in the process, it left the windows wide open for future intrusions of state power into Indian Country. The Court maintained that "essentially, absent governing Acts of Congress, the question has always been whether the state action infringed on the right of reservation Indians to make their own laws and be ruled by them."[21] This so-called "infringement test" gives states a form of jurisdictional leverage in Indian Country whenever non-Indians are involved and allows the state to "protect its interest up to the point where tribal self-government would be affected."[22] *Worcester* had erected a virtually impenetrable barrier to state authority in Indian Country because the Court viewed the tribe's sovereign authority as grounded within and extending throughout the tribe's territory. In *Williams,* however, the Court provided states with an entrance ramp into Indian Country that was tempered only by a reviewing court's application of the "infringement" test.

To be sure, much had changed on the ground in Indian Country between 1832 and 1959. Dramatic shifts in federal Indian policy like the Allotment Act of 1887 led to the arrival of large numbers of permanent non-Indian residents in Indian Country, thus making it inevitable that tribal sovereignty would be re-examined by the courts in light of the new conditions. The Supreme Court had already allowed intrusions of state law within Indian Country in cases involving only non-Indians;[23] the novelty in *Williams* was determining whether state law could reach Indians within Indian Country. The *Williams* dispute arose within the Navajo Nation, a reservation not directly touched by the disastrous allotment policies. Nonetheless, the Court echoed then-prevailing political sentiments that favored the termination of tribal sovereignty and noted, "Congress has followed a policy calculated eventually to make all Indians full-fledged participants in American society. This policy contemplates criminal and civil jurisdiction over Indians by any State ready to assume the burdens that go with it as soon as the educational and economic status of the Indians permits the change without disadvantage to them."[24]

Tribal sovereignty was not an insignificant consideration in *Williams,* however, as the Court found that allowing state courts to hear the case would "undermine the authority of the tribal courts over Reservation affairs and hence would infringe on the right of

Indians to govern themselves."[25] In directing Hugh Lee to tribal court to collect his debt from Paul and Lorena Williams, the Court deemed it inconsequential that Lee was a non-Indian: "He was on the Reservation and the transaction with an Indian took place there. The cases in this Court have consistently guarded the authority of Indian governments over their reservations."[26] Despite this affirmation of a territorial component to tribal authority, the Court did not explain precisely how or why tribal sovereignty was undermined in this case or provide interpretive rules for applying the infringement test in future cases, two factors that contributed to the ambiguity and challenge in refining the jurisdictional picture in Indian Country.

The modern Court holds that in cases not involving non-Indian citizens, state law generally will not apply within Indian Country unless federal legislation clearly permits it. Like the infringement test, this so-called federal "preemption test" was designed to help resolve disputes over "the boundaries between state regulatory authority and tribal self-government."[27] The preemption analysis relies primarily on the language of treaties and federal statutes and less on "platonic notions of Indian sovereignty"[28] to determine if state law can apply in Indian Country. The Court still considers tribal sovereignty to be an important consideration but does not view the doctrine as the deciding element in resolving jurisdictional conflicts. As noted by Justice Thurgood Marshall in *McClanahan* v. *Arizona State Tax Commission* (1973),[29] tribal sovereignty is significant "not because it provides a definitive resolution of the issues ... but because it provides a backdrop against which the applicable treaties and federal statutes must be read. It must always be remembered that the various Indian tribes were once independent and sovereign nations, and that their claim to sovereignty long predates that of our own Government."[30]

The *McClanahan* Court's reference to "platonic notions of Indian sovereignty" arose in a unanimous decision rejecting Arizona's efforts to impose the state's personal income tax on Rosalind McClanahan, a member and resident of the Navajo Nation whose entire income came from reservation sources. The Court's phrasing suggests some dilution in the force of tribal sovereignty, and perhaps more significantly, a retrenchment by the judicial branch of its commitment to honor the nation's promises to tribes. This reading may be unwarranted, especially if the *McClanahan* decision is considered in proper historical perspective. The Court heard arguments in this case in December 1972, just over two years after President Richard Nixon's landmark address to Congress that condemned the previous federal policy of "termination" and ushered in a new federal policy of self-determination for Indian tribes. The termination policies of the 1950s and 1960s gave rise to unilateral federal acts that severed the government's legal and political relationship with and responsibilities toward a large number of Indian tribes (notably tribes like the Menominee, the Klamath and a host of California tribes), leaving those communities largely subject to state authority. In his July 1970 message to Congress, President Nixon called on the federal government to reject "the extremes of termination and paternalism because it resulted in 'the erosion of Indian initiatives and morale.'"[31] In its *McClanahan* opinion, the Court echoed this policy shift in requiring close examination of applicable treaties and federal statutes in light of the nation's longstanding commitment to and recognition of tribal governmental authority as "once independent and sovereign nations."

The dramatic shift in federal Indian policy was also influenced by the rise of political activism in the 1960s among Indian groups around the country, including the work of the American Indian Movement (AIM), and tribal demands for greater respect and accountability in federal-tribal relations. In late fall 1972, just before the presidential election, Indian activists organized caravans of supporters who drove across the country bound for Washington, D.C., to call attention to the "Trail of Broken Treaties." Hank Adams, an Assiniboine and Sioux activist, provided political and intellectual context for the marchers by developing a "Twenty Points" plan for the reform of federal Indian policy. At its core, the plan called for greater federal respect of tribal sovereignty, including the restoration of treaty-making as the principal vehicle to conduct in-tergovernmental relations.[32] The march on Washington, D.C., cul-minated with activists taking over and occupying the Bureau of Indian Affairs in November 1972, a move that added an element of urgency to these events and served to capture, at least momen-tarily, national attention.[33] Federal policymakers and tribal leaders worked actively at this time to develop both the language and structure for giving practical effect to the meaning of tribal self-determination. The states were not disinterested parties in these developments and watched, perhaps with some alarm, as the tec-tonic plates of federal Indian policy were again set into motion. The states' longstanding opposition to recognized tribal territorial and political authority within state borders was most colorfully cap-tured by an 1886 Supreme Court opinion in these terms: "[The In-dian tribes] owe no allegiance to the states, and receive from them no protection. Because of the local ill feeling, the people of the states where they are found are often their deadliest enemies."[34]

As noted earlier, the author of the *McClanahan* opinion was Justice Thurgood Marshall, writing his first of a record number of Indian law decisions for any Supreme Court justice. Justice Mar-shall, perhaps more so than any prior (or subsequent) justice on the high court, knew well the challenge of translating the rights en-shrined in the Constitution and other federal laws into positive changes on the ground, especially for people who had experienced a history of marginalization and oppression that was sanctioned by law. He particularly understood the phenomenon of state intransi-gence in the face of federally mandated policy changes, notably in the epic struggle to eliminate "separate but equal" as the law of the land.[35]

In this broader historical context, *McClanahan*'s treatment of tribal sovereignty may reflect the Court's judgment that the doc-trine was still relevant in the modern era but insufficient, alone, to do battle against persistent state encroachments and other threats to tribal authority within ancestral homelands. Easily misinter-preted or ignored, like the shadows in Plato's cave allegory, tribal sovereignty would more likely command the attention, if not the respect, of its opponents if it were coupled with and enforced through federal law. In an interesting bit of historical circularity, this is quite close to the view expressed by the Court in *Worcester*, in which the Court referenced international law for the proposition that a "weak state, in order to provide for its safety, may place itself under the protection of one more powerful, without stripping itself of the right of government, and ceasing to be a state."[36] The American experience relating to tribal affairs underscored both the wisdom and the necessity of such political alliances.

IN GENERAL TERMS, then, this is the condition in which tribal sovereignty existed at the start of the so-called "self-determination" era. Major cases like *Williams* and *McClanahan* reveal the complexity behind the task of simply locating the proper governmental authority to resolve contemporary disputes in Indian Country. They also signal further changes in the Court's construction of the nature and scope of inherent tribal authority. Those changes were not long in coming. Five years after *McClanahan* was decided, the Court issued a trio of Indian law decisions that would significantly alter the legal landscape in Indian Country. The year 1978 would prove to be a watershed for Indian tribes and for the field of federal Indian law.

2

1978—A WATERSHED YEAR
IN INDIAN LAW

THE HISTORY OF tribal-federal relations has rarely seen a year as exceptional and as controversial as 1978. In that year, all three branches of the federal government produced legal rules that significantly affected the course of tribal sovereignty and the rights of Indian people. The impetus for some, though not all, of these important developments was the publication in May 1977 of the Final Report of the American Indian Policy Review Commission. This body was created by act of Congress in 1975 largely in response to the Indian political activism of the early 1970s, as exemplified by the 1972 march on Washington during the "Trail of Broken Treaties." The final report contained over two hundred recommendations to guide federal Indian policy for the future but it largely avoided taking on the broader challenges of reconciling the federal government's claims to vast power in Indian affairs—a power the Supreme Court has described as "plenary" or nearly absolute—with tribal sovereign authority.[1]

The United States Congress passed two measures in 1978, the Indian Child Welfare Act (ICWA)[2] and the American Indian Religious Freedom Act (AIRFA).[3] The ICWA was enacted to counter the extraordinarily high rates at which Indian children were being separated from their families by state agencies. Congress considered evidence showing that in the late 1960s and early 1970s, approximately one-third of all Indian children had been removed from their families and placed in alternative, usually non-Indian, custodial care.[4] In states like South Dakota, Indian children were placed in foster care at a rate sixteen times that of non-Indian children; Washington's adoption rate for Indian children was nineteen times that for non-Indian children.[5] Perhaps even more dispiriting than these extraordinary rates of child removal was the fact that state officials regularly accomplished these acts within Indian Country, areas that are usually off limits to state authority, on grounds that reflected considerable bias on the part of state social workers about the nature of Indian family values and organization.[6]

The ICWA employs a combination of jurisdictional and procedural rules along with substantive placement criteria to help restore a greater measure of tribal authority in child placement decisions and to otherwise guide such decisions when they occur in state proceedings.[7]

The AIRFA was enacted to counter an equally disturbing and longer history of government hostility toward traditional Indian religious practices. Throughout most of the nineteenth and early twentieth centuries, a "quasi-theocracy" reigned in Indian Country where federal policymakers worked hand in hand with Christian churches to impose Christianity among tribal members as part of the government's civilizing project. In the 1880s and 1890s, the government, in rather selective and inconsistent fashion, discouraged or imposed bans on many forms of traditional religious practices, including the Sun Dance, use of peyote in ceremonial settings and observance of potlatch rituals.[8] Some tribal religious practitioners modified elements of their traditional practices to appease white Christians. For example, some tribes modified features of the annual Sun Dance, a ceremony of renewal and spiritual reaffirmation, to omit the element of self-sacrifice (many participants observed the ritual of skin piercing), reduced the number of days for the ceremony from eight to two and otherwise emphasized the ceremony's social, rather than its religious, features.[9] These federal policies, of course, were in flagrant disregard of constitutional principles enshrined in the First Amendment as well as the tradition of separation of church and state. AIRFA was a modest, if long overdue, corrective step expressing "the policy of the United States to protect and preserve for American Indians their inherent right of freedom to believe, express, and exercise the traditional religions of the American Indian including but not limited to access to sites, use and possession of sacred objects, and the freedom to worship through ceremonials and traditional rites."[10] The act provided no substantive rights enforceable in court but it did lay an important foundation for subsequent legal developments that accorded more meaningful protections for tribal religious rights.[11]

In 1978, the executive branch, through its Department of the Interior, issued regulations governing the process by which Indian groups that currently lack federal recognition as tribal governments could establish that legal status.[12] For most "recognized" tribes, that legal status is confirmed as a result of ratified treaties, federal statutes or executive orders affecting the tribe. Federal recognition or acknowledgment of a tribe's legal status is characterized as a "formal political act" that confirms the tribe's governmental powers and activates the panoply of trust obligations owed to tribes and their members by the federal government.[13] While Congress retains its prerogative to recognize a tribe by formal act, most tribal groups proceed through the administrative process established in 1978.[14]

Finally, within the judicial branch, the United States Supreme Court issued three decisions that, in significant respects, were among the most important and controversial rulings in the history of federal Indian law. In *Oliphant* v. *Suquamish Indian Tribe,* the Court ruled that Indian tribes lack the inherent sovereign authority to exercise criminal jurisdiction over non-Indian defendants. In *United States* v. *Wheeler,* decided sixteen days after *Oliphant,* the Court held that successive prosecution of an Indian defendant by an Indian tribe and the federal government arising from the same incident is constitutional since the prosecutions are by separate and distinct sovereign bodies. Less than two months later, the Court handed down its decision in *Santa Clara Pueblo* v. *Martinez* holding that the federal courts are not open to persons alleging violations of rights under the Indian Civil Rights Act of 1968 except in the limited context of habeas corpus review. Each of these cases warrants a closer look.

OLIPHANT V. SUQUAMISH INDIAN TRIBE (1978)

In August 1973, Mark David Oliphant, a non-Indian permanent resident of the Suquamish Reservation in northwestern Washington, was arrested and charged by tribal officials with assaulting a tribal law enforcement official and resisting arrest. He applied for a writ of habeas corpus in federal court, challenging not the *exercise,* but the very *existence* of tribal criminal jurisdiction over non-Indians. The lower courts rejected his application, finding that preserving law and order within tribal lands was an indispensable attribute of inherent tribal sovereignty that had been neither surrendered through treaty nor removed by Congress under its plenary power. Judge Anthony Kennedy, now Justice Kennedy on the U.S. Supreme Court, dissented from this ruling, finding no support for the notion that only express withdrawals by Congress or treaty language could divest tribes of their retained sovereign powers. His review of congressional law and policy, coupled with the observation that "virtually no white man appears to have been tried by an Indian tribunal in the past century,"[15] convinced him that Congress did not intend for tribes to exercise criminal jurisdiction over non-Indians. The doctrine of tribal sovereignty was not "analytically helpful" in resolving this issue, according to Judge Kennedy, and in any event, was limited to those powers "essential to the tribe's identity or its self-governing status."[16]

The Supreme Court, in an opinion written by then Associate Justice William Rehnquist, reversed the lower courts and found that inherent tribal powers could be divested both *explicitly* (through congressional acts or treaties) and *implicitly* if found to be "inconsistent with their status" as domestic dependent nations. Stating it differently, the Court said that "upon incorporation into the territory of the United States, the Indian tribes thereby come under the territorial sovereignty of the United States and their exercise of separate power is constrained so as not to conflict with the interests of this overriding sovereignty."

Before *Oliphant,* the only inherent tribal powers deemed surrendered as a consequence of "incorporation" were the powers to freely transact property and to engage in foreign relations, both stemming from rulings by Chief Justice John Marshall in the formative years of the country. We can call these "framework limitations" because they represented the sort of overarching and necessary limits imposed (rightly or wrongly) by the national government to carry on the colonial project in the "New World" without interference from pre-existing indigenous populations. From the colonizing sovereign's perspective, and that of the United States as successor in interest, those plans could be readily compromised if Indian tribes were left free to transact in lands or engage in foreign relations without regard to the colonizer's asserted sovereign prerogatives. Framework limitations can be likened to the limitations imposed on the tenant of a structure who is precluded from making choices that might compromise the structural integrity of the owner's building. Knocking out a weight-bearing wall, for example, would be precluded but changing the color of the paint on the wall might be an acceptable alteration. Framework limitations, of the kind suggested by Chief Justice Marshall, emerged from the foundational clashes and the resulting alliances achieved between sovereign bodies that were considered long resolved in the formative years of this country.[17]

The *Oliphant* Court essentially elevated a local level conflict between a private citizen and an Indian tribe into a collision of framework interests between two sovereigns, and in the process revived the most negative and destructive aspects of colonialism as it relates to Indian rights. This is a principal reason the decision has attracted so much negative reaction. In short, *Oliphant* is controversial because it signaled that the project of imperialism is alive and well in Indian Country and that the courts can now get into the action. In the modern era, the weapon of choice is not the militia, the cavalry, religion, smallpox-infested blankets or even the raw exercise of political power but instead a subtle but lethal legal doctrine called "implicit divestiture" that lies at the hand of judges "like a loaded weapon ready for the hand of any authority that can bring forward a plausible claim of an urgent need."[18]

What was the "urgent need" in *Oliphant* that required the wholesale stripping away of tribal power to prosecute non-Indians? According to the Court, the intrinsic limitations on tribal powers to transfer lands or engage in foreign relations stemmed from the national sovereign's interest in protecting its territory. Similarly, the country's interest in protecting its citizens against "unwarranted intrusions on their personal liberty"[19] compelled the conclusion that Indian tribes, by submitting to the overriding sovereignty of the United States, "necessarily give up their power to try non-Indian citizens of the United States except in a manner acceptable to Congress."[20] The Court acknowledged that defendants appearing in tribal courts are entitled to all the due process guarantees contained in the Indian Civil Rights Act (ICRA) of 1968 but cautioned that those guarantees are not identical to the protections afforded under the Bill of Rights, which do not apply to Indian tribes.[21] The Court refused to countenance the idea that the ICRA itself constituted the "manner acceptable to Congress" that would allow tribes to exercise criminal jurisdiction over non-Indians.

Oliphant's impact on the development of federal Indian law and life on the ground in Indian Country has been nothing short of revolutionary. The opinion gutted the notion of full territorial sovereignty as it applies to Indian tribes.[22] The Court, drawing mostly from nineteenth-century precedents, revived the assimilation-era doctrine of *United States* v. *Kagama* (1886), in which the Court noted that "Indians are within the geographical limits of the United States. The soil and people within these limits are under the political control of the Government of the United States, or of the States of the Union. There exists in the broad domain of sovereignty but these two."[23] *Oliphant*'s conception of limited tribal territorial and sovereign rights stands in stark contrast to language in *Williams* (1959), in which the Court thought it immaterial that the non-Indian creditor was non-Indian: "He was on the Reservation and the transaction with an Indian took place there. . . . The cases in this Court have consistently guarded the authority of Indian governments over their reservations. . . . If this power is to be taken away from them, it is for Congress to do it."[24] The court simply ignored *Williams*; the *Oliphant* opinion nowhere even mentions the case. A facile distinction is that *Williams* involved civil authority while *Oliphant* involved criminal authority. But the Court had no difficulty later extending and applying *Oliphant*'s principles to civil cases.[25] Another distinction—though hardly sufficient to justify the Court's rationale—is that the reservations involved in the two cases were vastly different. The Navajo Nation—site of the *Williams* case—sprawls across the territories of three states in an area the size of West Virginia and is populated almost entirely by Navajo tribal members. The Suquamish Reservation, on the other hand, bears the scars of the legacy of allotment.[26] It consisted (at the time of *Oliphant*) of just over seven thousand acres of land, nearly two-thirds of which was owned by non-Indians, who composed the vast majority of the reservation population.[27]

The *Oliphant* opinion also introduced the concept of citizenship and the accompanying language of individual rights of personal liberty as a limiting principle on tribal powers. This functioned much like the "protective cloak" of nationality that early colonizers used to insulate themselves from the laws of indigenous peoples. As the political theorist Steven Curry explains, "This move was usually justified by the claim that settlers could not be subjected to the 'arbitrary' and 'primitive' laws of 'vengeance and the blood feud' practised by the original inhabitants as this would be unjust. The nationality that clung like a protective cloak to these settlers also brought with it the jurisdiction of their sovereigns wherever they happened to settle. They denied to indigenous communities the integrative power and territorial authority that they ascribed to their own communities so as to impose the extended power of their own states on the New World, rather than having that authority already present there imposed on them (as they would have expected if they settled in a different European state.)"[28]

The *Oliphant* opinion resurrects another nineteenth-century precedent, *Ex Parte Crow Dog* (1883), to make a similar point. In *Crow Dog,* the Court rejected the assertion of federal jurisdiction in a homicide case involving only Indians, in part because of the fundamental unfairness of trying Indians "not by their peers, nor by the customs of their people, nor the law of their land, but by . . . a different race, according to the law of a social state of which they have an imperfect conception."[29] Likewise, said the *Oliphant* Court, it would be equally unfair for Indian tribes to try someone like Oliphant "according to their own customs and procedure." The Court acknowledged that the Indian Civil Rights Act and improvements in tribal court systems generally reduced but did not eliminate "many of the dangers that might have accompanied the exercise by tribal courts of criminal jurisdiction over non-Indians only a few decades ago."[30] The Court specifically noted, for example, that non-members of the tribe could not sit on a jury in Suquamish court proceedings. The Court did not seem concerned that as a practical matter, Indian citizens are regularly tried before state or federal juries that rarely include Indian jurors.[31] *Oliphant*'s conception of tribal powers in relation to outsiders is really premised on frontier-era notions of interracial relations where the response to interracial conflict (real or imagined) was to separate settlers from the Indians. What the Jacksonians accomplished by way of geography—forcibly removing Indians away from white settlers—the *Oliphant* Court accomplished through legal fiction by declaring the tribe's criminal jurisdiction over non-Indians nonexistent.

Finally, *Oliphant* foists the courts and judges into policy-making roles that are normally thought to be reserved to the political branches. Courts are now free to determine the contours of tribal powers armed only with the "inconsistent with their status" language as their compass and rudder. The problems with that development are twofold. First, as *Oliphant* itself demonstrates, the implicit divestiture analysis is necessarily backward-looking in that it requires courts to rummage through the detritus of colonialism to see what, if anything, remains of tribal authority. This leaves little room for proper consideration of modern developments in tribal-federal relations and risks producing a "frozen in time" formulation of tribal authority. Second, this backward-looking perspective pushes tribes back into a colonial or frontier setting and puts considerable distance between that imagined perspective and the contemporary realities that typify tribal life on the ground today. From that perspective, the Indian tribes are the ones that appear out of step with contemporary notions of organized government, justice and individual rights. In short, while modern congressional Indian policy pulls away from the legacy of colonialism and toward a future of revitalized tribal governments, the Court heads the other way, reviving images of tribes as lawless, disorganized and conquered peoples unfit for the serious task of resolving constitutional interests like personal liberty.[32] *Oliphant*'s implicit divestiture theory exemplifies what legal scholar Philip Frickey described as law doing "double work, providing the glue holding the republic together while legitimating the displacement of indigenous institutions to make room for it."[33] Indeed, that Justice Rehnquist thought the Court had accomplished precisely that displacement is reflected in his comment during oral arguments in a 1981 tribal taxing case: "This court has retreated from the position that Indians are sovereigns."[34]

UNITED STATES V. WHEELER (1978)

In October 1974, Anthony Robert Wheeler, a member of the Navajo Nation, was prosecuted by his tribe and pleaded guilty to charges of disorderly conduct and contributing to the delinquency of a minor arising out of a sexual assault on a Navajo girl that took place on the tribe's reservation. He was sentenced to time in jail and a fine. Just over a year later, Wheeler was indicted by a federal grand jury on rape charges arising from the same incident. His lawyers sought to dismiss the indictment on grounds that successive prosecutions on charges arising from the same incident by the same sovereign violated his rights under the Constitution's double jeopardy clause.[35] The "same sovereign" argument was premised on the argument that tribal governments derive their authority from the federal government and thus the earlier tribal prosecution barred the subsequent federal prosecution. The lower courts agreed with this view and dismissed the federal indictment. The Supreme Court agreed to review the case to resolve a conflict between two federal appellate courts on this question.

The oral arguments before the Supreme Court in *Wheeler* and *Oliphant* were held within two days of each other in early January 1978. Less than a week following the *Wheeler* arguments, Justice Thurgood Marshall wrote the following memorandum to his fellow justices indicating he was inclined to agree with the lower courts on their conception of tribal authority:

> I tentatively vote to affirm the judgment of the Court of Appeals. While I believe that tribes retain certain rights of self-government through a residual sovereignty not deriving from the federal Constitution but pre-existing it, I do not at this time think that different sources of sovereignty necessarily require application of the "dual sovereign" doctrine. . . . What strikes me as peculiar about the relationship between the tribes and the federal government is the plenary nature of Congress' authority to act vis-à-vis the tribes. Unlike the states, whose sovereignty (and concomitant police power) is protected and recognized in the Constitution, the tribes continue to possess any criminal jurisdiction at all wholly at the sufferance of the federal government (absent limiting treaty language). . . .

  For these reasons, I am presently inclined to believe that the relationship between the tribes and the United States is more comparable to that of the territories and the United States or municipalities and states, than it is to that of the states and the federal government, which, as the [Solicitor General]'s office has conceded, are the only full sovereign powers in the United States. My vote is tentative, however, since the majority opinion in this case or developments in *Oliphant* or *Santa Clara* may persuade me otherwise.[36]

Ultimately, Justice Marshall joined the Court's unanimous opinion reversing the lower court. The *Wheeler* opinion confirmed that Indian tribes and the federal government each dipped into their own respective bucket of sovereignty when they prosecuted Wheeler. Since they derived their sovereign powers from different sources of authority, the successive prosecutions by the two sovereigns did not offend the provisions of the Constitution. The fact that tribal powers are subject to Congress's plenary power does not mean that Congress is the source of the tribal powers.

Justice Marshall's memo suggests that, notwithstanding the outcome in *Wheeler*, continued ambivalence still pervades the Court's thinking on the proper conception of Indian tribes within our constitutional democracy. The memo also illustrates how fluid these conceptions are from one case to another and shows how a shift in context can make a significant difference in the minds of some justices. Practical considerations also affected the result in *Wheeler* as the Court expressly sought to avoid a result that would somehow bar or limit the exercise of federal power in Indian affairs. The alternative conception of tribal powers adopted by the lower courts (and initially by Justice Marshall) would create a race to the tribal courthouse. The "prospect of avoiding more severe federal punishment," said the Court, "would surely motivate a member of a tribe charged with the commission of an offense to seek to stand trial first in a tribal court. Were the tribal prosecution held to bar the federal one, important federal interests in the prosecution of major offenses on Indian reservations would be frustrated."[37]

As important as these considerations are, they do not capture the true legacy of the case. *Wheeler* is noteworthy and controversial in federal Indian law for giving a name to the legal principle articulated in *Oliphant—implicit divestiture*—and for providing a fuller context and even greater reach for that principle. First, though, the Court articulated its conception of tribal powers in relation to federal authority:

> We have recently said that: "Indian tribes are unique aggregations possessing attributes of sovereignty over both their members and their territory. . . . [They] are a good deal more than 'private voluntary organizations.'" . . . The sovereignty that the Indian tribes retain is of a unique and limited character. It exists only at the sufferance of Congress and is subject to complete defeasance. But until Congress acts, the tribes retain their existing sovereign powers. In sum, Indian tribes still possess those aspects of sovereignty not withdrawn by treaty or statute, or by implication as a necessary result of their dependent status.[38]

Applying this framework to the problem at hand, the Court found no evidence that the Navajo Nation's power to prosecute one of its own members was surrendered through treaty or taken away by federal statute. It also concluded that this power was not among those implicitly divested by virtue of the tribe's dependent status.

> The areas in which such implicit divestiture of sovereignty has been held to have occurred are those involving the relations between an Indian tribe and nonmembers of the tribe. . . . *These limitations rest on the fact that the dependent status of Indian tribes within our territorial jurisdiction is necessarily inconsistent with their freedom independently to*

determine their external relations. But the powers of self-government, including the power to prescribe and enforce internal criminal laws, are of a different type. They involve only the relations among members of a tribe. Thus, they are not such powers as would necessarily be lost by virtue of a tribe's dependent status [emphasis added].[39]

The scope of federal legislative and judicial powers to shape, modify or *eliminate* inherent tribal powers *at will,* as reflected in these passages from *Wheeler,* is nothing short of breathtaking in its audacity, immorality and unconstitutionality. From the constitutional perspective, recall that Article I enumerates among Congress's powers the authority to "regulate Commerce . . . with the Indian Tribes." To be sure, the Supreme Court has long recognized that Article I's "necessary and proper" clause[40] provides a basis for recognizing an additional layer of implied powers that are ancillary to the enumerated powers. But those implied powers are not limitless. As the Supreme Court held in its celebrated decision in *McCulloch* v. *Maryland* (1819) construing this clause and the reach of implied federal powers: "Let the end be legitimate, let it be within the scope of the constitution, and all means which are appropriate, which are plainly adapted to that end, which are not prohibited, but consistent with the letter and spirit of the constitution, are constitutional."[41] Even with this broad articulation of implied federal power, it is inconceivable that the framers intended that the enumerated power to regulate commerce *"with"* the Indian tribes included the power to "extinguish" the existence of those tribes, at least in the political sense. As the noted constitutional law scholar Laurence H. Tribe noted, "If one believes, with most, that the limits on Congress' affirmative powers should be judicially enforced, then surely one cannot find acceptable a roadmap for the enforcing authority that contains no exits, no signs, no directions, and no boundaries."[42]

Wheeler breathed new life into the "dying Indian" thesis by recognizing that both Congress, through the exercise of unbridled plenary power, and now the Court, through its upgraded loaded weapon of implicit divestiture, can empire at will in Indian Country. One finds no mention of limiting principles that would check this exercise of power by either federal branch of government. The trust doctrine, for example, rooted in the "internal structures of sovereignty in the American system,"[43] is nowhere discussed. Similarly, no effort is made to clarify that the "external relations" limitations that the Court traces to rulings of Chief Justice John Marshall in the early nineteenth century were in fact carefully limited intrusions on tribal powers resulting from potential conflicts with and among sovereign bodies, not with or among *individuals* within those bodies.[44] The limitation on tribes' engaging in "external relations" was expanded from the sovereign-to-sovereign context to embrace any dealings between an Indian tribe and individuals who are not members of the tribe. This significantly narrows the scope of inherent tribal authority and calls into question the Court's assertion that tribes are "a good deal more than 'private voluntary organizations.'"

Finally, we should note the interesting and rather bizarre position that Mr. Wheeler and his lawyers were required to take in this case. In order to "win" a dismissal of the federal indictment, Mr. Wheeler essentially had to take a legal position calculated to diminish the sovereign authority of his own nation and that of all other Indian tribes. In affirming the tribe's inherent authority to prosecute its own members, the Court still managed to write an opinion that undercut the tribes' foundational authority to govern inside tribal lands while also securing the superior authority of federal power in Indian affairs.

Santa Clara Pueblo v. *Martinez* (1978)

Julia Martinez, a member of the Santa Clara Pueblo, challenged her own tribe's membership rules in federal court under the equal protection provisions of the Indian Civil Rights Act (ICRA) of 1968.[45] Congress wrote this law at the height of the civil rights movement and at a time when the courts were substantially involved in giving revitalized expression to the scope of individual rights enshrined in the Constitution. Since the Constitution expressly applies only to the federal and state governments, its provisions are not binding on tribal governments. Relying on its plenary authority in Indian affairs, Congress wrote the ICRA to impose most, though not all, of the Bill of Rights on Indian tribes to limit the exercise of their sovereign powers.

Ms. Martinez claimed that the tribe's membership ordinance dating from 1939 was discriminatory in "mixed marriage" settings like hers because it bestowed membership on the children of a male member, but not those of a female member, who married and had children with nonmembers of the Pueblo. Membership in the Pueblo was required to enjoy certain tribal political rights (e.g., voting in tribal elections, holding office), tribal material rights (e.g., land use rights) and a number of federal rights as well, including access to educational and health care benefits. The Martinez children were raised on the Pueblo, spoke Tewa, the traditional language, and observed the cultural practices of the community. As the lower court found, the children were for all practical purposes Santa Claran Indians. Martinez's efforts to enroll her children with the tribe dated back to 1946[46] and intensified in the late 1960s when the lack of enrollment papers led the federal Indian Health Service clinic to deny treatment for her daughter, Natalie (since deceased), for strokes associated with a terminal illness.[47]

Many tribes base membership decisions on lineal descent from a particular parent, on either a matrilineal or patrilineal basis. While there was some dispute among the parties in *Martinez* about whether the Pueblo had traditionally observed patrilineal descent, it was clear that federal policies flowing from the Indian Reorganization Act (IRA) of 1934 influenced the Santa Clara's particular rule to some extent.[48] In 1935, the Bureau of Indian Affairs urged Indian tribes that elected to organize under the IRA to develop rules limiting membership to "persons who reasonably can be expected to participate in tribal relations and affairs."[49] This echoed earlier federal policies from the late nineteenth century, particularly the allotment policies, that similarly imposed narrow tribal membership rules based on minimal blood quantum measures in order to limit, and eventually eliminate, the number of Indians (and tribes) eligible for federal benefits and services.[50] These federal policies illustrate how membership and enrollment rules (and the underlying policies giving rise to some of them) can operate without any regard to the social and cultural realities by which Indian people organize and perceive themselves as Indian people.

The lower courts in *Martinez* both agreed that people like Julia Martinez were entitled to have a federal court review claims of alleged violations of the ICRA, but they disagreed on whether the Santa Clara Pueblo had actually breached the statutory protections guaranteeing equal protection of the tribe's laws. The Supreme Court limited its review to the jurisdictional question and ruled that the ICRA did not provide for federal court review of tribal actions alleged to violate ICRA's substantive provisions outside the narrow remedy of habeas corpus petitions. Julia Martinez's remedy would have to come from the tribal courts, which, the Court acknowledged, "have repeatedly been recognized as appropriate forums for the exclusive adjudication of disputes affecting important personal and property interests of both Indians and non-Indians."

The Supreme Court's analysis was largely taken up with the history of the ICRA and determining Congress's intent regarding federal review of ICRA-related claims. The ICRA was enacted to guard individuals against "arbitrary and unjust actions of tribal governments." In an earlier case, *Talton* v. *Mayes* (1896), the Supreme Court had determined that Indian tribes, though subject to Congress's paramount authority, were not subject to the particular provisions of the Constitution or the Bill of Rights.[51] In 1968, Congress imposed limitations on inherent tribal powers that were comparable but not identical to limitations contained in the Bill of Rights and the Fourteenth Amendment that limit federal and state governmental powers. Congress adjusted the ICRA limitations to "fit the unique political, cultural, and economic needs of tribal governments. . . . Thus, for example, [ICRA] does not prohibit the establishment of religion, nor does it require jury trials in civil cases, or appointment of counsel for indigents in criminal cases."[52] As a point of historical interest, the Supreme Court during the 1960s actively reviewed claims contending that various provisions of the Bill of Rights applied to state governments via the Fourteenth Amendment's due process guarantees. For example, the right to a lawyer in state prosecutions was not assured as a constitutional matter until the Court's 1963 decision in *Gideon* v. *Wainwright*.[53] Similarly, the famous "Miranda rights" often depicted in television and cinema police dramas—"You have the right to remain silent . . ."—date only from 1966, the year of the Court's decision in *Miranda* v. *Arizona*.[54] In short, increasing federal concern with individual civil rights led both Congress and the Supreme Court to examine and rewrite the rules respecting limits on tribal and state powers.

In the ICRA, the Supreme Court found that Congress actually pursued two goals—providing enhanced protections for individual civil rights and promoting tribal self-government. In providing only one express route to federal court—the habeas corpus provisions that allowed Mark Oliphant to jump from tribal court into federal court—Congress intended to make a limited (though significant) intrusion on tribal sovereignty. The Court refused to aggravate that intrusion by recognizing an implied right to seek federal review of tribal actions. The Court never questioned whether Congress was actually empowered to write a law like the ICRA in the first place, and it put words into the mouth of the *Talton* Court when it stated that "Congress has plenary authority to limit, modify or eliminate" a tribe's sovereign powers. *Talton* said no such thing, but given the assimilationist policies of its day, that sentiment likely pervaded the Court's thinking. Unlike *Oliphant,* the *Martinez* opinion relied extensively on both the language and policy concerns underlying the Court's *Williams* v. *Lee* decision, particularly its "infringement test," to underscore the point that allowing federal review here would undoubtedly "unsettle a tribal government's ability to maintain authority."[55]

The leading treatise in federal Indian law, the *Cohen Handbook,* notes that the ICRA, as interpreted in *Martinez,* has attracted considerable criticism from all sides, from those "who believe it went too far and those who believe it did not go far enough in constraining tribal actions."[56] ICRA's critics see it as yet another example of government-imposed ideology—this time, an ideology of individual rights—running roughshod over tribal social and cultural institutions that have endured over centuries. ICRA's supporters view the law as an important check on tribal governmental excesses that *Martinez,* in their view, undermined when it rejected federal court review of tribal court ICRA rulings outside the habeas corpus context.[57] From the ICRA supporters' perspective, checks on tribal powers are particularly critical when the rights involved are those recognized by the dominant society as fundamental individual rights. That was the problem in *Martinez,* in which the tribe's membership rule appeared on the radar of the federal courts as a gender-based discriminatory rule. In other situations—e.g., employment disputes, allocation of such benefits as housing or land rights—the nexus between traditional tribal practices and broader individual rights may not be so clear. Although *Martinez* appeared to have settled the matter on choice of forum and law for these questions, doubts persist about the ability or capacity of tribal courts to render justice in particular cases. As recently as 2004, a federal appeals court expressed deep concerns about the administration of justice in one tribal community and explicitly urged Congress to "consider giving this Court power to act."[58] On the other hand, there is evidence that tribal courts are actually doing quite well in mediating claims arising under the ICRA.[59] The history of federal Indian policy, however, suggests that even isolated concerns may lead to dramatic curtailment of a tribe's powers by either Congress or the courts. *Oliphant* is the best reminder of that danger.

AS THE DISCUSSION above suggests, the Court's opinions in *Oliphant, Wheeler* and *Martinez* laid the groundwork for a fundamental realignment of the nature and scope of tribal sovereign powers. Tribal leaders were quick to recognize the impact these decisions would have on their capacity to govern on the ground, and in short order, they organized a national conference in Washington, D.C., in June 1978. The keynote speaker, Senator Edward Kennedy (Democrat, Massachusetts), drew attention to the cases and noted, "They all helped draw the boundaries of tribal self-determination which will guide the cause of Indian and non-Indian relationships in the decades to come."[60]

Placing the Court's 1978 Indian law decisions alongside the work of Congress and the executive branch for the same year highlights the sharp divisions that emerged among the federal branches in understanding the nature of tribal sovereignty and in charting the course of federal Indian policy. The added historical perspective from our first chapter shows how the federal branches actually reversed positions from the days of Chief Justice John Marshall, when it was the Court that served as principal guardian of the nation's historical legal promises to Indian tribes. Today, the "least dangerous branch" poses the greatest challenges to supporters of tribal sovereignty. The final chapter in Part One will highlight how the Court's modern teachings on tribal sovereignty have been applied in more recent cases and helped contribute to a fairly dramatic clash among the branches over the nature of tribal-federal relations.

3

CREEPING CONSTITUTIONALISM
FROM THE TEMPLE

At bottom, the Court needs a contemporary comfort level with the proposition that tribes are governments, not voluntary membership associations; it is surely discomfort with this conclusion that has led the Court to impose a creeping constitutionalism in federal Indian law.
—Professor Philip P. Frickey, "A Common Law for Our Age of Colonialism," 109 Yale L.J. 1, 82 (1999)

THE BUSINESS OF locating the sources and limits on *tribal* governmental power is quite different from that of similar inquiries involving the federal or state governments. In the latter situation, the Constitution serves as the touchstone document through which the Court determines the proper limits of governmental action. This is true even for situations in which the interests of tribes or Indian people might be involved, even indirectly. For example, in the early 1970s, a non-Indian federal employee named Carla Mancari brought one of the earliest challenges to federal affirmative action policies. She challenged a federal employment preference system within the Bureau of Indian Affairs that favored similarly qualified members of federally recognized Indian tribes in hiring and promotion decisions. Her legal argument rested on the Constitution, which she contended prohibited the federal government from engaging in racial discrimination among its citizens.[1]

In *Morton* v. *Mancari* (1974), the Court rejected her claim, stating that the hiring and promotion preferences reflected a political, not racial, classification in light of the tribes' unique sovereign status and Congress's special responsibilities to Indian tribes.[2] As a result, federal legislation of this sort would be valid so long as it was "tied rationally to the fulfilment of Congress' unique obligations towards the Indians."[3]

In cases in which individuals are challenging the legitimacy of *tribal* power, the Constitution is not available as a check against alleged unlawful government acts.[4] Individuals within the tribe's jurisdiction must rely instead on the limits imposed by the federal Indian Civil Rights Act (ICRA) and other limitations derived from federal or tribal law. In setting limits on tribal jurisdiction based on an individual's status as a member or nonmember of the tribe, the Court in 1978 essentially declared tribal justice systems to be presumptively inappropriate and inadequate for nonmembers. Unable to wield the Constitution against the tribes, the Court nonetheless embraced constitutional values like personal liberty to announce further limits on the scope of inherent tribal powers using the theory of implicit divestiture.[5] Employing the methods of this "creeping constitutionalism," the Court soon extended the *Oliphant* rule into other settings—notably the civil and regulatory area—to impose further restraints on inherent tribal authority.

IN *MONTANA* V. *UNITED STATES* (1981),[6] the Court considered a challenge to the Crow tribe's power to regulate hunting and fishing by nonmembers on lands located within the reservation but held in fee simple by nonmembers. At the time this case was filed, nonmembers owned nearly 30 percent of Crow reservation lands, another product of the allotment policies. The Court readily agreed that the tribe could regulate nonmembers hunting and fishing on tribal lands—that is, lands within the reservations belonging to the tribe or held in trust by the United States for the tribe. But reaching nonmembers on their own fee lands within the reservation was another matter. This represented an attempt by the tribe independently to determine their "external relations," which was inconsistent with the tribe's "dependent status." According to the Court, the "exercise of tribal power beyond what is necessary to protect tribal self-government or to control internal relations is inconsistent with the dependent status of the tribes, and so cannot survive without express congressional delegation."[7] This rule was expressly derived from *Oliphant* and its theory of implicit divestiture: "Though *Oliphant* only determined inherent tribal authority in criminal matters, the principles on which it relied support *the general proposition that the inherent sovereign powers of an Indian tribe do not extend to the activities of nonmembers of the tribe*" (emphasis added).[8]

Earlier precedents had, of course, upheld tribal power over nonmembers of the tribe in civil matters, including cases like *Williams* v. *Lee*. In *Montana,* the Court purported to reconcile these earlier cases by treating them as exceptions to the "general proposition" that fall into two categories:

> A tribe may regulate, through taxation, licensing, or other means, the activities of nonmembers who enter consensual relationships with the tribe or its members, through commercial dealing, contracts, leases, or other arrangements. A tribe may also retain inherent power to exercise civil authority over the conduct of non-Indians on fee lands within its reservation when that conduct threatens or has some direct effect on the political integrity, the economic security, or the health or welfare of the tribe.[9]

Since no "consensual relationships" existed between the Crow tribe and the non-Indian sportsmen, and the tribe had not alleged that hunting and fishing by nonmembers of their fee lands would "imperil the subsistence or welfare of the Tribe,"[10] the Court held that the Crow tribe could not apply its regulations to nonmembers on their fee lands.

By extending *Oliphant*'s implicit divestiture rule into the civil and regulatory area, the Court in *Montana* unleashed a new wave of litigation that challenged anew, not the particular *exercise* of a tribe's inherent governmental power, but the very *existence* of that power over nonmembers. Described by the Court as "the path-marking case concerning tribal civil authority over nonmembers"[11] and "the most exhaustively reasoned of our modern cases address-ing [inherent tribal sovereignty],"[12] *Montana* effectively provided a double edge to *Oliphant*'s implicit divestiture theory that functions like a Sword of Damocles, ready to drop on tribal governmental powers that extend beyond *Montana*'s elusive boundaries and even on the Court's own precedents that do not conform to *Montana*'s limiting principles.

In *Strate* v. *A-1 Contractors* (1997),[13] the Court relied on *Montana*'s general rule to hold that a tribal court lacked inherent power to hear a private lawsuit between two non-Indians involved in a two-vehicle collision that occurred on a state-managed highway running through the Fort Berthold Indian Reservation. The Court first had to clear some "jurisprudential brush" in order to reach this conclusion. In other words, the Court had to find a way to reconcile *Montana*'s limiting principles on tribal sovereignty with some of its other cases that spoke more generously and liberally about the scope of tribal governmental power, especially over nonmembers of tribes. In two particular cases—*National Farmers Union Ins. Co.* v. *Crow Tribe* (1985)[14] and *Iowa Mutual Ins. Co.* v. *LaPlante* (1987)[15]—the Court accorded significant weight to tribal court decision-making power for events occurring in Indian Country, suggesting that tribal *adjudicatory* power (i.e., the authority of tribal courts to hear and resolve disputes) was broader than its *regulatory* or legislative power (the subject of *Montana*). These two decisions are best known for allowing nonmembers of the tribe to enter federal court to chal-lenge tribal court jurisdiction over them, usually after they've first "exhausted" tribal court remedies. The *Strate* Court flatly rejected the notion that tribal adjudicative power was somehow broader in scope than a tribe's regulatory power: "As to nonmembers, we hold, a tribe's adjudicative jurisdiction does not exceed its legislative juris-diction."[16] The Court found neither of *Montana*'s exceptions appli-cable and, indeed, cautioned that *Montana*'s main rule—that tribal inherent powers do not extend "beyond what is necessary to protect tribal self-government or to control internal relations"—must tem-per the application of *Montana*'s second exception, the so-called "negative effects" test.[17] Otherwise, the exception would swallow the rule. Thus, while recognizing that "those who drive carelessly on a public highway running through a reservation endanger all in the vicinity, and surely jeopardize the safety of tribal members," the Court still concluded that opening the tribal court to the plaintiff (whose husband and children were tribal members) was "not neces-sary to protect tribal self-government."[18]

Similarly, in *Atkinson Trading Company* v. *Shirley* (2001)[19] a unanimous Court relied on *Montana* to strike down a tribal tax imposed on nonmembers for activities (operating a hotel) occur-ring on fee lands owned by the nonmembers within the Navajo Reservation. As in *Strate*, the Court first had to prune some its own opinions in this area, notably its decision in *Merrion* v. *Jicarilla Apache Tribe* (1982).[20] In upholding the tribe's power to tax non-Indian oil and gas lessees operating on tribal trust lands, the *Mer-rion* Court described the taxing power as "an essential attribute of Indian sovereignty because it is a necessary instrument of self-government and territorial management."[21] While *Merrion* in-volved nonmember activities on tribal trust lands, the Court in that case explicitly recognized that the tribe's taxing power reached nonmember activities on their own fee lands as well: "Neither the United States, nor a state, nor any other sovereignty loses the power to govern the people within its borders by the existence of towns and cities therein endowed with the usual powers of municipali-ties, *nor by the ownership nor occupancy of the land within its territo-rial jurisdiction by citizens or foreigners*" (quoting from *Buster* v. *Wright* (8th Cir., 1905) (emphasis in original).[22] Indeed, *Montana* itself listed *Buster* v. *Wright* as among the cases within the "consen-sual relations" exception that supported the tribe's retained power over nonmembers "even on non-Indian fee lands."[23] Moreover, another Court precedent, *Brendale* v. *Confederated Tribes and Bands of the Yakima Indian Nation* (1989),[24] upheld a tribe's zoning powers over nonmember-owned fee lands in areas predominantly held and managed as tribal lands. In *Atkinson,* the Navajo Nation asserted that 99.74 percent of the 13.5 million acre reservation is held in trust for the tribe or its members.[25]

In *Atkinson,* Chief Justice Rehnquist's opinion gave *Merrion* short shrift and limited it to its facts. "An Indian tribe's sovereign power to tax—whatever its derivation—reaches no further than tribal land."[26] What about *Merrion*'s reliance on *Buster* and *Montana*'s citation of *Buster* as evidence of retained tribal taxing authority even on fee lands? The Court simply stated, "We have never endorsed *Buster*'s statement that an Indian tribe's 'jurisdiction to govern the inhabitants of a country is not conditioned or limited by the title to the land which they occupy in it.'" According to the Court, *Buster* was merely illustrative of the kinds of consensual relationships that would support tribal authority under *Montana*'s first exception, but it was otherwise "not an authoritative precedent."[27] In truth, the cases are not that easily reconciled; *Atkinson* effectively pruned back *Merrion* to make it conform to *Montana*'s limiting principle "that Indian tribes lack civil authority over nonmembers on non-Indian fee land."[28]

Applying *Montana* "straight up," the Court found neither exception applicable. On the consensual relations prong, the Court discounted evidence that the trading post relied substantially on a variety of tribal services, including fire, police, medical and health protection. The Court viewed the "generalized availability" of such tribal services as "patently insufficient" to uphold the tribe's taxing power. The exception requires that "the tax or regulation imposed by the Indian tribe have a nexus to the consensual relationship itself."[29] Any broader reading of the exception would risk swallowing the rule and would ignore "the dependent status of Indian tribes and [subvert] the territorial restriction upon tribal power."[30] Likewise, the Court rejected the "negative impacts" argument, stating, "The exception is only triggered by *nonmember conduct* that threatens the Indian tribe; it does not broadly permit the exercise of civil authority wherever it might be considered 'necessary' to self-government. Thus, unless the drain of the nonmember's conduct upon tribal services and resources is so severe that it actually 'imperil[s]' the political integrity of the Indian tribe, there can be no assertion of civil authority beyond tribal lands"[31] (emphasis in original). This is an unprecedented formulation of *Montana's* second exception and suggests that tribal power over nonmembers on fee lands would only be justified to "avert catastrophic consequences."[32] The Court also interpreted its ruling in *Brendale* so narrowly as to be practically useless to tribes operating in the real world. Under that case as interpreted in *Atkinson,* tribal authority to regulate nonmembers on their fee lands exists only if development (or other nonmember activities) would "place the entire area 'in jeopardy.'"[33] The Court's analysis in *Atkinson* illustrates that case precedents, like statistics, can be tortured to say just about anything.

On the Cameron Trading Post's website—the same non-Indian business involved in *Atkinson*—one finds this phrase on several pages: "The More Things Change . . . the More They Stay the Same." *Atkinson* repeats an unfortunate chapter in the history of federal-Indian relations where law is the agent used to put distance between Indian tribes and nonmembers of the tribe and to diminish the scope and effectiveness of tribal governmental power. Justice Thurgood Marshall expressed a similar sentiment in a draft opinion in the earlier *Merrion* case, which opened with this sentence: "The boundaries of Indian land and the scope of Indian sovereignty often are disputed by those seeking for themselves the benefits of resources within Indian dominion."[34] One of the supreme ironies in *Atkinson* is that the Cameron Trading Post promotes itself as one of the last trading posts of the Old West. It capitalizes on and exploits its position in Indian Country to sell native-made arts and crafts with a workforce that is nearly 80 percent Navajo.[35] It relies on the Navajo Nation to provide a wealth of governmental services. It broadcasts proudly on its website the history of longstanding mutually beneficial relations between the founders of the post and the neighboring tribes: "As traders, the [founding] brothers were more than merchants. Understanding local dialects and customs, they were trusted by the local Native American people in matters concerning confusing new American legal and social systems." With a substantial assist from a unanimous Supreme Court, the current owners of the Trading Post revealed the truth in Justice Marshall's words and successfully rebuffed the taxing power of the very tribal nation whose culture and traditions they exploit for money on a daily basis.

The *Atkinson* case contained other ironies that embraced the lawyers and lower court judges in the case. As a private attorney, Bruce D. Black represented one of the plaintiff companies in *Merrion*. In 1995, he was appointed to the federal bench by President Bill Clinton. He was the trial judge who presided over and ruled in favor of the tribe in *Atkinson*. Recalling his experience litigating *Merrion,* Judge Black noted, "I lost both sides of the case. The Supreme Court converted me in *Merrion* and then converted me back in *Atkinson*."[36] At the appellate court level, Judge Monroe G. McKay wrote a concurring opinion supporting the tribe's position in *Merrion* and later wrote the majority opinion in *Atkinson*—the one reversed by the Supreme Court. He offered this assessment of the high court's work in federal Indian law:

> I think *Atkinson* in the Supreme Court was a major retreat from the Court's own opinions. It had not come home to me how seriously the trend away from *Merrion* was until the *Atkinson* decision. While I was not surprised that it was decided against the Tribe, I was surprised at the unanimous court in *Atkinson*. It was nine to zero. We weren't wrong. . . . The Supreme Court has begun to erode its earlier decisions and emasculate the idea of tribal sovereignty. The Court built a body of law of tribal sovereignty under the aegis of Congress. The current Court is

in the process, and has been for nearly two decades, of eroding those protections of the power of tribes to govern their own affairs within their territorial borders.[37]

The *Montana-Strate-Atkinson* line of cases provides the legal framework for assessing the scope of tribal civil or regulatory power over nonmembers on fee lands in Indian Country (or the equivalent of fee lands where tribal control over the lands has been largely surrendered). At the same time, the Court expressly recognized the existence of tribal power over nonmembers for their conduct on tribal trust lands (as it did in *Montana* and *Atkinson*) or it carefully left the matter open for future cases. In *Strate,* for example, the Court noted, "We express no view on the governing law or proper forum when an accident occurs on a *tribal road* within a reservation" (emphasis added).[38] In short, the legal status of the land in question as tribal or trust lands mattered significantly in understanding the jurisdictional framework because in those areas, the Court recognized a greater measure of tribal authority over nonmembers.

In a recent case, *Nevada* v. *Hicks* (2001),[39] the Court needlessly muddied the waters on this issue. The Court rejected the tribal court's authority to hear a lawsuit brought by a tribal member against state law enforcement officials for alleged civil rights violations that took place on reservation trust lands. Suspecting Mr. Hicks of having committed an off-reservation crime (killing a California bighorn sheep), the state officials entered the reservation to execute a search warrant on Mr. Hicks's property. In rejecting the tribe's authority to hear Hicks's lawsuit, the court aligned *Montana*'s general rule with its legal progenitor, *Oliphant*, and stated, "*Oliphant* itself drew no distinctions based on the status of the land. . . . The ownership status of land, in other words, is only one factor to consider in determining whether regulation of the activities of nonmembers is 'necessary· to protect tribal self-government or to control internal relations.'"[40] While the Court was remaking legal history, it went one step further in characterizing state sovereignty in relation to tribal power:

Our cases make clear that the Indians' right to make their own laws and be governed by them does not exclude all state regulatory authority on the reservation. State sovereignty does not end at a reservation's border. Though tribes are often referred to as "sovereign" entities, it was "long ago" that "the Court departed from Chief Justice Marshall's view" that "the laws of [a State] can have no force" within reservation boundaries. "Ordinarily," it is now clear, "an Indian reservation is considered part of the territory of the State." [41]

Attaching great significance to the state's interests in pursuing alleged violators of state law, the Court concluded that the asserted tribal authority over state officials in the context of this case was simply "not essential to tribal self-government or internal relations."

The Court was careful to limit its holding to the unique facts of the case and left open the broader question of tribal civil jurisdiction over nonmember defendants generally. At least three sitting justices—Justices Souter, Kennedy and Thomas—have already signaled that they view *Montana*'s general limiting principle (that inherent tribal sovereign powers do not extend to nonmembers) as applying broadly regardless of the legal status of the land.[42] Justice Scalia is a likely fourth vote for this position. A fifth vote (perhaps from one of the more recently appointed justices, Chief Justice John Roberts or Associate Justice Samuel Alito) would constitute a majority holding and would extend *Oliphant*'s gutting of territorial sovereignty in civil cases where tribes would presumptively lack jurisdiction over nonmembers for conduct occurring *anywhere* in Indian Country unless one of the *Montana* exceptions applies. These developments feed suspicions about the Court's overall purpose or intent in these cases, as reflected in the following commentary from a federal district court judge in 2005: "This court has not yet grown so cynical as to infer that the *Montana* analysis was concocted merely as a device to be used to diminish Indian tribal sovereignty 'one case at a time,' though some argue quite convincingly that such has been its actual effect, intended or not."[43]

THE *MONTANA-STRATE-ATKINSON* line of cases illustrates the significant changes *Oliphant* inspired in the nature and scope of inherent tribal *civil* jurisdictional powers. *Oliphant* also inspired further changes in the Court's understanding of inherent tribal *criminal* jurisdictional powers. In 1990, the court ruled in *Duro* v. *Reina* that Indian tribes lacked inherent sovereign authority to prosecute nonmember Indians.[44] In an opinion by Justice Kennedy (the dissenting judge in *Oliphant* when that case was before the federal court of appeals), the Court likened Albert Duro to Mark Oliphant in terms of his national citizenship and his status as a political outsider to the Salt River Pima-Maricopa Indian Community, the tribe that tried to prosecute him for illegal firing of a weapon in connection with a homicide. In draping the United States flag around Duro, the same protective cloak of nationality given to Mark Oliphant, the Court declared:

> We hesitate to adopt a view of tribal sovereignty that would single out another group of citizens, nonmember Indians, for trial by political bodies that do not include them. As full citizens, Indians share in the territorial and political sovereignty of the United States. The retained sovereignty of the tribe is but a recognition of certain additional authority the tribes maintain over Indians who consent to be tribal members. Indians like other citizens share allegiance to the overriding sovereign, the United States. A tribe's additional authority comes from the consent of its members, and so in the criminal sphere, membership marks the bounds of tribal authority.[45]

The Court hinted that the Constitution would preclude even Congress from altering this conclusion through a delegation of authority to tribes: "Our cases suggest constitutional limitations even on the ability of Congress to subject American citizens to criminal proceedings before a tribunal that does not provide constitutional protections as a matter of right."[46]

This is a remarkable analysis. In the course of reaffirming the United States' territorial and political supremacy, the Court reclaimed the foundational supremacy of the modern nation-state, at least in its early forms. A prominent feature of that development, according to political theorist Steven Curry, was the extension of uniform laws throughout the sovereign's territory: "There simply could not be land anywhere within the state taken to be held of some other source than from the legal will of the sovereign. The very possibility of the constitutional achievement of civic equality depended upon this change. . . . Territorial integrity was to go hand in glove with political integrity."[47] Within this framework, of course, any competing claim to territorial or political authority simply would not be tolerated. And in *Duro*—it wasn't. More remarkable still was the Court's imposition of Western political philosophy— particularly its reliance on consent theory—to describe the nature and scope of indigenous systems of self-governance. In a dissenting opinion, Justice Brennan challenged the Court to explain why a consent requirement was deemed particularly salient in a criminal context when it was not required in a civil context. Furthermore, said Justice Brennan, there was no precedent for requiring participation in the political process as a prerequisite for a sovereign's exercise of criminal jurisdiction. If it were otherwise, "A State could not prosecute nonresidents, and this country could not prosecute aliens who violate our laws."[48]

As in the follow-up to the 1978 triumvirate of cases, tribal leaders and supporters of tribal sovereignty organized quickly to counter the effects of *Duro*. Of particular concern was the jurisdictional void in law enforcement authority created in the wake of the Court's decision that exacerbated problems of rising rates of violent crime in Indian Country.[49] United States statutes provide for federal law enforcement power in Indian Country, but only if the offender, the offense and the location of the crime fit the particular terms of the Major Crimes Act[50] or the Indian Country Crimes Act.[51] State law enforcement power over Indians in Indian Country exists only if authorized by Congress.[52] In seeking support from Congress to overturn the Court's *Duro* ruling, tribal officials and their supporters advocated legislation that would affirm the tribe's inherent authority to prosecute nonmember Indian defendants. Delegation of this authority from Congress would likewise have filled the jurisdictional void, but tribal authority in that context would be constrained by the Constitution. The tribal effort here was not to skirt any form of external limits on tribal powers; the Indian Civil Rights Act of 1968 already functioned in that way. It was to recognize that different systems of justice, not lesser forms of justice, operated in Indian Country.[53] Moreover, the tribes' advocacy efforts were limited to overturning the result in *Duro,* not *Oliphant.* That decision was necessitated by political pragmatism: "Tribal officials [did] not seek to overturn *Oliphant,* not because they [did] not wish to exercise criminal misdemeanor jurisdiction over non-Indians, but because they [were] sufficiently pragmatic to accept that the white majority in this country [would] never countenance the return to tribes of jurisdiction over non-Indians."[54]

In October 1991, the tribes' advocacy efforts were realized when Congress amended the Indian Civil Rights Act to provide that tribal powers of self-government included "the inherent power of Indian tribes, hereby recognized and affirmed, to exercise criminal jurisdiction over all Indians."[55] In effect, Congress responded to an organized national tribal advocacy effort and reasserted its constitutional authority in Indian affairs in direct reaction to a decision of the United States Supreme Court. Almost immediately, questions arose about whether Congress was actually empowered to override the Court's rulings on the limits of inherent tribal sovereignty. The lower federal courts ultimately produced conflicting rulings on the constitutionality of the so-called "*Duro*-fix" legislation and a showdown in the Supreme Court was inevitable.

In *United States* v. *Lara* (2004),[56] the Supreme Court upheld

Congress's actions. The case involved a challenge by Billy Jo Lara, an enrolled member of the Turtle Mountain band of Chippewa Indians in North Dakota, to a federal prosecution for assault on a federal officer that followed on the heels of a tribal court prosecution on a similar charge arising out of the same incident. The tribal court in question was the judicial court of the Spirit Lake tribe on whose reservation Lara resided with his family. Lara pleaded guilty to the tribal charges but argued that the subsequent federal prosecution was barred by the Constitution's double jeopardy provision. In essence, Lara claimed that Congress's *"Duro*-fix" legislation imbued tribes with *federal* authority to prosecute nonmember Indian defendants; having had their one bite at the defendant through the medium of a tribal prosecution, the federal government was precluded by the Constitution's double jeopardy provision from taking another crack at the defendant for the same conduct.

The Court's majority opinion in *Lara,* authored by Justice Stephen Breyer, characterized the decisions in *Oliphant, Wheeler* and *Duro* as "judicially made" federal Indian law, not constitutional rulings. Congress is free to make adjustments in the former category of cases but not the latter, since the Supreme Court is the final arbiter of the Constitution.[57] The Court affirmed that Congress's "plenary power" in Indian affairs, rooted in the Indian Commerce Clause of the Constitution, supported the conclusion that "Congress does possess the constitutional power to lift the restrictions on the tribes' criminal jurisdiction over nonmember Indians as the statute seeks to do."[58] On whether this restored tribal authority represented delegated federal power or inherent tribal power, the Court held that "the Constitution authorizes Congress to permit tribes, as an exercise of their *inherent tribal authority,* to prosecute nonmember Indians." (Italics added)[59] In the process, the Court specifically left open Lara's additional objections to federal prosecution based on the Constitution's due process and equal protection clauses. Consequently, Billy Jo Lara, the nonmember Indian defendant who had already pleaded guilty to an offense in the Spirit Lake Sioux

Tribal Court, could be prosecuted by the federal government without offending the Constitution's double jeopardy limitations since the successive prosecutions were brought by separate and distinct sovereign bodies.

The majority decision provoked a number of other interesting opinions, including one by Justice Kennedy, who concurred in the judgment but disagreed strongly with the breadth of the Court's holding. As he did in his *Duro* opinion, Justice Kennedy expressed serious doubts about whether Congress was authorized under the Constitution to subject United States citizens "within our domestic borders, to a sovereignty outside the basic structure of the Constitution."[60] For Justice Kennedy, the constitutional limitations spring not only from expressly stated guarantees like the equal protection and due process clauses, but from the "constitutional structure" itself. "The political freedom guaranteed to citizens by the federal structure is a liberty both distinct from and every bit as important as those freedoms guaranteed by the Bill of Rights. The individual citizen has an enforceable right to those structural guarantees of liberty, a right which the majority ignores."[61] This argument is reminiscent of Justice Rehnquist's opinion in *Oliphant,* in which the Court discovered limitations on inherent tribal powers emanating from their status as dependent sovereigns. I called these "framework limitations." Justice Kennedy's analysis seems to find similar "framework limitations" on Congress's powers that are rooted in the Constitution. The argument seems to anticipate the possibility that Congress might one day overturn *Oliphant*; if so, Justice Kennedy's "structural limitations" argument will surely weigh heavily in the balance.

Justice Clarence Thomas, however, produced the most interesting opinion of the bunch. Justice Thomas also concurred in the judgment but expressed great frustration with the Court's inability or unwillingness to confront the great contradictions that exist in federal Indian law. Characterizing federal Indian policy as "schizophrenic," Justice Thomas highlighted the tensions inherent in two longstanding but contradictory principles in federal

Indian law: Congress's plenary power in Indian affairs, on the one hand, and inherent tribal sovereignty, on the other. On the former principle, Justice Thomas stated, "The Court utterly fails to find any provision of the Constitution that gives Congress enumerated power to alter tribal sovereignty. The Court cites the Indian Commerce Clause and the treaty power. I cannot agree that the Indian Commerce Clause 'provide[s] Congress with plenary power to legislate in the field of Indian affairs.' At one time, the implausibility of this assertion at least troubled the Court, and I would be willing to revisit the question."[62] On the latter principle relating to tribal sovereignty, Justice Thomas noted, "The sovereign is, by definition, the entity 'in which independent and supreme authority is vested.' It is quite arguably the essence of sovereignty not to exist merely at the whim of an external government."[63] He further noted that the Court's distinctions between tribal authority over "internal matters" and "external matters" (and by extension, members and nonmembers) made sense as a matter of federal common law but were not distinctions rooted in or dictated by the Constitution. In short, Justice Thomas (finally) gave voice to a perennial challenge and frustration in federal Indian law—how and why the construction of the tribe's sovereign authority functions differently in relation to and in comparison with that of the states and federal government. From the constitutional standpoint, Justice Thomas noted that treaty-making, not unilateral statutory rules, was the "one mechanism that the Constitution clearly provides for the Federal Government to interact with sovereigns other than the States."[64] And yet, Congress unilaterally ended treaty-making in 1871, in a statute Justice Thomas characterized as "constitutionally suspect."

The *Lara* opinion reveals a Supreme Court still divided on fundamental elements of federal Indian law. While it is unlikely that the Court will seriously take up Justice Thomas's call to provide a definitive answer on the nature of Congress's power in Indian affairs, it is clear the questions about the nature and scope of inherent tribal sovereignty will come before the Court again. It remains to be seen whether the Court will continue to deploy its implicit divestiture theory without regard to the clear contemporary signals from Congress that support broad expressions of inherent tribal authority. As one federal court noted, "The full extent of implicit divestiture has yet to be determined, resulting in no small amount of uncertainty and confusion as to the scope of tribes' inherent civil authority over non-Indians and leading to frequent litigation of that question in cases such as this one."[65]

GUIDED BY THIS general overview of the legal landscape facing today's legal and political actors working in Indian Country, it is appropriate to return to the four scenarios described in Chapter One that each raised jurisdictional challenges to the authority of tribal governments. Each of these scenarios arose from real controversies that have been litigated in tribal or federal court and required its decision makers to confront and resolve the immediate dispute before it in accordance with the complex system of legal principles and federal policies described above.

LUMMI NATION: *ALVARADO* V. *WARNER-LAMBERT COMPANY* (TRIBAL COURT, 2003)

In *Alvarado* v. *Warner-Lambert Company* (May 2003), the Lummi Tribal Court affirmed its jurisdiction over the nonmember drug manufacturer. The Lummi Tribal Code confers personal jurisdiction over individuals who "enter" the reservation. Since that term was not defined in the code, the court chose to interpret the term narrowly, mindful of the defendant's due process rights. The court ruled that a physical entry into the reservation was required to support personal jurisdiction. The evidence showed that the defendant's agents regularly entered the reservation for face-to-face meetings with Lummi Nation medical personnel to encourage sales of their company's drug products.

The Lummi Tribal Code also provides for subject matter

jurisdiction over all suits involving residents of the Lummi Reservation and other actions where a party's consent to tribal court jurisdiction is apparent or where the events giving rise to the action took place within reservation territory. In applying these provisions, the Lummi Tribal Court examined federal Indian law precedents to test the limits of its jurisdictional power over this particular case. Although all the reservation-based activities with the company's agents took place on reservation trust lands, the court still applied *Montana*'s general rule and its exceptions, based largely on its view that *Nevada* v. *Hicks*'s "strained" analysis had largely eliminated the trust lands/fee lands distinction governing application of *Montana*'s rule. The court noted that under *Montana,* the tribal court "is presumed to lack jurisdiction over non-Indians, subject to two exceptions." The court held that since both exceptions applied in this case, it could properly exercise jurisdiction over the lawsuit. The consensual relations exception was fulfilled on evidence that the drug company agents' regular presence within the reservation led directly to the sale of pharmaceutical products to the Lummi Health Center, which were then used to fill the decedent's prescription. On the "negative effects on tribal self-government" exception, the court first noted that the Lummi Nation had taken control of health services from the federal government under the Tribal Self-Governance Demonstration Project. It then stated:

> Providing adequate health care to its population is a vital role for any government. The court can think of no better example of preserving the health and welfare of the tribe than protecting its borders from the distribution of potentially unsafe drugs to its members. It is a basic tenet, universally accepted, if debated, that a vital mechanism for checking the sale and distribution of unsafe products is to allow private causes of action for injury claims. Certainly providing a forum for individuals to seek compensation should they suffer the effects of unsafe drugs is part of the tribe's self-governance.[66]

It should be noted that the Navajo Nation Supreme Court also issued an opinion in 2003 that upheld tribal jurisdiction in a similar suit involving the same drugs. In *Nelson* v. *Pfizer, Inc.* (2003), the Navajo Supreme Court refused to apply the *Montana* limiting principles, since the activities in question all occurred on tribal trust lands. The court did not hesitate to register its concerns with the *Montana* analysis and made clear its position that it will not readily participate in rule-making that effectively surrenders tribal power:

> The implications of *Montana* for the Navajo Nation's power over its territory are clear. A rule requiring the application of *Montana* to all land restricts judicial authority over non-Indian conduct. We take judicial notice of the fact that trust land and tribally-owned fee land comprise virtually all land within the Navajo Nation. There are many non-Indian actors who impact the Navajo Nation in various and significant ways that may escape the authority of the Navajo Nation if our courts are required to apply the *Montana* exceptions to every civil case involving non-Indians. Judicial resources would be stretched if every case brought against a non-Indian required a detailed analysis of the various consensual relationships or direct effects on the Navajo Nation merely to establish jurisdiction. Further, application of *Montana* to every civil case with a non-Indian defendant undermines the federal policy encouraging the development of tribal courts. . . . Finally, our responsibility to protect the sovereignty of the Navajo Nation counsels that we not surrender authority unnecessarily.[67]

There is no reported decision to indicate whether the defendants appealed the tribal court rulings in either Lummi tribe or the Navajo Nation cases.[68]

NORTHERN CHEYENNE TRIBE: *McDonald v. Means* (UNITED STATES COURT OF APPEALS, NINTH CIRCUIT, 2002)

In this case, Kale Means (a minor), a tribal member, was driving on a tribally maintained reservation road when he collided with McDonald's horse, which had wandered onto the road. McDonald, an enrolled member of the Oglala Sioux tribe, lived on fee lands within the Northern Cheyenne reservation. Means filed suit in tribal court through his mother. Before the tribal court could even rule on jurisdiction, the defendants entered federal court, exercising (some might say exploiting) rights recognized by the Supreme Court in the *National Farmers–Iowa Mutual* line of cases, to challenge tribal jurisdiction. The federal district court found against tribal jurisdiction but a divided panel of the Ninth Circuit Court of Appeals reversed this (the federal courts of appeals typically hear cases in panels of three judges). The court of appeals focused attention on the fact that the accident in question occurred on a Bureau of Indian Affairs road running through the reservation over which the tribe exercised significant responsibilities. This factor was sufficient to distinguish the case from *Strate*, in which the accident occurred on a state highway over which the tribe had substantially relinquished management responsibilities. Moreover, the court interpreted *Hicks*'s holding as limited to its facts, i.e., to suits against state officers engaged in enforcing state law within tribal lands. Given these distinctions, the court held that the *Montana* presumption against tribal authority was not triggered at all, thus preserving the tribal government's authority over the lawsuit. The court took note of the *Duro*-fix legislation and found that "the tribal court in this case is merely exercising civil jurisdiction over a defendant whom it could prosecute criminally."[69] The dissenting judge offered the view that *Hicks* had effectively extended the *Montana* rule throughout Indian Country, including Indian trust lands.

The accident in this lawsuit occurred on May 2, 1998. The decision of the federal court of appeals affirming tribal court jurisdiction was handed down (in amended form) on October 18, 2002—well over four years following the accident. Unfortunately, securing one's day in court is often a lengthy affair in the American legal system, but Ms. Means waited over four years just to find out *which* court would hear her child's case.

NAVAJO NATION: *FORD MOTOR COMPANY* V. *TODECHEENE*
(UNITED STATES COURT OF APPEALS, NINTH CIRCUIT, 2005)

An on-duty tribal police officer was killed when the Ford Expedition patrol car she was driving on a tribally maintained road rolled over, allegedly because of a product defect. The lawsuit began in the Navajo Tribal Court where the court, applying *Montana*, upheld tribal jurisdiction. The Ford Motor Company, exercising rights recognized in the *National Farmers–Iowa Mutual* line of cases, entered federal court to challenge the tribal court's ruling on the jurisdictional issue. A strongly divided federal court of appeals affirmed the federal district court's opinion holding against tribal jurisdiction.[70] This is the same court of appeals, with a different panel of judges, which decided the *McDonald* case discussed above. As in *McDonald*, the tragic events in *Todecheene* occurred on tribal lands. A straightforward application of *McDonald* would mean that the *Montana* rule would not even be triggered. However, a majority of the appeals court judges distinguished *McDonald* as being out of step with the "consistently articulated direction from the Supreme Court that tribal jurisdiction does not automatically track the reservation boundaries" with the result that "tribal jurisdiction is to be limited, rather than expanded."[71] The court noted that the issue of land ownership, which *Hicks* said might be dispositive on the jurisdiction question, helped tilt the *McDonald* court in favor of tribal authority because there, the defendant's horse had actually intruded onto reservation roads, whereas here, there was no comparable trespassory interest.

Applying *Montana*, then, the court's majority found neither exception applicable. The consensual relations exception did not apply since the Todecheenes were not parties to the tribe's contract with Ford and the tribe was not seeking to enforce the forum selection clause in the lease-purchase agreement. In any event, the contract seemed to cover contract disputes, not tort actions. Further, the court rejected the argument that regulation through tort litigation constituted an acceptable means of regulating consensual relations "through taxation, licensing, or *other means*." (Italics added) The negative effects on tribal self-government exception did not apply either, since, however tragic, "There is no indication in the record that the death of this tribal police officer in a rollover accident in any way prevented the Tribe from enacting or being governed by its laws."[72]

The dissenting judge would have adhered to *McDonald* in supporting tribal court jurisdiction. Viewing *Hicks* as limited to its facts, the dissenting judge reiterated that the *Montana-Strate-Atkinson* line of cases all considered the jurisdictional questions in the context of events occurring on nontribal lands. *McDonald,* on the other hand, was "explicitly based on the fundamental principle contained in Supreme Court case law that '[t]ribes maintain considerable authority over the conduct of both tribal members and nonmembers on Indian land, or land held in trust for a tribe by the United States.' "[73] Expressing incredulity at the majority's dismissal of the tribal interests, the dissent countered,

> This is not just a product liability case. It is, instead, a case in which the defendant allegedly designed and manufactured a fatally defective vehicle; the defendant sold that vehicle to the tribe for use by its police officers; and the vehicle rolled over and killed one of the tribe's police officers. Not only is this a case about the safety of the tribe's roads. Not only is this a case about the safety of products sold to tribal members. This is also a case about the ability of a tribe to ensure the safety of its police officers as those officers drive on tribal roads, protecting tribal members and enforcing tribal law. Under the weighing process prescribed in *Hicks,* we must weigh the self-government interest of the tribe in ensuring the safety of its roads and the safety of tribal police officers while driving on those

roads against the interest of the defendant in escaping the tribal court's civil jurisdiction. The majority concludes that the tribe's interest in self-government is greater in a case arising out of an accident involving a stray horse than in a case arising out of the death of a tribal police officer caused by an allegedly defective vehicle.[74]

NAVAJO NATION: *RUSSELL MEANS* v. *NAVAJO NATION* (UNITED STATES COURT OF APPEALS, NINTH CIRCUIT, 2005)

In December 1997 Russell Means allegedly assaulted two Indian men, including a Navajo tribal member, while on the Navajo Reservation. In another life, Means was a founding member of the American Indian Movement, an activist organization from the 1960s and 1970s that advocated reform in Indian affairs and greater recognition of Indian treaty rights. The proceedings in the tribal courts were put on hold or "stayed" while Means challenged the tribe's criminal jurisdiction over him. The federal appeals court confronted the questions expressly reserved by the Supreme Court in *Lara,* i.e., whether a tribal prosecution of a nonmember Indian under the *Duro*-fix legislation violates the equal protection and due process clauses of the federal Constitution.[75]

The court acknowledged that Means's equal protection argument had "real force" but ultimately rejected it. In amending the Indian Civil Rights Act (ICRA) to affirm tribal criminal jurisdiction over "all Indians," Congress imposed the same definition of "Indian" as the one embraced under the federal Major Crimes Act. That definition only encompasses individuals who are Indian by political affiliation (enrolled members or otherwise "*de facto*" tribal members), not all who may be ethnically Indian. Under the teaching of *Morton* v. *Mancari,* that sort of classification is a political, not a racial, one and will be upheld if rationally related to Congress's unique obligations to Indian tribes. The court found Congress's action amending the ICRA passed the rational tie standard since it furthered the tribe's governmental interests in criminal law enforcement.

Means's twofold due process argument was similarly rejected. The court rejected as premature Means's "as applied" argument (where a person claims that rights were actually violated in the course of legal proceedings), since criminal proceedings in Navajo tribal courts were stayed pending resolution of the jurisdictional battles. The court also rejected Means's "facial" challenge (where a person claims that a law even before it is applied contains flaws of constitutional dimension). The ICRA and the Navajo Bill of Rights provided Mr. Means with all the constitutional protections he would otherwise receive "despite being tried by a sovereign not bound by the Constitution." The Navajo Bill of Rights, for example, provides for appointed counsel.

THESE FOUR CASE scenarios provide a glimpse of tribal sovereignty operating on the ground today. They reveal the complexity, the confusion and the incoherence that plague the field of federal Indian law and bring into high relief the serious challenges confronting today's Indian Country actors—lawyers, judges, tribal leaders, private citizens, corporations and state and federal government employees—who work earnestly to resolve contested claims about tribal governmental power. The impulse of many tribal advocates is to recall the foundational principles from Chief Justice John Marshall's era when the Court clearly recognized full territorial sovereignty as the primordial right of Indian tribes memorialized in sacred treaties, constrained only by those few "framework limitations" that preserved the overarching dominance of the national power. Unfortunately, the legal landscape from Marshall's era to the present is scarred with the legacy of broken treaty promises and shifting federal policies that were often fueled by beliefs or convictions that Indians were inherently inferior to whites or were soon to pass away from the national scene altogether.

The modern era of self-determination represents the first time since the early nineteenth century that Indian tribes have enjoyed sustained support and cooperation from the Congress and the executive branch to engage in meaningful government-to-government relations. By "meaningful," I mean that government relations typically proceed on terms that take seriously the concerns, interests and values of Indian tribes. In earlier periods, the federal government's policies on Indian affairs were largely dictated by federal interests and values, which presumed to know what was in the Indians' best interests. The monkey wrench in the modern tribal-federal relationship is the Supreme Court and its recent batch of Indian law cases that show little tolerance for anything but the most limited expression of tribal sovereignty. The Court's distaste for a more robust "John Marshall version" of tribal sovereignty stems from its concern for the rights of nonmember citizens in Indian Country and the Court's growing sympathy for state claims to have unfettered control within state boundaries. On occasion, the Court's Indian law cases also revive the legacy of colonialism and its associated racism. The *Montana* decision best reveals this tendency in embracing the "dying race" thesis to support a diminished form of tribal sovereignty, one that will rarely reach non-Indians living on fee lands in Indian Country. In choosing to give effect to Congress's repudiated allotment policies, the Court gave new life to outmoded policies that were designed to eliminate all traces of tribalism, all for the purpose of keeping non-Indians safely beyond the reach of tribal law. Here's how the Court explained this result in its *Montana* opinion:

> There is simply no suggestion in the legislative history that Congress intended that the non-Indians who would settle upon alienated allotted lands would be subject to tribal regulatory authority. Indeed, throughout the congressional debates, allotment of Indian land was consistently equated with the dissolution of tribal affairs and jurisdiction. It defies common sense to suppose that Congress would intend that non-Indians purchasing allotted lands would become subject to tribal jurisdiction when an avowed purpose of the allotment policy was the ultimate

destruction of tribal government. And it is hardly likely that Congress could have imagined that the purpose of peaceful assimilation could be advanced if feeholders could be excluded from fishing or hunting on their acquired property.

The policy of allotment and sale of surplus reservation land was, of course, repudiated in 1934 by the Indian Reorganization Act. But what is relevant in this case is the effect of the land alienation occasioned by that policy on Indian treaty rights tied to Indian use and occupation of reservation land.[76]

Montana exposes the broader tensions and contradictions that pervade federal Indian law. No legal precedent required the Court to give effect to long-abandoned federal policies, and yet that is precisely what *Montana*'s rule produces today. The scope of inherent tribal sovereignty is now vulnerable to further narrowing by the courts because *Montana* embraced the "dying race" thesis for Indian people, and effectively advanced the interests and expectations of non-Indians at the expense of Indian tribes and their rights to self-government. Indian tribes and their advocates were not the only ones who expressed dismay over the Court's approach in *Montana*. A federal appeals court offered this stinging critique of the high court's opinion only one year after *Montana* was handed down:

It may well be that non-Indians who acquired land inside the reservation never expected to be subjected to regulation by the Indians. But likewise the Indians themselves never expected . . . that reservation land opened without their consent to non-Indians would be removed from their jurisdiction. The Indians' expectations rest on the explicit guarantees of a treaty signed by the President and Secretary of State and ratified by the Senate. The non-Indians' expectations rest not on explicit statutory language, but on what is presumed to have been the intent underlying the allotment acts—a policy of destroying tribal government to assimilate the Indians into American society. It is difficult to see why there should be an overriding federal interest in vindicating only the latter expectations—especially when the anti-tribal policy on which they rest was repudiated over fifty years ago.[77]

In light of these developments, it may be fair to ask how Indian tribes managed to persist as distinct cultural groups and as distinct political bodies with powers of self-government. The answers are complicated and vary with the different historical experiences of tribes across the landscape of Indian Country. There are, however, common characteristics in the strategies of resistance employed by Indian people. First, Indians did not and do not live their lives in accordance with some unwritten statute of limitations that sets an end point to "being Indian." Even at the height of the federal government's assimilation policies, the historical record is replete with strategies of adaptation that permitted the expression of traditional cultural values, albeit in muted or subtle forms. In short, despite years of imposed policies designed to "kill the Indian, save the man," Indian people did not stop being Indian. The Acoma Pueblo poet Simon Ortiz expressed it more eloquently in saying that "because of the insistence to keep telling and creating stories, Indian life continues, and it is this resistance against loss that has made that life possible."[78]

Second, tribal leaders actively and persistently (if not always successfully) resisted threats to their political and territorial rights by regularly engaging with the American political and legal systems. These legal forms of resistance served as a historical looking glass to an American democratic system whose commitment to the rule of law was selective at best. The renaissance of Indian tribes as governments in the modern era is thus a story about the tenacity of Indian people to preserve their distinctive cultures and their persistence in seeking to honor the rule of law.

Tribal efforts to protect the integrity of their governmental status has necessarily marched arm in arm with efforts to preserve their ancestral homelands, the legally protected spaces within which they exercise their governmental authority. Tribal ancestral homelands historically have served as the cultural and political spaces within which tribalism is sustained and nurtured. Threats to the integrity of Indian tribal homelands, like threats to tribal sovereign authority, date back to this nation's founding and reveal the same patterns of indigenous cultural tenacity and persistence in trying to secure the promises contained in ancient treaties and other legal agreements. The legal conflicts that emerged in the nineteenth and early twentieth centuries involving Indian tribes were largely related to struggles over territory and the natural resources contained therein. Many of those struggles continue today, often in the form of conflicts over governmental control of certain territories or resources. Given these inextricable connections between tribal rights to self-government and preservation of tribal ancestral homelands, it is appropriate that we now consider in more detail how federal law has responded to tribal efforts to preserve, protect and enhance tribal ancestral homelands. Part Two considers these efforts in the context of efforts to define and preserve homeland boundaries, to safeguard the natural resources contained within those boundaries and to revitalize the economic and development capacity of these tribally controlled areas.

PART TWO

TRIBAL HOMELANDS

4

IDENTIFYING THE CONTOURS
OF INDIAN COUNTRY

THE COVER OF *Yankee* magazine's September 1998 issue featured a lovely photo of New England's fabled fall foliage to mark the natural rhythms of nature's changing seasons. The headline on that cover also signaled another turnabout in the region, this one relating to Indian affairs. The headline read, "Indian Landgrab in Connecticut?" and was connected to a feature story entitled "This Land is Whose Land? A territorial dispute between Indians and 'settlers' in Connecticut." The story focused on several non-Indian residents of towns neighboring the lands of the Mashantucket Pequot tribe, who had organized to resist the tribe's efforts to expand its reservation land base through an aggressive "annexation" plan.

Like other northeastern tribes in the 1970s, the Pequots sought to reclaim a portion of their former territories by arguing that earlier transactions for those lands lacked the approval of the federal government as required by a 1790 federal law.[1] In the Pequots' case, their land claims were ultimately resolved through an act of Congress in 1983 that accorded the tribe federal recognition and helped secure a land base of about 1,250 acres. That is a far cry from the days when the Pequot tribe numbered over eight thousand members and occupied an area of about 250 square miles in south-eastern Connecticut, making them one of the most dominant military, economic and political forces in the region during the first encounters with Europeans.[2] The more recent encounter noted in the *Yankee* article focused on the tribe's efforts to expand its reservation land base beyond the terms of the settlement act. The driving force underlying this conflict was the tribe's burgeoning casino operation at Foxwoods and the claimed negative impact on the surrounding towns. Framing the struggle as a modern-day David and Goliath mismatch, the article noted, "The residents who oppose annexation don't see reverence for ancestral streams and woods in the Pequots' quest for a bigger reservation. They see simple greed, a rich tribe using a flawed federal policy to get richer."[3] In other words, the dispute was less about land than it was about concern over the Pequots' resurgence as an economic and political force in the region. This echoes what the legal scholar Milner S. Ball observed years ago regarding disputes over territory: "Territoriality is a way of organizing and talking about power. The problem is one of power, not space. There is plenty of the latter."[4] On the subject of power, the antiannexation residents found receptive political power brokers, including U.S. Senator Joseph Lieberman (Independent, Connecticut), who denounced tribal land acquisition by the Pequots as "welfare for the rich," and advocated legislation to eliminate that option among wealthy tribes. "Tribes like the Pequots," said Lieberman, "have reached the point where land annexation is not about preserving a culture or achieving self-sufficiency. It is about expansion of an already successful business in a way that harms their neighbors."[5]

Disputes over land dominated the course of United States–Indian relations in the early years of this nation, especially in treaty-making. The federal law noted above, the 1790 Non-Intercourse Act (more formally, the Trade and Intercourse Act of 1790), sought to achieve some of the same objectives advanced by the British Crown in its Proclamation of 1763. Both acts sought to centralize the process of Indian land transactions by insisting on Crown (and later, congressional) approval to legitimize such deals as a means of minimizing frontier conflicts that were both costly and disruptive to the colonial project. The United States' land acquisition efforts, launched under the policy banner of "expansion with honor," were designed to accommodate a burgeoning non-Indian population and to create territorial "buffers" between non-Indian settlements and Indian communities. The rationale for acquiring Indian lands through purchase rather than force was best expressed by George Washington:

> I repeat it, again, and I am clear in my opinion, that policy and economy point very strongly to the expediency of being upon good terms with the Indians, and the propriety of purchasing their Lands in preference to attempting to drive them by force of arms out of their Country; which as we have already experienced is like driving the Wild Beasts of the Forest which will return as soon as the pursuit is at an end and fall perhaps on those that are left there; when the gradual extension of our settlements will as certainly cause the Savage as the Wolf to retire; both being beasts of prey tho' they differ in shape.[6]

It is important to note that the European colonial powers and, later, the United States government engaged in treaty-making with the Indian tribes for decades before any definitive ruling emerged from the Supreme Court about the precise nature of the tribe's legal interests in property. Washington's statement, however, reflects the sentiments prevailing among the founding leaders that Indian tribes, at that time a force to be reckoned with, would inevitably fall under the sway of civilization. The "dying race" thesis was a factor in these early territorial disputes with Indian tribes and suggested that tribal connections to land, whatever their precise legal nature, represented only a temporary impediment to the national expansion project. When the Supreme Court finally did rule on the nature of tribal property interests in 1823, it coupled the "Indians as savage" rhetoric with heavy doses of Christian ideology to make straight the path of conquest and expansion in the New

World. Over time, those legal policies and ideology contributed to the radical breakup of Indian ancestral homelands. Today, the Indian land base consists of about 55.7 million acres of trust lands—an area slightly larger than the state of Utah—managed through the federal Bureau of Indian Affairs,[7] and another 45 million acres of land held by Native Alaskan state-chartered corporations under the terms of the 1971 Alaska Native Claims Settlement Act.[8] For jurisdictional purposes (i.e., clarifying the primacy of tribal, federal or state sovereign authority in a particular controversy), "Indian Country" includes all lands that are located within an Indian tribe's reservation (including lands owned in fee simple by non-Indians), all allotted lands still owned by Indians and held in trust for them by the United States or subject to restrictions on alienation, and a category of lands called "dependent Indian communities," which originally embraced only Pueblo lands but now include any lands set aside for Indians by the federal government and managed under federal superintendence.[9] The federal role in creating and sustaining these Indian Country lands generally means that tribes have recognized property interests that may, in certain circumstances, have constitutional protection against government takings. Land claims lawsuits like that of the Pequots, along with federal laws dating from the 1930s Indian Reorganization era, have helped a number of tribes re-establish and even enhance the size of their ancestral homelands.

This latest development, expansion of the tribal land base, stands in sharp contrast to the predominant historical experience in Indian Country where federal policy worked to eliminate or diminish the tribal land base or effect an exchange of tribal lands (often forcibly) for lands further removed from white settlements. In other words, the history of diminished Indian rights to their ancestral homelands worked in parallel with the history of diminished inherent tribal sovereign powers. That is why stories of tribal renaissance create such a stir in the broader society. The resurgence of Indian tribes exercising meaningful sovereign powers within their own homelands confounds the expectations of the non-Indian society. This strikes at the heart of stories like the one in *Yankee* magazine that involve tribes long thought to be extinct. A sidebar to the article, entitled "Out of the Ashes . . . The Rebirth of the Pequots," highlights the conflict known as the Pequot War of 1637. After leading the raid on Pequot villages and ordering the massacre of hundreds of Pequot men, women and children, English captain John Mason proclaimed that he had vindicated God's judgment, quoting the Psalms: "Thus, were the stout-hearted spoiled, having slept their last sleep, and none of their men could find their hands. Thus did the Lord judge among the heathen, filling the place with dead bodies."[10] The *Yankee* sidebar concludes, "Thus Foxwoods arose from the ashes of a tribe that Captain Mason was certain that Providence had snuffed out."[11]

The *Yankee* article captures many of the historical elements that characterize the development of law in Indian lands disputes. In invoking familiar biblical imagery, the article inadvertently recalls the role that Christianity played in early Court decisions that paved the way for dispossessing Indian tribes of the vast majority of their ancestral homelands. Further, in calling attention to proposed national legislation that would eliminate the rights of tribes "like the Pequots" to enlarge their land base, the article underscores the fragility and impermanence of tribal land rights in federal law. Finally, in rebuking the Pequots for turning their backs on their traditional "reverence for ancestral streams and woods," the article treats the Pequots' cultural evolution and adaptation as an abandonment of traditional values, a development that implicitly undermines the integrity of the tribe's claim to territory and even their Indian identity. Each of these elements informs our understanding of territorial disputes involving Indian tribes and merits closer scrutiny.

CHRISTIANITY, LAW AND TRIBAL LAND RIGHTS

The first major Supreme Court decision involving questions of tribal land rights did not consider traditional Indian perspectives of land as a life-giving and life-sustaining force or address how those perspectives could be squared with the prevailing European view of land as a resource or a commodity and a source for wealth generation. In fact, the first Supreme Court decision on Indian land rights did not even involve Indians as parties to the lawsuit. The Court's landmark decision in *Johnson* v. *McIntosh* (1823)[12] involved only non-Indian parties who apparently colluded in bringing this "controversy" before the Court in hopes of confirming the title of aggressive land speculators who were operating in Indian Country without federal approval.[13] The case required a ruling on the nature of Indian property interests to determine which of the non-Indian parties held superior title to the lands in dispute. The side represented by Johnson claimed that their "ancestors in title" had acquired title directly from the Indian tribes who originally occupied the lands, the Illinois and Piankeshaw nations, in transactions dating back to 1773 and 1775. The side represented by McIntosh claimed their title through a grant from the U.S. government, which had acquired the same lands through a treaty with the tribes after defeating them in the Battle of Fallen Timbers (1794).

In an opinion written by Chief Justice John Marshall, the Court relied on the European doctrine of discovery to hold that the United States, as successor to England's sovereignty, acquired the former "discovering" nation's "absolute ultimate title" in the "discovered lands" subject only to an Indian title of occupancy. The discovery doctrine was a rule developed and observed by the Christian colonizing powers of Europe to help manage their collective ambitions to empire around the world. The doctrine created a right of "first dibs" in favor of the discovering nation to acquire the soil—through purchase or conquest—from the native inhabitants. As described by Chief Justice Marshall, "Discovery gave title to the government by whose subjects, or by whose authority, it was made, against all other European governments, which title might be consummated by possession."[14] In short, the doctrine of discovery made Indian tribes guests in their own ancestral homelands, whose invitation could be revoked unilaterally by the new hosts. But until the sovereign revoked that invitation, the Indians' right of occupancy was to be honored and protected in law. Marshall recognized an Indian right of occupancy that fell somewhere in between the opposing positions urged by the parties on the nature of the Indians' rights to land. One party (the Johnson side) maintained that Indian tribes—before European colonization—"held the country in absolute sovereignty, as independent nations, both as to the right of jurisdiction and sovereignty, and the right of soil,"[15] while the other party (the McIntosh side) argued that Indian tribes were in a "state of nature, and have never been admitted into the general society of nations."[16] Marshall's decision imbued the tribes with a sufficient measure of legal stake in their lands to support and justify their alienation through treaties with European nations and later with the United States government.

Only Christian colonizers in their encounters with non-Christian peoples could invoke the discovery doctrine. An indigenous seafaring tribe, by contrast, could not plant a flag in the British Isles or on the beaches of Normandy and make comparable claims to England or France under the doctrine. Chief Justice Marshall noted that as "early as the year 1496, [England's] monarch granted a commission to the Cabots, to discover countries then unknown to *Christian people*, and to take possession of them in the name of the king of England" (emphasis in original).[17] Discovery under these terms gave Christian colonizers the "right to take possession, notwithstanding the occupancy of the natives, who were heathens, and, at the same time, admitting the prior title of any Christian people who may have made a previous discovery."[18] The Indians' "character and religion . . . afforded an apology for considering them as a people over whom the superior genius of Europe might claim an ascendency. The potentates of the old world found no difficulty in convincing themselves that they made ample compensation to the inhabitants of the new, by bestowing on them civilization and Christianity, in exchange for unlimited independence."[19] Noting "the tribes of Indians inhabiting this country were fierce savages, whose occupation was war," the Court sounded the theme of the "dying race" thesis when it stated, "Frequent and bloody wars, in which the whites were not always the aggressors, unavoidably ensued. European policy, numbers, and skill, prevailed. As the white population advanced, that of the Indians necessarily receded. The country in the immediate neighbourhood of agriculturists became unfit for them. The game fled into thicker and more unbroken forests, and the Indians followed."[20]

Years later, the *Johnson* case figured prominently in *Tee-Hit-Ton* v. *United States* (1955), in which the Court (for the first time) distinguished Indian title from "recognized" title and concluded that since the former was not "property" under the Constitution, Congress could extinguish the Indian title without making just compensation to the tribes.[21] This holding effectively created a different class of property rights for certain Indian land claims to avoid triggering the legal obligation imposed on government by the Constitution's Fifth Amendment, which states, in pertinent part: "Nor shall private property be taken for public use, without just compensation."

The Indian title was essentially worthless when the United States (as the sovereign succeeding the discovering European nations) acted to extinguish it. There is nothing in the *Johnson* case or in any other Supreme Court precedent that suggests this astonishing conclusion. Only nine months after the Court's landmark decision in *Brown* v. *Board of Education*,[22] a majority of the justices in *Tee-Hit-Ton* reverted to *Johnson*'s "Indians as savages" rhetoric in an attempt to provide some support for the "no just compensation" rule: "The Tee-Hit-Tons were in a hunting and fishing stage of civilization, with shelters fitted to their environment, and claims to rights to use identified territory for these activities as well as the gathering of wild products of the earth. We think this evidence introduced by both sides confirms the Court of Claims' conclusion that the petitioners' use of its lands was like the use of the nomadic tribes of the United States Indians."[23] The Court summed up the history of Indian land disputes in this way: "Every American schoolboy knows that the savage tribes of this continent were deprived of their ancestral ranges by force and that, even when the

Indians ceded millions of acres by treaty in return for blankets, food and trinkets, it was not a sale but the conquerors' will that deprived them of their land."[24] In addition to these dubious rationales, the Court hinted that financial considerations also influenced its decision against the tribe. A contrary ruling on the tribe's property interest would have triggered an award of interest on top of money damages for the value of the property taken. The Court acknowledged that then-existing Indian land claims against the United States with interest could exceed $9 billion.[25]

The noted scholar of federal Indian law Robert A. Williams, Jr., has called *Johnson* v. *McIntosh* "the most important Indian rights opinion ever issued by any court of law in the United States."[26] The decision rationalized the dispossession of a continent from its original owners by creating a legal framework that, at its core, assumed the racial inferiority of Indian people. Professor Williams states, "No one presently sitting as a justice on the Supreme Court seems to have the least problem with *Johnson*'s legalized presumption of Indian racial inferiority, its incorporation into U.S. law of a European colonial-era legal doctrine of conquest and colonization, its use of an antiquated racist judicial language of Indian savagery to define Indian rights, or its declaration that the justices can unfortunately do nothing about the resulting white racial dictatorship imposed upon tribes."[27] *Johnson*'s right of occupancy theory has influenced the development of indigenous land rights in other commonwealth nations, such as Australia,[28] New Zealand,[29] and Canada.[30]

As recently as 2005, the Supreme Court cited *Johnson*'s discovery doctrine without revealing a trace of discomfort with its underlying rationale. In that case, *City of Sherrill, New York* v. *Oneida Indian Nation of New York* (2005), the Court noted, "Under the 'doctrine of discovery,' fee title to the lands occupied by Indians when the colonists arrived became vested in the sovereign—first the discovering European nation and later the original States and the United States."[31] *Johnson*'s status as a cornerstone precedent in United States property law essentially allows modern courts to adopt a sanitized version of the discovery doctrine without having to re-state its assumptions about Indian racial inferiority and non-Christian standing.

In the *Sherrill* case, the Oneida Indian Nation argued that its purchase in the late 1990s of former reservation lands now included within the City of Sherrill made those lands exempt from the city's property taxes. In rejecting the tribe's argument that it could unilat-erally "revive its ancient sovereignty" over these parcels, the Court highlighted the tribe's long delay in seeking relief from the courts (these lands had last been occupied by tribal members in 1805), the disruptive effect on local governance that a shift in sovereign au-thority would cause and the "justifiable expectations" of non-Indians who were accustomed to state regulatory authority.[32] The Court seemed concerned that the Oneidas (who, like the Pequots, have a thriving casino operation and hence growing economic clout) were unfairly capitalizing on the increased local property values generated by generations of non-Indian settlers: "Moreover, the properties here involved have greatly increased in value since the Oneidas sold them 200 years ago. Notably, it was not until lately that the Oneidas sought to regain ancient sovereignty over land *converted from wilderness* to become part of cities like Sherrill" (em-phasis added).[33] The Court noted that the tribe could have accom-plished its objective of enlarging its land base through a congressionally authored process founded in the 1934 Indian Reor-ganization Act.[34] The process essentially authorizes the secretary of the interior, at the tribe's request, to take newly acquired lands into trust. The conversion into trust lands is the "magical act" that trans-forms the lands into Indian Country and effectively places the lands outside the reach of state control, including state taxing power. Having survived a number of recent constitutional challenges,[35] the process requires the secretary to weigh a number of factors, includ-ing the tribe's need for more lands and the impact on state and local governments, before taking lands into trust. No unilateral tribal ac-tion could otherwise serve to displace state authority. In essence, the *Sherrill* Court teaches that only the restorative legal magic of one legal fiction—the federal "lands into trust" process—can counter the destructive magic of another legal fiction, the loss of tribal lands through "discovery."

Fragility of Tribal Land Rights

The treaties' agreements and statutes which the federal government issued in the past generally created "recognized" property interests in the lands, and were often accompanied by federal promises that tribes would hold the lands permanently and exclusively. The allotment policies of the late nineteenth century wreaked havoc on the territorial integrity of tribal homelands, with Indian land holdings falling from about 138 million acres in 1887 to about 48 million acres in 1934, the year Congress ended the allotment system.[36] Tribes faced immense pressure from the federal government during this period to cede lands to accommodate white settlers moving into territories promised to Indian tribes. In those moments, tribal leaders pulled out the treaties that memorialized the terms by which further land cessions could be made. Tribal insistence on playing by the treaty rules frustrated federal lawmakers who were intent on opening the West to white settlers to hasten the arrival of civilization and Christianity at the tribal doorstep. Since 1896, for example, the federal government had campaigned aggressively to acquire additional lands from the Crow Indians, who withheld their treaty-required consent until the government complied with their demands to be paid market rates. One "apoplectic Congressman," according to historian Frederick Hoxie, demanded to know how the Indian could "have more than a possession of title simply by making moccasin tracks over it with his bow and arrow."[37] Other tribes joined with the Crow tribe in withholding their consent to further land cessions, at least until the Supreme Court opened the floodgates in 1903 with its decision in *Lone Wolf* v. *Hitchcock*.[38] In holding that Congress had the power unilaterally to break or "abrogate" its treaty promises with Indian tribes, the Court removed tribal consent as a factor in federal efforts to acquire more Indian lands. Beginning with the Rosebud

Sioux Act in 1904, Congress quickly enacted other laws opening up the lands of other tribes in Montana, Utah and Wyoming.[39] As Professor Hoxie notes, however, "The methods used to effect those openings revealed that the process at work was not [Senator Dawes's] original scheme. The Rosebud bill had established a new pattern for allotment and staked out a new approach to Indian land policy. The initiative for dividing each reservation into homesteads had come from Congress and had not been delayed by negotiations."[40]

As the legal precedent unleashing this federal power, *Lone Wolf* merits a closer look.[41] Three tribes, the Kiowa, Comanche and Apache, challenged the constitutionality of a congressional law that purported to embody the terms of an "agreement" between the tribes and the federal government on the allotment of their tribal lands. The tribes maintained that the agreement was invalid as it was obtained by fraud and lacked the requisite number of signatures by consenting tribal members as required by an earlier treaty, all in violation of the tribes' property rights under the Constitution's Fifth Amendment. In a remarkably brief opinion, the Court rejected the tribes' claims by recognizing a near-absolute federal power in Indian affairs that was essentially free of judicial review, tempered only by those aspects of the trust relationship that reflected "considerations of justice as would control a Christian people in their treatment of an ignorant and dependent race."[42] Upholding the tribes' insistence on consent-based transactions would effectively put a legal straitjacket on Congress in its "care and protection of the Indians," and would deprive Congress "in a possible emergency, when the necessity might be urgent for a partition and disposal of the tribal lands, of all power to act, if the assent of the Indians could not be obtained."[43] The Court nowhere described the "emergency" or "necessity" that existed to justify Congress's actions in this case but it offered a hint in the following passage: "As with treaties made with foreign nations (*Chinese Exclusion Case*, 130 U.S. 581), the legislative power might pass laws in conflict with treaties made with the Indians."[44] The hint is the curious parenthetical reference to a case, *Chae Chan Ping* v. *United States* (1888), that upheld Congress's authority unilaterally to break its treaty commitments with China on immigration policy. The Court in the *Ping* case offered a transparent description of the reasons underlying Congress's abrupt change in Chinese immigration policy:

> The differences of race added greatly to the difficulties of the situation. . . . [The Chinese] remained strangers in the land, residing apart by themselves, and adhering to the customs and usages of their own country. It seems impossible for them to assimilate with our people or to make any change in their habits or modes of living. As they grew in numbers each year the people of the coast saw, or believed they saw, in the facility of immigration, and in the crowded millions of China, where the population presses upon the means of subsistence, great danger that at no distant day that portion of our country would be overrun by them unless prompt action was taken to restrict their immigration. The people there accordingly petitioned earnestly for protective legislation.[45]

This pattern of immigration was in stark contrast to that of European immigration, or such was the observation of a congressional supporter of the Chinese exclusion laws: "No voice is raised against the immigration from across the Atlantic because we feel ourselves akin to the people who thus come to our shores. They are the offspring of the nations from which the founders of the Republic, its defenders, and heroes sprang. They are not only of our race, but allied in moral and religious sentiments, in the degree of culture attained. . . . By contrast, [t]he Chinaman is neither socially, nor politically fit to assimilate with us."[46]

Lone Wolf's parenthetical reference to the *Ping* case suggests that Indian resistance to federal allotment policies represented the same sort of cultural, social and political threat to American society as that posed by Chinese immigration. Beyond legal challenges like *Lone Wolf*, organizations like the Four Mothers' Society in the Indian Territory rose up to challenge the allotment policies. The government labeled opponents of allotment as "irreconcilables" and subjected them to arrest, incarceration and forced apportionment of land under the allotment acts.[47] The resistance of Indian people to forced assimilation, coupled with unprecedented waves of immigrants from southern and eastern Europe between 1880 and 1920, presented increasingly pressing challenges to the assumed cultural superiority of America's "founder" Anglo-Saxon race.[48] The Court's language in both *Lone Wolf* and *Ping* reinforced this assumed cultural superiority in condoning the radical domestic land policies against Indians and the immigration policies against Chinese nationals in order to preserve the country as an "Anglo-Saxon polity."[49]

Beyond advancing the rule that Congress has power unilaterally to break Indian treaties, the *Lone Wolf* Court also suggested that the allotment acts actually did not deprive the tribes of any recognized property interests. Congress had effected "a mere change in the form of investment of Indian tribal property, the property of those who, as we have held, were in substantial effect the wards of the government."[50] This language found its way into a modern Supreme Court decision, *United States* v. *Sioux Nation of Indians* (1980)[51] in which the Court created a unique test applicable only to Indian tribes to determine whether they are entitled to just compensation when Congress alters their land holdings. As noted earlier, the government may, consistent with the Constitution's Fifth Amendment, take private property for public use so long as it makes just compensation to the owner (usually at the fair market value of the property plus interest from the time of the "taking"). This is typically known as the governmental power of eminent domain. In the Indian context, however, a court must first determine if Congress acted under its eminent domain powers or under its trustee powers before determining whether just compensation must be paid to tribes. The "test" approved in *Sioux Nation* is the following: "Where Congress makes a good faith effort to give the Indians the full value of the land and thus merely transmutes the property from land to money, there is no taking."[52] The Sioux Nation ultimately succeeded in their century-long lawsuit to establish the wrongful taking of their lands, including the sacred *Paha Sapa* or Black Hills, but, to date, have not claimed the money judgment confirmed by the Supreme Court in *Sioux Nation*.[53] That money judgment with accrued interest is well over $500 million and sits in the United States Treasury because the Sioux maintain that the action all along has been to recover their ancestral lands. This position reveals another dramatic contrast between Indian and Western views of land and property rights. From the Indian perspective, the relationship with their ancestral lands operates in the form of a sacred covenant between the community and the land, in which Indian people regularly minister to the land as stewards and the land reciprocates by supporting, nurturing and teaching the community to live in proper balance with its surroundings. The Kiowa writer N. Scott Momaday expressed similar sentiments when he challenged Western society, and American society in particular, to embrace a "moral comprehension" of the earth and air embodied within the principles of a land ethic. The alternative "is that we shall not live at all."[54] This is in stark contrast to the Western view of land, expressed in the *Lone Wolf* and *Sioux Nation* cases, which sees land as a fungible commodity, a resource that serves as a foundation for the creation of personal wealth. The *Sherrill* opinion (2005) echoed this view when the Court spoke disparagingly about the Oneidas' efforts to reclaim sovereignty over their former lands that had long since been "converted from *wilderness*" by the more productive non-Indian citizens of New York.

Lone Wolf's rule on treaty abrogation is still the law of the land and functions as an ever-present reminder of the precarious nature of Indian land tenure. Additionally, the allotment policy itself—condoned in *Lone Wolf*—continues to reveal the fragility of Indian land rights. The allotment policy was the key plank in the government's assimilation efforts of the late nineteenth and early twentieth centuries designed to bring an end to the distinct cultural and political existence of Indian tribes. These policies

were repudiated in 1934 with passage of the Indian Reorganization Act, but their aftershocks continue to be felt in modern-era
clashes over jurisdiction in lands that were opened up to non-
Indian settlers. The Supreme Court has addressed these conflicts
in a series of cases by trying to divine Congress's plan for how the
executive branch should carry out the allotment policy in particular reservation communities. The key jurisdictional consideration
has been whether Congress intended to preserve or to diminish the
original reservation boundaries when it opened Indian lands to
non-Indian settlers. A finding of "diminishment" means that those
lands may no longer qualify as "Indian Country" lands and are
consequently out of tribal political control.

One of the more problematic "diminishment" cases from the
modern Court is *South Dakota* v. *Yankton Sioux Tribe* (1998).[55]
The jurisdictional conflict stemmed from a decision by several
counties to locate a solid waste facility on lands the tribe considered
part of its reservation. A finding that the lands were still within
"Indian Country" would mean that the solid waste facility would
remain subject to federal environmental standards and would entail (among other things) the installation of a costly synthetic com-
posite liner to help prevent leakage into tribal water aquifers.[56] A
contrary finding against "Indian Country" would mean that the
state would exercise primary authority over the lands and the construction of the facility.

The tribe maintained that their 1892 agreement with the federal government (confirmed in an 1894 statute) to cede surplus Indian lands expressly preserved all their rights under an earlier
treaty. The agreement's so-called "savings clause" provided that
nothing in the agreement "shall be construed to abrogate the treaty
[of 1858]" and that "all provisions of the said treaty . . . shall be in
full force and effect, the same as though this agreement had not
been made."[57] The tribe argued that this language served to confirm the reservation boundaries as memorialized in the 1858 treaty.
The United States—the other party to the treaty and the subsequent agreement—joined in the lawsuit on behalf of the tribe to

confirm and support the tribe's interpretation of the agreement's terms. The Court rejected the tribal/federal governments' arguments finding that such a "literal construction" of the savings clause would "impugn the entire sale" made in 1892. The Court pointed to other historical materials that suggested the savings clause was only designed to ensure the continuation of annuities promised in the earlier treaty but that otherwise Congress clearly intended to diminish the physical size of the reservation in the subsequent agreement. According to the Court, this finding was supported by other contemporary developments, including the rather dramatic alteration of the demographic makeup in the area, with the Yankton Sioux population declining quickly and replaced by a surge of non-Indian settlers. The Court explicitly recognized the resulting tension in giving effect to a long-repudiated federal policy but felt powerless to alter the course or effects of that history:

> The allotment era has long since ended, and its guiding philosophy has been repudiated. Tribal communities struggled but endured, preserved their cultural roots, and remained, for the most part, near their historic lands. But despite the present-day understanding of a "government-to-government relationship between the United States and each Indian tribe," we must give effect to Congress' intent in passing the 1894 Act. Here, we believe that Congress spoke clearly, and although "[s]ome might wish [it] had spoken differently . . . we cannot remake history."[58]

The Court offered no justification for why it "must give effect" to the tribal-assimilation-minded Congress of 1894 instead of the tribal-sovereignty-minded Congress of 1934. In 1989, Associate Justice Harry Blackmun challenged the Court on precisely this point. In a case challenging the limits of tribal authority to zone lands within the reservation, Justice Blackmun reminded his fellow justices that the allotment policies had long been repudiated and that in considering the question of tribal zoning authority, "This Court should direct its attention not to the intent of the Congress that passed the Dawes [Allotment] Act, but rather to the intent of the Congress that repudiated the Dawes Act, and established the Indian policies to which we are heir. This 1934 Congress, as definitively interpreted by the Executive Branch at the time, intended that tribal civil jurisdiction extend over 'all of the lands of the reservation, whether owned by the tribe, by members thereof, or by outsiders.'"[59]

The supreme irony is that the Court's decision in cases like *Yankton Sioux* makes both the tribes and Congress prisoners of an imposed history and deprives the Congress of power and flexibility to act in light of changed circumstances in Indian Country—the very flexibility the Court deemed so vital in *Lone Wolf*. That imposed history is again dominated by reference to and perpetuation of the "dying race" thesis, something the Court explicitly adopts in the early passages of the *Yankton Sioux* case: "Within a generation or two, it was thought, the tribes would dissolve, their reservations would disappear, and individual Indians would be absorbed into the larger community of white settlers. With respect to the Yankton Reservation in particular, some Members of Congress speculated that 'close contact with the frugal, moral, and industrious people who will settle [on the reservation would] stimulate individual effort and make [the tribe's] progress much more rapid than heretofore.'"[60]

The Image of "Indians" in Indian Land Rights

The language of the *Lone Wolf* decision reflected the prevailing national sentiments about Indian people as an ignorant race, dependent upon the beneficence and guidance of a superior civilization to achieve even the semblance of a progressive society. It also reflected the prevailing expectation that the Indians' cultural distinctiveness would vanish under the weight and influence of civilized white society. Ironically, there was keen interest among white policymakers during this same period to present publicly or otherwise capture the last vestiges of this cultural distinctiveness before all traces of it disappeared. As historian Patricia Nelson Limerick observed, once Americans embraced the mythology of conquest, it was easy to indulge in a bit of sympathy for the Indians—even to laud some of their qualities as a critique of the excesses of modern civilization. Limerick writes, "Since there was no chance of reversing the conquest, it was safe to regret it. Discontent with modern industrial society led to an interchanging of the usual terms: white Americans were the barbarians, savage and unprincipled, possessed by primitive greed; Indians were the genuinely civil people, who lived with an ecological wisdom and saintliness that made white Americans look like childish brutes."[61] These more "positive" aspects of the noble savage inspired a journalist to note in 1981 that at her confirmation hearings, Supreme Court nominee Sandra Day O'Connor "sat before her questioners, erect, like an American Indian."[62]

The major national and international expositions and fairs held in the United States during the late nineteenth and early twentieth centuries included representations of Indian culture as among the world's "backward races" along with Ainus from Japan and African pygmies.[63] With a touch more benevolence, the noted photographer Edward S. Curtis began publishing in 1907 a massive collection of photographs that captured Indians "in an idealized, imagined past, the romantic survivors of a 'vanishing race.' "[64] With the support of powerful industrialists like J. P. Morgan who profited from the opening up of Indian lands and resources, Curtis produced a body of work that was both lauded for its technical and artistic achievements and criticized for its portrayals of Indian people in stereotyped, "frozen in time" settings. Curtis, like most of his non-Indian contemporaries, subscribed to the "dying race" thesis, a belief that supplied a primary motivation for his massive project. In 1898, Curtis expressed these sentiments in a letter to his mentor, conservationist George Bird Grinnell: "I don't know how many tribes there are west of the Missouri, Bird—maybe a hundred. But I want to make them live forever—in a sort of history by photographs. . . . You and I know, and of course everyone does who thinks of it, the Indians of North America are vanishing. They've crumbled from their pride and power into pitifully small numbers, painful poverty and sorry weakness. There won't be anything left of them in a few generations and it's a tragedy—a national tragedy."[65] Curtis relied on techniques like photo cropping, lighting, posing and retouching of negatives to produce images that adhered to the wider public's popular image of traditional Indian people. For example, in one well-known case, the photo negative of a print entitled "In a Piegan Lodge" showed a clock positioned between two sitting tribal men; in the published print contained in Curtis's *The North American Indian,* the negative was retouched to remove the clock.[66]

In similar ways, court opinions also "construct" images of Indians that comport with popular conceptions or views of Indian people, whether those images reflect reality or not. The significant difference, of course, is that judicial opinions have the force of law with the potential to unleash both productive and destructive effects in the lives of individuals and communities. The late legal scholar Robert M. Cover expressed it best when he wrote: "A judge articulates her understanding of a text, and as a result, somebody loses his freedom, his property, his children, even his life. Interpretations in law also constitute justifications for violence which has already occurred or which is about to occur."[67]

The Supreme Court's early precedents are replete with constructed images of Indian people that at one end, condemn them as incorrigible, inferior, war-loving savages, and at the other, laud them for being environmentally friendly and culturally cohesive societies. More often than not, it is the former negative image that dominates the Court's narratives on Indian law and life. The Court relied on that negative image in *United States* v. *Sandoval* (1913)[68] to conclude that the Pueblo Indians and their lands were indeed subject to Congress's plenary power notwithstanding the fact that they owned their lands in fee simple title. The Court noted:

The people of the pueblos, although sedentary rather than nomadic in their inclinations, and disposed to peace and industry, are nevertheless Indians in race, customs, and domestic government. Always living in separate and isolated communities, adhering to primitive modes of life, largely influenced by superstition and [fetishism], and chiefly governed according to the crude customs inherited from their ancestors, they are essentially a simple, uninformed and inferior people. [T]hey have been regarded and treated by the United States as requiring special consideration and protection, like other Indian communities.[69]

Similarly, then associate justice William Rehnquist relied on the negative image of Indians to express his dissenting views in *United States* v. *Sioux Nation*, the land claims lawsuit discussed above. His opinion raised important "separation of powers" arguments in terms of the role Congress played in keeping the Sioux's land claims case alive. But the Rehnquist dissent also devoted much attention to challenging the Court's reliance on "revisionist" historical accounts that magnified the culpability of the United States while ignoring that "the Indians did not lack their share of villainy either." In support of his "Indian as villain" thesis, Justice Rehnquist turned to American historians like Samuel Eliot Morison, quoting the following from Morison's *Oxford History of the American People* (1965):

The Plains Indians seldom practiced agriculture or other primitive arts, but they were fine physical specimens; and in warfare, once they had learned the use of the rifle, [were] much more formidable than the Eastern tribes who had slowly yielded to the white man. Tribe warred with tribe, and a highly developed sign language was the only means of intertribal communications. The effective unit was the band or village of a few hundred souls, which might be seen in the course of its wanderings encamped by a watercourse with tipis erected; or pouring over the plain, women and children leading dogs and packhorses with their trailing travois, while gaily dressed braves loped ahead on horseback. They lived only for the day, recognized no rights of property, robbed or killed anyone if they thought they could get away with it, inflicted cruelty without a qualm, and endured torture without flinching.[70]

Having "established" that both parties to the treaty controversy in *Sioux Nation* had blood on their hands, Justice Rehnquist turned to Christian teachings to proclaim, "Both settler and Indian are entitled to the benefit of the Biblical adjuration: 'Judge not, that ye be not judged.'"[71]

But it is the decision in *Brendale* v. *Confederated Tribes and Bands of the Yakima Indian Nation* (1989)[72] that best illustrates the tendency of even modern justices to employ constructed images of Indian people and, more important, to rely on those constructed images to develop legally binding rules of law. In *Brendale*, two non-Indian residents of the Yakama[73] Reservation who owned lands in fee simple challenged the tribe's inherent power to regulate land use through zoning ordinances. One individual's land was located in the reservation's forested areas largely closed to development while the other individual's land was in the relatively more populated and developed "open" area of the reservation. The justices were hopelessly split in this case, as revealed by three distinct opinions that ultimately recognized the tribe's authority to regulate land use in the closed section but not in the open area. Of particular interest here are the opinions authored by Associate Justices John Paul Stevens and Harry Blackmun.

Starting with the premise that zoning represents a community's effort to define its "essential character," Justice Stevens voted to uphold tribal authority in the closed section but not in the open section of the reservation. Given the massive demographic changes wrought by the Allotment or Dawes Act, Justice Stevens concluded that the tribe was no longer empowered to exclude non-members in the broad areas where Congress had encouraged their active settlement (in the open area). Since the tribe was divested of the greater power to exclude nonmembers from their fee lands, it followed—for Justice Stevens at least—that they were divested of the lesser power to define the essential character of the area. Conversely, since the tribe retained the right to exclude nearly everyone from the closed area, it retained the power to maintain that area's "pristine, wilderness-like character."

Justice Blackmun lamented the "checkerboard" jurisdictional picture that emerged from the other *Brendale* opinions and found that tribal governments retained full authority to regulate land use throughout the reservation. He criticized Justice Stevens for relying on stereotypical images of Indians and Indian life to limit tribal governmental powers:

> To the extent that Justice Stevens' opinion discusses the characteristics of a reservation area where the Tribe possesses authority to zone because it has preserved the "essential character of the reservation," these characteristics betray a stereotyped and almost patronizing view of Indians and reservation life. The opinion describes the "closed area" of the Yakima Reservation as "pristine," and emphasizes that it is spiritually significant to the Tribe and yields natural foods and medicine. The opinion then contrasts this unadulterated portion of the reservation with the "open area," which is marked by "residential and commercial developmen[t]." In my view, even under Justice Stevens' analysis, it must not be the case that tribes can retain the "essential character" of their reservations (necessary to the exercise of zoning authority) only if they forgo economic development and maintain those reservations according to a single, perhaps quaint, view of what is characteristically "Indian" today.[74]

In the development of their respective draft opinions, the two justices traded sharply worded letters debating the points above. Justice Stevens fired the first salvo in a private memo to Justice Blackmun in which he noted that "the references to the fact that the reservation is 'pristine' and that the closed area has spiritual significance to the Tribe and yields natural foods and medicines all come out of the district court's findings, based on evidence produced at the trial by lawyers representing the Tribe. I guess its 'heads I win, tails you lose' if one shows respect for certain traditions that are obviously of importance to the Tribe." Justice Blackmun responded quickly the same day: "I seem to have ruffled your feathers. One always regrets that, and I certainly do this time." He made minor changes in his draft opinion but retained the criticism of Justice Stevens's stereotyped and patronizing analysis.[75]

Consciously or not, Justice Stevens's *Brendale* opinion shares a quality with Justice Rehnquist's *Oliphant* opinion in relying on the power of images of Indian people and reservation life to develop binding legal rules. For Justice Stevens, the preservation of "pristine wilderness-like" areas went hand in hand with tribal power to zone their lands; the legal rule fit comfortably with the popular conception of Indians living in a state of nature without the trappings (or burdens) of modern civilization and development. Despite Justice Stevens's private protestations to Justice Blackmun, it is inconceivable that the Yakama would have equated the scope of their sovereign land use powers with only that power necessary to preserve reservations as protected Indian wilderness zones. In Justice Rehnquist's *Oliphant* opinion, the image of Indian lands as lawless frontier spaces influenced the Court's development of a broad and devastating rule putting non-Indians completely beyond the reach of the tribe's criminal jurisdiction. Since there was no question that the reservation boundaries were preserved intact in both *Brendale* and *Oliphant*, it was not open to the non-Indian parties to argue that the tribal land base itself had been diminished. Instead, the strategy was to find other limitations on the scope of tribal powers even within their protected lands. The language of the decisions canvassed above suggests that those legal limitations on tribal powers were heavily influenced by the lasting power of images of Indians and reservation life. This confirms observations made by historian Robert F. Berkhofer, Jr., in 1978:

> Since Whites primarily understood the Indian as an antithesis to themselves, then civilization and Indianness as they defined them would forever be opposites. Only civilization had history and dynamics in this view, so therefore Indianness must be conceived of as ahistorical and static. If the Indian changed through the adoption of civilization as defined by Whites, then he was no longer truly Indian according to the image, because the Indian was judged by what Whites were not. Change toward what Whites were made him ipso facto less Indian.[76]

THE "DOMESTIC DEPENDENT" legal status of tribes casts a long shadow in Indian law and has provided the courts and Congress wide berth to shape the contours of Indian Country and Indian political authority in ways that pose minimal threat or disruption to the broader society. As noted above, this is why stories like the *Yankee* article profiled at the beginning of this chapter provoke such primal reactions among non-Indians. The story of the Pequots' territorial expansion challenges one of America's most enduring mythologies—the myth of the "vanishing Indian." The "enduring and thriving" or "rich and powerful" Indian tribe is not a familiar or comfortable concept in the popular imagination. The Pequots and many other tribes are claiming for themselves the colonizer's prerogative to enlarge their territorial estate and to move with confidence to influence the terms by which economic, commercial and political transactions will take place.

In short, tribes have proven themselves to be remarkably

resourceful and adept at securing meaningful levels of legal protections for their homelands. They have been particularly successful in securing recognition of their authority to protect and enhance their reservations' environmental and natural resource assets as well as their authority to develop their homelands as viable economic centers that support and sustain tribal life. We turn to each of these general areas in the next two chapters of this section.

5

STEWARDS OF THE NATURAL WORLD

THE *LONE WOLF* and *Sioux Nation* cases discussed in the previous chapter highlight fundamental differences between Indian and Western philosophies on the relationship between people and the surrounding natural environment. Stated simplistically, the former perspective views the relationship in terms of a sacred covenant between the people and the land while the latter perspective views land as a fungible commodity to be exploited for personal gain. These perspectives are admittedly drawn broadly to underscore the historical points of tension in the development of federal Indian land policy. The lines of distinction have blurred over the years, with tribes often pursuing economic development activities that necessarily involve some exploitation of natural resources, while non-Indian society has increasingly embraced the wisdom of an environmental ethic to limit growth and development. Nonetheless, United States Indian land policy in the nineteenth and early twentieth centuries, expressed in the forcible removal of tribal communities from their homelands, extinguishment of Indian title to vast areas of land and the imposition of individual allotments, was designed to fracture the unique bonds between tribal communities and their ancestral homelands to make way for national expansion and the development of lands and natural resources by white settlers. In the words of Raymond Kane, a White Mountain Apache elder, the loss of ancestral tribal lands in these ways was akin to an "unanesthetized amputation."[1]

In light of this history, it is all the more surprising that Indian tribes often point to environmental stewardship as the legal field within which they have experienced the most positive and meaningful recognition of their sovereign authority in the modern era. Environmental stewardship for our purposes is a broad concept and embraces developments in treaty-based hunting and fishing rights, control of natural resources (e.g., water, timber and minerals), protection of sacred lands and primacy in enforcing environmental laws in Indian Country. Each of these areas alone merits book-length treatment that is beyond the scope of this chapter or this book. We can, however, review overarching trends and principles that operate in these subfields to assess the tribal experience as governmental steward of the natural environment. Beginning with a brief look at tribal perspectives on the relationship between humans and their natural environment, we will look at how federal law has responded to tribal environmental and natural resource claims as grounded in tribal sovereignty, treaties, the federal Constitution and the Indian trust doctrine.

TRIBAL PERSPECTIVES ON THE NATURAL WORLD

One of the foremost Indian activists for tribal fishing rights in the modern era, Billy Frank, Jr., of the Nisqually Nation in Washington, offered this perspective on tribal world views and environmentalism: "I don't believe in magic. I believe in the sun and the stars, the water, the tides, the floods, the owls, the hawks flying, the river running, the wind talking. They're measurements. They tell us how healthy things are. How healthy we are. Because we and they are the same. That's what I believe in."[2] He also famously quipped that his role in the long battles for the recognition of tribal treaty fishing rights in the Northwest was not as a "policy guy [but] a getting-arrested guy."[3]

In the Southwest, Ronnie Lupe, leader of the Ndee people, or White Mountain Apache, pointed to a single Ndee word to capture a marvellously complex tribal philosophy on living in proper relation with one's surroundings. The same Ndee word— *ni'* —is used to capture the concept of "land" and "mind," a powerful expression of the unity between sacred landscapes and one's state of being or identity.[4] Through the magic of the discovery doctrine, tribal ancestral lands once occupied exclusively by the Ndee were claimed by the federal government and "restored to the public domain."[5] Government policies that stripped the Ndee of millions of acres of lands caused lasting social and cultural trauma to the fabric of Ndee traditional life. The newly arrived white settlers worked quickly to exploit the natural bounty from within and upon the land without showing, from the Ndee perspective, any respect for the natural world: "Because the new arrivals moved from place to place as they depleted and sometimes destroyed the land, the Ndee viewed the newcomers as landless and thus, from all appearances, mindless."[6]

The Ndee philosophy captures well what N. Scott Momaday, the noted Kiowa writer, meant by coming to a "moral comprehension" of the earth and air, and living in accordance with a land ethic.[7] A similar land ethic is found among the Anishinabe (Ojibwe) people of the upper Midwest and Great Lakes regions. Noted Anishinabe writer and activist Winona LaDuke points to her people's natural law or *mino bimaatisiiwin,* (meaning "good life" or "continuous rebirth") as the source for this land ethic. This ethic relies principally on the value of reciprocity, a sort of covenant chain, between people and the natural world. LaDuke says, "Within this act of reciprocity is also an understanding that 'you take only what you need and leave the rest.' Implicit in the understanding of Natural Law is also the understanding that most of what is natural is cyclical: whether our bodies, the moon, the tides, seasons, or life itself. Within this natural cycling is also a clear sense of birth and rebirth, a knowledge that what one does today will affect us in the future, on the return."[8]

Of course, the challenge of the modern era is not recovering Indian perspectives on stewardship of natural resources, but rather identifying and removing the legal, political and economic barriers that obstruct those perspectives from being deployed in actual practices. This form of "sovereignty on the ground" would allow for a true and profound expression of the recognized unity between Indian identity and the tribes' surrounding landscapes.

TRIBAL SOVEREIGNTY AND ENVIRONMENTAL STEWARDSHIP

When it comes to regulating use of natural resources located in Indian Country, tribal governments possess inherent sovereign authority to regulate the activities of all persons, including nonmembers, when those resources are located on tribal trust lands.[9] Certain activities may be off limits to tribes (and states for that matter) as a matter of federal law, including most matters having to do with the nuclear power industry.[10] Tribal inherent sovereign authority also extends to nonmembers on fee lands within the reservation to the extent the nonmembers' activities meet either of the exceptions recognized in *Montana* v. *United States* (1981). An interesting application of the *Montana* test arose in a recent dispute between the Hoopa Valley tribe in northern California and a non-Indian permanent resident of the reservation. In the mid-1990s, Roberta Bugenig challenged the tribe's authority to prohibit timber cutting on reservation lands she owned in fee simple. The tribe adopted a timber-harvesting plan in 1995 that included a buffer zone to protect culturally significant sites. Specifically, the ban prohibited timber cutting in areas used to perform the White Deerskin Dance, a ceremony of renewal that occurs every two years. Ms. Bugenig's property, purchased shortly after the tribe passed its timber-harvesting plan, was located entirely within an area considered the most significant for the ceremonial dances, which scientific evidence at trial suggested may be among the oldest continuously used indigenous dance sites in the

United States. The tribal court, relying on *Montana*, upheld the tribe's inherent authority to regulate Ms. Bugenig's activities, noting that the tribe "has the power and the authority to define areas of sacred significance and, through establishment of the buffer no-cut zone in the Bald Hill area, has exercised that power."[11] In short, the tribal court's ruling affirmed that threats to a tribe's spiritual and cultural well-being were embraced within the "health and welfare" portions of *Montana*'s second exception. The federal courts affirmed the tribe's authority over Ms. Bugenig but under the separate legal theory that Congress had in fact delegated authority to the tribe over all persons within the reservation.[12]

Beyond these developments in the courts, tribal assertions of their sovereign prerogatives on Indian lands influenced natural resource policy in the federal government's executive branch. In 1994, the White Mountain Apache tribe in Arizona and the U.S. Fish and Wildlife Service negotiated a landmark agreement on resource management, specifically, enforcement of the Endangered Species Act (ESA) on the reservation. In the early 1990s, concerned that federal officials would unilaterally declare large portions of the tribe's reservation critical habitat for threatened or endangered species, the tribe adopted a resolution barring any federal or state agency official from entering its lands to conduct studies related to natural resource management. While the tribe worried about the impact habitat designations could have on its various economic ventures (e.g., its ski resort, sawmill and various wildlife management enterprises), it based its resolution on the affront to tribal sovereignty. In testimony before the U.S. Senate in 1995, tribal chairman Ronnie Lupe recounted the tribe's efforts to rebuild its reservation following decades of mismanagement by federal bureaucrats and offered these thoughts on the ESA:

> Despite the damages we have sustained, our reservation remains a refuge for many endangered and sensitive species, both listed and unlisted. Although the Endangered Species Act was passed in 1973, our Tribe had very little

involvement with the Act or its implementation until recent years. Initially, we viewed the challenges by environmental groups and the regulatory actions of the U.S. Fish & Wildlife Service regarding endangered species as total hypocrisy. Those who sought to impose the ESA upon our Tribe and our aboriginal lands, made their challenges from cities where they had long ago exterminated native animals and plants and had erected cities of concrete and steel where prairies, wetlands and other wildlife habitat once existed. The species found on our reservation that are listed as "endangered" are rare because there are few healthy habitats elsewhere. Our reservation is home to many of these plants and animals because we have managed our lands well.[13]

The 1994 accord between the White Mountain Apache and the U.S. Fish and Wildlife Service served as a template for a broader bilateral agreement between two cabinet-level departments and Indian tribes on enforcement of the ESA. In 1997, the secretaries of commerce and the interior issued joint Secretarial Order 3206: American Indian Tribal Rights, Federal-Tribal Trust Responsibilities, and the Endangered Species Act, which provides a bilateral federal-tribal framework for enforcement of the ESA on Indian lands, with primacy accorded to the tribe's enforcement role.[14]

A decade earlier, in 1984, the Environmental Protection Agency became the first federal agency to articulate a formal policy on Indian tribes in light of the federal government's broader objectives to enhance tribal self-determination.[15] The EPA viewed the tribal role in environmental regulation as primary within Indian Country, and it advocated amendments to the major federal environmental statutes to give its policy real teeth. In the mid-1980s, Congress began amending a number of environmental acts expressly to provide a regulatory role for tribes in environmental matters, including amendments to the Clean Water Act, the Clean Air Act, the Safe Drinking Water Act and the Superfund Act (more formally known as the Comprehensive Environmental Response, Compensation and Liability Act or CERCLA).[16] These amendments, and the tribal actions subsequently taken under them, provoked numerous legal challenges over the years that negatively affected the number of tribes actually electing to participate in the administration of federal environmental programs.[17] For example, although the Clean Water Act was amended in 1987 to accord tribes treatment as states (or TAS), just over twenty tribes operate EPA-approved programs for water quality standards in Indian Country.[18]

On the other hand, tribes that overcame the legal and economic barriers to run such regulatory programs have realized significant benefits on the ground (or in the water, as the case may be). For example, the Isleta Pueblo in New Mexico became the first tribe accorded TAS treatment in 1992 and, shortly thereafter, the first tribe to gain federal approval of its water quality standards for the Rio Grande flowing through the pueblo. The very next year, it became the first tribe involved in litigation that challenged the entire federal-tribal environmental regulatory scheme. In a suit brought by the City of Albuquerque, the federal court upheld the EPA's authority to make the Isleta's water quality standards binding upon the city.[19] The Court specifically noted that the tribe's inherent sovereign authority allowed it to set standards more stringent than those required by the federal government. The tribe was particularly concerned about achieving water quality levels in the Rio Grande that would protect its members' use of waters for religious and ceremonial purposes.[20] The city ultimately upgraded its wastewater treatment facilities at a cost of over $60 million so that its discharges into the Rio Grande complied with Isleta's stringent water quality standards.[21] Admittedly, without the authority of the federal Clean Water Act, the tribe's sovereign authority would not extend outside the reservation boundaries. Nonetheless, the TAS system for environmental regulation, as with the joint secretarial order on enforcement of the Endangered Species Act, reveals how tribal and national interests can be advanced meaningfully through policies that embrace, rather than reject, the tribe's sovereign authority to serve as an environmental steward.

Tribes can also exercise sovereign prerogatives as environmental stewards through their beneficial ownership and management of natural resources located on their lands through leasing (subject to federal approval) and taxation. According to the *Cohen Handbook* (2005), Indian lands contain approximately 30 percent of the nation's coal west of the Mississippi, about a third of the nation's uranium and about 16 million acres of forested land, nearly half of which is rated suitable for commercial production.[22] The federal government generally manages the revenue derived from these trust assets on behalf of tribes and individual tribal members, though its success in carrying out that responsibility efficiently and accurately has been sharply contested and is currently the subject of one of the largest class action lawsuits against the government in United States–tribal history.[23] Beyond these hard resources, many Indian tribes are actively involved in harnessing the power of wind to generate electrical energy for local consumption and for transmission off the reservation. Three of the top five "wind rich" states (North Dakota, South Dakota and Montana) contain large areas of Indian Country, and several tribes within these areas have already developed extensive wind turbine operations on their lands.[24] Other Indian tribes, like the Nez Perce in Idaho, manage their forest resources as carbon sequestration units. Companies that emit carbon dioxide essentially pay the tribes to "sequester" the CO_2 within their forests.[25]

Of course, tribes are not immune to external market and political forces that can cause disruptions in the management and development of their natural resources. In December 2005, Peabody Coal's enormous operations at the Black Mesa Mine in Arizona ground to a halt when its largest (and only) coal customer, Mohave Generating Station in Nevada, elected to shut down indefinitely after it failed to implement environmental upgrades to reduce toxic air emissions under a federally approved consent decree. The shutdown cost nearly two hundred people, mostly Navajo and Hopi tribal members, their jobs, which paid upward of eighty thousand dollars a year in wages and benefits. The coal operation had always attracted controversy among tribal people anyway because of the tension between preserving fragile ecosystems, notably precious aquifers underlying Navajo and Hopi lands, and providing high-paying jobs on reservations where unemployment is rampant. The operation itself used massive amounts of water to drive grounded coal through slurry pipelines to the power plant over 270 miles away. Former Hopi tribal chairman Vernon Masayesva criticized the mining operation as wasteful of precious and finite water resources. According to Masayesva, "Wasting water is criminal in our culture. It is the tribe's covenant with the earth, and we broke it."[26]

Tribes face formidable obstacles, both internal and external, in carrying out their role as environmental stewards, but recognition of their sovereign status provides them an important seat at the table in the national conversation over the wise, efficient and moral uses of natural resources.

TREATY RIGHTS TO NATURAL RESOURCES

In surrendering their rights to millions of acres of ancestral home-lands in return for "recognized" reservation lands, tribes often insisted on treaty language that would secure their continued access to and a share of natural resources located off their reserved lands. Over the years, the courts have had numerous occasions to interpret the meaning of these treaty promises, including those expressly stated in the treaties and those that were implied. In doing so, courts often employed the so-called "canons of treaty interpretation" derived from the era of Chief Justice John Marshall, which require treaty terms to be construed in a manner that reflects how the Indian people would naturally have understood them. A state court opinion from Idaho's Supreme Court provides a simple, yet powerful, illustration of the importance of these interpretive principles. In *State* v. *Tinno* (1972), the court interpreted the treaty term "to hunt" as embracing the fishing rights of the Shoshone and Bannock tribal members. The court found it significant that neither of the indigenous languages had separate words for "hunting" and "fishing." Since the Shoshone word *tygi* and the Bannock word *hoawai* meant "to gather wild food," the court interpreted the treaty term "to hunt" liberally so as to capture the tribes' understanding of the concept.[27]

The most commonly litigated express treaty promises dealing with natural resources were those guaranteeing tribal fishing, hunting and gathering rights off the reserved lands. The 1855 treaty with the Yakama—the one signed by Kamiakin and his fellow tribal leaders—contained the following express guarantee:

> The exclusive right of taking fish in all the streams, where running through or bordering said reservation, is further secured to said confederated tribes and bands of Indians, as also the right of taking fish at all usual and accustomed places, in common with the citizens of the Territory, and of erecting temporary buildings for curing them; together with the privilege of hunting, gathering roots and berries, and pasturing their horses and cattle upon open and unclaimed land.[28]

This language, with slight but important variations for other tribes,[29] became fairly standard in the treaties with tribes of the Northwest and Great Lakes regions. The Yakama confederated tribes were among the first tribes to go to court to defend their treaty rights against encroachment by non-Indian settlers and newly emerging states. In *United States* v. *Winans* (1905), the Supreme Court offered an eloquent and surprisingly strong affirmation of the Yakamas' off-reservation fishing rights: "The right to resort to the fishing places in controversy was a part of larger rights possessed by the Indians, upon the exercise of which there was not a shadow of impediment, and which were not much less necessary to the existence of the Indians than the atmosphere they breathed."[30] The Court acknowledged that "new conditions" in the form of newly arrived non-Indian settlers required an accommodation, but not the elimination, of rights that the Indians once enjoyed exclusively. "In other words," said the Court, "the treaty was not a grant of rights to the Indians, but a grant of right from them,—a reservation of those not granted."[31] The treaty effectively created a property right in favor of treaty fishermen that functioned as a legal right of way on the land; Indians therefore had rights to enter and occupy private lands that contained their "usual and accustomed [fishing] places" in order to exercise their treaty fishing rights.

The state of Washington, on the other hand, was openly hostile to the idea of honoring treaty-based fishing rights. Notwithstanding the emphatic language of the Supreme Court in *Winans*, the Washington Supreme Court rejected the argument that the Yakamas' express treaty fishing rights shielded individual members from state prosecution for fishing in violation of state law. In *State* v. *Towessnute* (1916), the state high court left no doubt about prevailing local attitudes toward Indians and Indian treaty rights:

> The premise of Indian sovereignty we reject. The treaty is not to be interpreted in that light. At no time did our ancestors in getting title to this continent ever regard the aborigines as other than mere occupants, and incompetent occupants, of the soil. Any title that could be had from them was always disdained. . . . Only that title was esteemed which came from white men.
>
> The Indian was a child, and a dangerous child of nature, to be both protected and restrained. In his nomadic life, he was to be left, as long as civilization did not demand his region. When it did demand that region, he was to be allotted a more confined area with permanent subsistence.
>
> These arrangements were but the announcement of our benevolence which, notwithstanding our frequent frailties, has been continuously displayed. Neither Rome

nor sagacious Britain ever dealt more liberally with their subject races than we with these savage tribes, whom it was generally tempting and always easy to destroy and whom we have so often permitted to squander vast areas of fertile land before our eyes.[32]

The state of Washington maintained its posture of opposition toward Indian treaty fishing rights well into the modern era. In a series of federal cases from the 1960s and 1970s (including a number of appeals to the United States Supreme Court), Washington openly defied judicial precedent, federal treaty law and a growing activist Indian community in challenging the nature and scope of treaty-protected fishing rights. This posture contributed to the spread of open conflicts on the ground between treaty opponents and treaty supporters. Legal scholar Charles Wilkinson poignantly linked the clashes over treaty fishing rights with the civil rights movement of the 1950s and 1960s: "In time, the banks of the Nisqually [River] merged with the schoolhouse steps of Little Rock, the bridge at Selma, and the back of the bus in Montgomery."[33]

The volatile controversy once again landed before the United States Supreme Court, and the Court, in 1979, again used surprisingly strong language to endorse the tribes' treaty rights and equally strong language to chastise the state for its unfounded opposition to the exercise of those rights. In *Washington* v. *Washington State Commercial Passenger Fishing Vessel Association* (1979), the Court confirmed that treaty language guaranteeing the tribes "the right of taking fish, at all usual and accustomed grounds and stations . . . in common with all citizens of the Territory" meant that tribes had rights to an equal share of available fish runs.[34] In stark contrast to the Court's language in *Wheeler* (1978), in which the Court stated that tribal sovereignty was subject to "complete defeasance" by Congress, the fishing case affirmed that "a treaty, including one between the United States and an Indian tribe, is essentially a contract between two sovereign nations. When the signatory nations have not been at war and neither is the vanquished, it is reasonable to assume that they negotiated *as equals* at arm's length" (emphasis added). The dramatic turnabout in language, at least as it relates to the Court's characterization of tribal sovereignty, is best explained as the Court's attempt to (re)assert the federal government's constitutional supremacy in Indian affairs as a check against the state's "widespread defiance" of federal authority. The Court drew analogies between the fishing controversy and the earlier school desegregation cases to highlight its displeasure with the state's actions: "Except for some desegregation cases . . . the district court has faced the most concerted official and private efforts to frustrate a decree of a federal court witnessed in this century."[35]

The *Washington* fishing case placed important limits on treaty rights that have influenced later cases. The Court noted that the tribe's treaty share represented a maximum but not a minimum allocation of the harvest. In the Court's words, the treaty "secures so much as, but no more than, is necessary to provide the Indians with a livelihood—that is to say, a moderate living."[36] Changes in the tribe's numbers or their means of support could lead to subsequent adjustments in their share of the fish harvest. In a recent case, the federal courts rejected Washington's argument that the "moderate living" principles required a downward adjustment in the tribes' treaty allocations because of the tribes' added revenue sources from casino operations.[37] The Court pointed to evidence showing that despite the new revenue sources, Washington tribal members still ranked far below non-Indians on most socioeconomic measures.

Treaty rights protecting off-reservation rights to fish, hunt and gather will generally continue in perpetuity unless Congress extinguishes the rights in language that clearly and plainly reflects that intention.[38] Since the treaty-protected natural resource rights are regarded in law as property rights, tribes are typically entitled to compensation under the Constitution's Fifth Amendment.[39] That compensation may be long in coming, as the Skokomish Indians in Washington have learned. The tribe is still battling the federal, state and local governments over the ecological damages wrought by the Cushman Dam project built in the 1930s.[40] Beyond the devastating impact on their fishing resources, the tribe experiences annual flooding on their lands, which has prompted some local tribal members to joke that their reservation is the "only place in the world where salmon are 'road kill.' "[41]

The courts have not been entirely consistent in determining what constitutes evidence of clear intention to abrogate treaty rights. The Supreme Court itself has drawn different conclusions on whether tribal agreements that cede all interests in former tribal lands but are otherwise silent as to hunting and fishing rights are sufficient to abrogate the tribes' natural resource rights on the ceded lands. At times, the Court has shown greater concern for the impact such retained rights would have on the *state's* interests in reclaiming full authority over those ceded lands. That was precisely the argument urged by the late associate justice Byron White in 1984 in a case involving the Klamath tribe in Oregon. The lower federal court had ruled in favor of the Klamath's retained hunting and fishing rights on their ceded lands after finding no clear language indicating that Congress intended to extinguish those rights. The Supreme Court initially voted to deny a review of the case, which prompted Justice White to circulate a memo to his fellow justices urging them to reconsider. He first noted that the lower federal courts had arrived at different interpretations of earlier Supreme Court precedents that could only be resolved by the high court's action in the present case. He then voiced the following additional concern:

The question presented by this case is one of some importance: *the decision below deprives the State of Oregon of full authority to enforce its fish and game laws in almost 1,000 square miles of its territory.* The Ninth Circuit's decision [is] at least debatable, and the conflict between the Ninth Circuit's reasoning and that of the Eighth Circuit on a question concerning Indian treaty rights—a subject in which this Court has traditionally taken great interest—indicates a need for guidance from this Court [emphasis added].[42]

Less than a week after Justice White's memo, the Court agreed to review the case. By the following summer, the Klamath's hunting and fishing rights were extinguished and the state's "full authority" over the ceded lands was restored.[43] Justices Brennan and Marshall dissented from the Court's ruling and faulted the Court for failing to abide by the longstanding canons of treaty interpretation when faced with ambiguous treaty language.

WHEREAS FISHING AND hunting rights dominate the natural resource battles in the context of *express* treaty promises, water rights take center stage in disputes involving *implied* federal promises. The Supreme Court's landmark decision in *Winters* v. *United States* (1908)[44] affirmed that when Congress created Indian reservations, it implicitly reserved rights to water sufficient to fulfill the purposes of the reservation. The doctrine of federally reserved water rights operates within, but sometimes in tension with, the state system of "prior appropriation" that governs water allocation in most of the western United States. Given the relative scarcity of water in the region, the prior appropriation system assigns water rights to the first person applying water to some continuous beneficial use. In periods of water shortages, the most senior (i.e., earliest in time) appropriators get their full allocation of water (based on amounts actually applied to a beneficial use), which may leave the junior (later in time) appropriators with little or no water. Tribal reserved water rights are included in this hierarchy of users. But their priority date in times of shortage is not based on the date they began to put water to beneficial use, for example, to develop irrigation systems, but generally the date that their reservation lands were actually set aside for them, whether by treaty, agreement, statute or executive order.[45]

Had tribes been able to put their "*Winters* water rights" to actual use, they would have deprived many junior appropriators of their allocation of water. Those conflicts were largely avoided, however, because of the federal government's allotment policies that were aimed at dismantling the reservations and opening them up to large-scale resettlement by non-Indians. The government built massive irrigation projects using tribal funds in order to attract and sustain white settlement in the newly opened arid western lands.[46] The Bureau of Reclamation, formed in 1902 and located within the Department of the Interior, where it joined the Bureau of Indian Affairs (BIA), facilitated the watering of the West at the expense of Indian tribal rights to land and water. In the six decades after 1902, tribes could count on one hand the number of times the BIA rose to defend their federally reserved water rights in court.[47] In *Winters* itself, the Court acknowledged that "it was the policy of the government, it was the desire of the Indians, to change those habits and to become a pastoral and civilized people."[48] Federal policy effectively thrust Indian tribes and members into the "use it or lose it" arena of competition for scarce water resources. As historian Frederick Hoxie noted, "Like an imperial power, the American government would 'develop' native property by opening it to white farmers and businessmen, 'freeing' the Indians to participate in the process as they could. Natives who adapted quickly might survive under the new regime; those who didn't deserved their fate."[49]

Winters did not quantify the amount of water a tribe could claim under its reserved rights beyond that required to fulfill the government's purpose of converting the Indians into "a pastoral and civilized people." Over a half century later, in *Arizona* v. *California* (1963), the Supreme Court affirmed that Indian lands set aside for these agricultural pursuits were entitled to an allocation of water measured by the practicably irrigable acreage (PIA) within those Indian lands.[50] Once an allocation is made using the PIA standard, and assuming a tribe can actually divert waters so that its "paper water rights" are converted to "wet water rights," a tribe is typically free to use its allocation for purposes other than agricultural ones. The waters used to fulfill the tribe's allocation may come from surface or groundwater sources, whether located on or off the reservation.[51] While the PIA standard provides a measure of certainty over competing standards, such as a tribe's reasonably foreseeable needs, it is not without controversy. Critics on both sides charge that the PIA standard provides far too much or too little water to meet actual tribal needs.[52] Even more fundamentally, the standard is criticized for linking water rights to the outmoded aims of the allotment era that sought to impose the model of the yeoman farmer on individual Indian tribal members. In more recent lawsuits, the issue is often framed as a struggle to define the purposes for which the reservation was created and to attach water rights in accordance with those purposes.[53]

In 1989, the Supreme Court itself accepted the state of Wyoming's invitation to reconsider the PIA standard. In an unpublished opinion by Justice Sandra Day O'Connor, the Court elected to reaffirm its allegiance to the PIA standard but provided important limiting guideposts to help make water allocations under the standard. Since Justice O'Connor recused herself from the case before the decision was formally handed down, her opinion for the Court was never released. The remaining justices were evenly divided, which allowed the Wyoming Supreme Court's opinion to stand as the law of the case. In short, even though Justice O'Connor's opinion never saw the light of day, it is noteworthy for the changes it would have brought into existence and signals the Court's possible shift in a future case on this critical issue. The opinion, discovered among the papers of the late Justice Thurgood Marshall, contained language that would have severely curtailed the nature and scope of tribal reserved water rights. For instance, Justice O'Connor endorsed the state's view that quantification of tribal water rights should be narrowly construed to show "sensitivity" to the rights of prior appropriators. In effect, this view would subject tribal water allocations to the same limiting scrutiny that is applied for water allocations on other federal reservations, such as national parks or forests, ignoring the significant distinction that tribal lands serve as homelands for a people.[54] Justice O'Connor further noted that the "sensitivity doctrine" would require courts to employ some "degree of pragmatism" in assessing the "reasonable likelihood" that tribal communities would actually construct the facilities necessary to divert water resources for reservation use.[55] The draft opinion rejected the notion that the federal government had any legal obligation to construct these facilities on behalf of Indian tribes. The Court overlooked (or ignored) the massive federal expenditures to build the irrigation projects that enabled white settlers to take over Indian lands in the early twentieth century and stated that circumstances facing the federal government and tribes are far different today: "If money were plentiful, a finding of economic feasibility might suggest that the [irrigation] project in question will be built. But massive capital outlays are required to fund irrigation projects . . . and in today's era of budget deficits and excess agricultural production, government officials have to choose carefully what projects to fund in the West."[56]

Shortly after Justice O'Connor circulated this draft opinion, Justice Byron White, a westerner, like Justice O'Connor, wrote to applaud the draft opinion's refinements on application of the PIA standard, especially its use of the sensitivity doctrine. Given the relative paucity of Supreme Court opinions on the nature and scope of tribal reserved water rights, it is important to note what Justice White said in his letter's concluding passages:

> The prevailing rule in the West is that water in the stream is not subject to private ownership; it is not like oil or coal in the ground. There is a right to use water for specified purposes, but unused water belongs to the stream. On fully adjudicated streams, it is expected that water unused by those with senior rights is subject to use by holders of junior rights. In this case, if the reservation is to be granted rights to water that won't be used unless additional irrigation works are built some time in the future, until that

time comes such water should be available, without charge, to holders of state water rights, upstream or down. That would mean that such excess water would not be subject to annual sale or lease to the highest bidder. I realize that these issues are not before us, but I would take care not to hint at their resolution.[57]

Tribes are in a catch-22 when it comes to reserved water rights. They typically have senior rights to water but often lack the financial resources to apply those rights to practical uses on their lands. Many forms of economic development on western Indian lands inevitably require water resources that, in most cases, require the tribes (on their own or with federal assistance) to construct the facilities to divert and store water on tribal homelands. Selling or leasing the tribe's superior water rights, even if legal impediments were overcome, is not a viable option when—as even Justice White noted—junior appropriators can currently use those waters at no charge.

As a result of the expense, time and uncertainty of litigation, coupled with the economic and political complexities noted above, many tribes pursue some form of negotiated settlement to confirm definitive claims to their water rights and to secure the commitment of financial resources to help convert those rights into "wet water."[58] While far from perfect, the negotiated settlements do offer a practical, if compromised, option for tribes to fulfill the historic treaty promises of building viable homelands for their people.

THE U.S. CONSTITUTION AND PROTECTION OF SACRED GEOGRAPHY

As the *Bugenig* case revealed, tribes can exercise their sovereign prerogatives to provide meaningful protection to lands considered sacred when those lands are located within a reservation or in Indian Country generally. Tribes encounter far more difficult problems when they seek to protect sacred lands and other natural features that are located outside Indian Country, typically on federally protected public lands. In those instances, they typically must rely on the Constitution and assorted other federal statutes that might constrain the federal government in conducting activities that could negatively affect the sites and the tribal religious and cultural practices associated with those sites.

Indian claims based on the free exercise clause of the Constitution's First Amendment have not fared well in the courts. In *Lyng* v. *Northwest Indian Cemetery Protective Association* (1988),[59] tribal members from the Yurok, Tolowa and Karok tribes relied unsuccessfully on that constitutional provision to stop the United States Forest Service from completing a road under its forest management plans. The tribes asserted that the government's activity would "virtually destroy" their members' ability to exercise their religious rights. Tribal religious leaders and elders testified at trial that the proposed government road would slice through and devastate the pristine quality of lands and mountain peaks they regarded as their sacred "high country." Religious practitioners gathered plants and other natural resources to use in ceremonial activities while other tribal members regularly visited sacred praying sites from which they solicited the Creator's protection for humanity. The Court readily conceded that the tribal members had shown an "actual" burden on their religious freedom rights, but it found that they had failed to show the requisite "legal" burden on those rights. In other words, the religious practitioners had failed to show that the government activity somehow coerced them into doing something contrary to their religious beliefs or penalized them in some demonstrable way for acting in conformity with those beliefs. In her opinion for the Court, Justice Sandra Day O'Connor resisted the tribes' claims that would create "religious servitudes" on federal public lands. Justice Brennan issued a strong dissenting opinion that criticized the Court for misapplying precedent in the religious freedom cases and for ignoring the unique federal obligations to safeguard the integrity of tribal religious and cultural practices.

The political branches were a bit more responsive to tribal claimants seeking protection of sacred spaces. In 1993, Congress enacted the Religious Freedom Restoration Act or RFRA[60] to provide an additional layer of legal protection to individuals whose religious practices were "substantially burdened" by government laws, regulations or activities. In these instances, the government's activities could be pursued only if it demonstrated that the burden on religious practice was the least restrictive means of furthering a compelling governmental interest. The RFRA was written in response to the Supreme Court's decision in *Employment Division, Department of Human Resources of Oregon* v. *Smith* (1990)[61] in order to restore the measure of legal protection for religious practice formally accorded under the Constitution's First Amendment. In *Smith*, the Supreme Court held that the First Amendment's free exercise of religion clause did not prohibit states from enforcing laws of general applicability, such as criminal laws, even if they substantially burdened an individual's religious practices. In *Smith*, an Indian member of the Native American Church was denied unemployment compensation benefits following his termination as a substance abuse counselor for consuming peyote in religious ceremonies. Since Oregon law criminalized the use and possession of peyote, Smith's acts of "misconduct" justified the denial of unemployment compensation benefits. In subsequent developments, the Supreme Court held RFRA unconstitutional as applied to state and local governments, but to date, it has not invalidated the statute's application to the federal government.[62]

The RFRA recently served as the legal cornerstone for a number of tribes challenging the National Forest Service's plans to permit certain upgrades to the Snow Bowl ski resort in Arizona's San Francisco Peaks. Six tribes, including the Navajo, Hopi, Havasupai and Hualapai tribes, objected on religious and cultural grounds to the ski operators' plan to use reclaimed water in snowmaking operations on the peaks. One tribal leader expressed concern that the reclaimed waters could include wastewater from mortuaries or hospitals that risked infecting tribal members with "ghost sickness."[63] Other religious leaders noted that the reclaimed water would contaminate the plant life and other natural resources that were gathered and used in ceremonies. One tribal leader likened the contamination of the mountains with reclaimed wastewater to poisoning an individual: "If someone were to get a prick or whatever from a contaminated needle, it doesn't matter what the percentage is, your whole body would then become contaminated. And that's what would happen to the mountain." In March 2007, a federal appeals court ruled in favor of the tribes on their RFRA claim, finding that the government failed to show that the proposed upgrades to the ski resort served a compelling governmental interest by the least restrictive means.[64] Before the trial of this action, the tribes had already secured a concession from the federal government through the consultation process—a reform initiated by the Clinton administration—to prohibit night lighting on the San Francisco Peaks in response to the tribes' cultural and religious concerns that the peaks be allowed to rest.[65]

The enhanced consultation requirements noted above were part of broader federal efforts to fortify protections for Indian religious and cultural practices. For example, during the 1990s, Congress and the president acted to bolster (or restore) protections for Indian religious use of peyote, as well as access to and use of endangered or threatened animal parts otherwise prohibited under federal law, and augmented religious rights for Indian inmates.[66]

FEDERAL TRUST OBLIGATIONS AND TRIBAL NATURAL RESOURCES

There are a few instances where the federal government itself retains significant responsibility for the management and stewarding of a tribe's natural resources such that it may be open to a lawsuit by the tribe for money damages when it breaches those legal obligations. The Supreme Court has set a fairly high and narrow threshold for the circumstances that will trigger this legal obligation. The federal government's generalized role as trustee is insufficient to activate that obligation. A tribe must be able to point to a "substantive source of law that establishes specific fiduciary or other duties, and allege that the Government has failed faithfully to perform those duties."[67] Furthermore, having crossed that threshold, the question is whether the substantive law "can fairly be interpreted as mandating compensation for damages sustained as a result of a breach of the duties [the governing law] impose[s]."[68]

In *United States* v. *Mitchell (II)* (1983),[69] the Supreme Court interpreted the vast regime of federal statutes and regulations governing the management and development of tribal forests and timber resources as sufficiently specific to open the government to a suit for compensation for breaching its fiduciary obligations. The Court found it significant that the statutory and regulatory regime placed the federal government in control of nearly every phase of the tribal forestry enterprise. There are some indications that this particular federal obligation may still be actionable even as tribes gain more responsibility for the management of their own forest and timber resources.[70]

In *United States* v. *Navajo Nation* (2003),[71] the Navajo Nation sued the federal government for breach of fiduciary obligations based on the vast network of federal statutes and regulations governing coal development on Indian lands. A particular point of contention was the tribe's evidence that the secretary of interior unfairly influenced the negotiations of royalty rates for the tribe's coal by meeting privately with representatives of the coal company without the tribe's knowledge. The Supreme Court found that the coal laws did not impose specific federal obligations of the kind found in the forestry statutes and thus rejected the tribe's claim for damages. As to the private communications, the Court emphasized that nothing in the laws prohibited such contact and that, in any event, the tribe could have invoked more formal procedures that would have precluded these so-called "ex parte communications." This surprisingly wooden approach not only served to insulate the national treasury against tribal claims, but it effectively shifted the blame onto the tribes for failing to anticipate or counter the "Washington power play" involving the secretary of interior and the coal executives. From the tribe's perspective, the argument was not simply a case of federal neglect but one of intentional interference with the tribe's efforts to negotiate a fair rate for its natural resource. Any fair-minded reading of federal fiduciary obligations should be broad enough to encompass those sorts of acts as well. As Justice Oliver Wendell Holmes famously quipped, "Even a dog distinguishes between being stumbled over and being kicked."[72]

TAKEN AS A WHOLE, federal law has produced meaningful spaces for the expression of tribal values regarding the use, development and management of natural resources. Those protections are most visible within tribal lands and even those private lands that are embraced within the terms of historic treaties. It is difficult to pinpoint precisely why this area of law has produced a more robust form of tribal sovereignty or an enlarged measure of protection for tribal rights generally as compared with other areas of federal Indian law. A general answer would point to the convergence in the streams of respect accorded the natural world by both the Indian and non-Indian societies, at least within the past four decades. Modern society wages an ambivalent struggle between the forces of development and conservation, but it is ever mindful of the limits of growth and the capacity of the planet to tolerate the whims of its current human inhabitants.

As the eminent biologist Edward O. Wilson noted: "If there is any moral precept shared by people of all beliefs, it is that we owe ourselves and future generations a beautiful, rich, and healthful environment."[73] Indian people have long observed a covenant with the natural world, an environmental philosophy that recognizes inextricable and mutually sustaining links between a place and a tribal community. As stewards of the natural world, Indian tribes are seen as advancing both a philosophy and a way of life that has peculiar resonance with the dominant society. In this sense, active encouragement of a tribal governmental role and recognition of unique tribal treaty rights may appear consistent with, or, at least, not threatening to non-Indian values and practices. William H. Rodgers, Jr., one of the nation's preeminent scholars of environmental law, believes Indian tribes fully merit this active encouragement as environmental stewards:

> Count me among the believers that the U.S. Indian Tribes are the most creative and effective agents for positive environmental change in play today. Evidence is everywhere. Tribes have the better laws and they expect more of them. They are uniquely positioned to combat the corrosive influences that have undermined the modern environmental laws.[74]

6

REVITALIZING TRIBAL
ECONOMIES

LIKE THEIR NATIONAL and state counterparts, tribal governments work actively to stimulate their local economies to enhance
the community's standard of living and to generate the resources
needed to support government services. They do this by using the
regular tools of government, such as the power to tax individuals
and businesses operating within Indian Country. They also often
take a more active, proprietary role in commerce by designing and
operating the business entities that offer services, produce products
and employ people on tribal lands. The tribe's roles as government
and business operator are often confused and have led to numerous
legal challenges about whether tribes should be permitted to operate
in either capacity. Lurking behind these challenges is the ever-present
argument among non-Indian and state actors that federal law should
not accord "special rights" to Indian people and tribes or otherwise
compromise the nation's commitment to equal treatment before the
law. These concerns are particularly sensitive in the area of economic
development, given the likelihood that tribal economic policies and
activities within their lands can reverberate beyond the boundaries

of Indian Country and affect commerce outside the tribe's jurisdiction. There is nothing novel about this, however, especially when you consider that states offer widely differing governmental policies to stimulate economic growth and development, from tax exemptions to special economic incentives designed to attract particular forms of development. Historically, however, tribes have encountered great resistance from non-Indians (both private and public actors) when the heat from tribal economic competition and success becomes too intense. As Indian activist Suzan Shown Harjo (Cheyenne) once noted, "Indians can't win too big without some attempt at retribution."[1] In disputes over economic development in Indian Country, the three core areas of legal disputes—power, money and respect—interact in a particularly volatile manner and pose substantial challenges for tribal governments working to reverse the centuries-long cycles of poverty and oppression within their communities.

We should start, however, with a brief snapshot of socioeconomic conditions prevailing in Indian Country today. One of the most significant developments in this area, of course, is the proliferation of gambling activities inside Indian Country. That story is told in a bit more detail below, but for now, it's important to note that the benefits of gambling, while largely positive for many tribes, are not as dramatic or as diffused throughout Indian Country as popular media accounts might suggest. Perhaps the bigger story is that socioeconomic conditions in Indian Country, as revealed through census data from 1990 and 2000, show dramatic improvements in nearly all census-measured indexes. This was evident despite the fact that federal per capita spending for the Indian population declined, sometimes dramatically, during the past two decades.[2] Researchers from the Harvard Project on American Indian Economic Development confirmed (again) that the key factor in improving the socioeconomic conditions in Indian Country was the presence of a strong, effective and culturally sensitive tribal government:

Indeed, the progress evident among *non-gaming* tribes in the 1990s suggests that it is not so much gaming that is driving the socioeconomic changes evident across Indian America as it is a broader policy of Indian self-government. Jurisdiction over the gaming choice is part, but hardly the entirety, of that policy.

Prior research repeatedly indicates that devolution of powers of self-rule to tribes can bring, and has brought, improvements in program efficiency, enterprise competency, and socioeconomic conditions. The reasons are to be found in the fact that self-rule brings decision making home, and local decision makers are held more accountable to local needs, conditions, and cultures than outsiders.[3]

Despite the measurable gains of the past few decades, tribal communities are still trying to recover from centuries of misguided federal policies that radically altered the nature and extent of tribal land holdings while crippling their indigenous forms of self-government. The 2000 census shows that Indians living in Indian Country had per capita incomes that were less than half the levels in the general U.S. population, median household incomes that were slightly more than half the national levels, unemployment rates that were more than double the national rate, poverty rates that were three times the national rate and a proportion of Indian adults with college degrees that was half that of the comparable proportion for the national population.[4]

The mix of good and bad news is evident in other areas of contemporary Indian life. In health care, for example, while solid advances can be seen in reduced mortality rates for infants and their mothers, the broader Indian population remains at significantly higher risk for a broad range of diseases and experiences higher death rates, especially among the younger members of the Indian community.[5] Federal spending on Indian health care has declined both in real dollars and as a percentage of the national health care budget for populations directly served by the federal government (e.g., veterans, Medicare and Medicaid and federal prisoners); indeed, federal inmates received more in per capita health care spending than Indian citizens in fiscal 2003.[6]

If overcoming centuries' worth of poverty and oppression were not challenging enough, tribal governments must also deal with other social and economic deficits that hamper efforts to revitalize tribal economies. Tribal governments typically operate in locations far removed from the major centers of commerce. They must contend with such infrastructure deficits as poor roads, deficient or obsolete telecommunications systems and substandard housing conditions, along with social deficits such as a poorly trained or inexperienced workforce and the challenge of the "brain drain," with the tribe's most promising younger members often electing to seek employment opportunities outside Indian Country. Tribes also operate within the shadows of a federal bureaucracy accustomed to operating in paternalistic mode, the product of a legal system that still requires federal approval of contractual obligations involving the tribe and any transactions relating to tribal lands or other tribal property held in trust. These factors present enormous challenges for even the most talented and well-equipped tribal governmental system.

The research suggests, however, that tribes are up to the challenges if supported by the federal government in the exercise of their sovereign authority. That authority, however, as noted in Part One, is under constant challenge on many fronts, with no clear signs of abatement. This development, exacerbated by the recent trend of declining federal per capita spending in Indian programs, would seriously undermine, if not negate, the promising gains made by tribes in their struggle to break the cycle of poverty in Indian Country.

Of course, there is nothing new about Indian people encountering resistance in their efforts to build, and rebuild, their tribal economies. A telling story comes from the Cherokee Nation in the latter third of the nineteenth century, following the tribe's forced removal from their ancestral lands in Georgia to their newly reserved lands in what is now Oklahoma. The Cherokee shared the conundrum of many other tribes that were blessed with natural resources within their reserved lands but lacked the capital to develop the resources. Potential investors or developers from outside Indian Country bided their time in hopes that the relocated Cherokee Nation would eventually dissolve. As historian William McLoughlin explains, "Whites in the neighboring states expected that sooner or later the Cherokee land would fall into their hands, and they would not invest to enrich the Cherokees and keep them independent."[7] An enterprising Cherokee named Elias C. Boudinot, backed by his uncle Stand Watie, founded a tobacco company on Cherokee lands in the 1860s and soon turned it into a profitable business. An express provision in the treaty of 1866 between the federal government and the Cherokee Nation exempted such businesses from all taxation. Rival businesses challenged the Cherokees' tax exemption on the basis of an 1868 federal revenue law that purported to impose a federal tax on various articles, including tobacco, "produced anywhere within the exterior boundaries of the United States." In the *Cherokee Tobacco* case (1870),[8] the United States Supreme Court sided with the Cherokees' business rivals; had Congress intended to exempt Indian lands from the 1868 law, it would have expressly said so. More generally, the Court ruled that "a treaty may supersede a prior act of Congress, and an act of Congress may supersede a prior treaty."[9] This ruling effectively cleared the way for Congress to make a full frontal assault on treaty-making with all Indian tribes, and in March 1871, Congress ended the practice. Two justices dissented in *Cherokee Tobacco* on the basis that precisely the opposite rule should have applied, i.e., that laws of general applicability do not apply to Indian territories unless Congress expressly so provides.

The success of the Watie and Boudinot tobacco venture ultimately led to significant changes in the rules of the game for operating in Indian Country, including those governing economic development. As summarized by McLoughlin:

Boudinot's experience demonstrated that white business-people in the United States were not prepared to accept competition from Indians. When Indians demonstrated the ability to make money in a competitive business, they were not praised for learning the rules of capitalist enterprise and exhibiting business acumen. If an Indian nation's ambiguous status gave it any competitive edge, the advantage was promptly taken away by unilateral action; tariffs against foreign competition served the same end for overseas competitors. American free enterprise was quick to define "unfair competition" by others.[10]

In the modern era, the Supreme Court has done its share of erasing any competitive edge that might result from the tribes' "ambiguous status." In the very active and complex area of taxation powers, the Court has produced rules that have increasingly narrowed the scope of the tribe's taxing authority and broadened the reach of state taxing authority inside Indian Country. As recently as 1982, in *Merrion v. Jicarilla Apache Tribe,* the Court characterized tribal taxing authority as "a fundamental attribute of sovereignty" and expressly confirmed the view that tribal taxing powers extended throughout the reservation, even on lands owned by non-Indians in fee simple.[11] Less than two decades later, the court confined *Merrion* to its facts and ruled that any exercise of inherent tribal taxing power in Indian Country beyond trust lands would have to meet one of the two *Montana* exceptions to be enforceable against non-Indians on their fee lands.[12]

Perhaps more damaging from an economic perspective, the Court has gradually allowed the state's taxing power to enter Indian Country to reach individuals who are not tribal members and corporate entities that are not affiliated with the tribe. In cases where both the state and the tribes are authorized to tax the same activity—e.g., oil and gas production in Indian Country—the spectre of "double taxation" may cause tribes either to forgo their taxes or to reduce their tax rates so as not to dissuade developers from doing business on the reservation.[13] To be sure, the Court has repeatedly affirmed as a categorical rule that absent Congress's permission, the state's taxing power does not reach Indian tribes or their members within tribal lands.[14] Further, where the "legal incidence" of the state taxes falls on non-Indians (or nonmember Indians), the Court will only uphold the tax if its application in Indian Country is otherwise supported by federal law. As we'll see shortly, this has occurred most regularly in the context of tribal sales of cigarettes (and motor fuels) on the reservations. In these instances, the Court often relies on an "interests-balancing" test that weighs the interests of all three sovereigns to "determine whether, in the specific context, the exercise of state authority would violate federal law."[15]

The modern-day tobacco wars have provided numerous opportunities for the Court to rehearse and apply these legal principles. Beginning in the early 1970s, several tribes established tribally owned or member owned "smokeshops" on tribal lands offering cigarettes at discount prices to reflect the absence of a state tax. The tribes have, and often exercise, the legal authority to impose their own taxes on sales made to all customers, including non-Indians.[16] Even in these formative years, revenues from cigarette sales and taxes represented hundreds of thousands of dollars of new revenue for tribes seeking to stem the cycle of poverty in Indian Country. States, however, reacted quickly to stem the cigarette trade in Indian Country, fearful of losing their own grip on the lucrative state tax revenues derived from cigarette sales. As in the *Cherokee Tobacco* case a century before, the tribes' competitors (here, the states) argued that the tribes were unfairly exploiting their "ambiguous status" to divert cigarette tax dollars from the state's coffers into Indian hands. Perhaps not surprisingly, the Court agreed with the states. Indian tribes were effectively denied the opportunity to exercise the same sovereign prerogative as the states to employ tax exemptions and other taxing schemes to stimulate or respond to market forces. In 1980, in *Washington* v. *Confederated Tribes of the Colville Indian Reservation,* the Court offered the following instruction on the limits of tribal authority to set reservation economic policy, particularly in the face of state opposition:

> It is painfully apparent that the value marketed by the smokeshops to persons coming from outside is not generated on the reservations by activities in which the Indians have a significant interest. What the smokeshops offer these customers, and what is not available elsewhere, is solely an exemption from state taxation. The Tribes assert the power to create such exemptions by imposing their own taxes or otherwise earning revenues by participating in the reservation enterprises. If this assertion were accepted, the Tribes could impose a nominal tax and open chains of discount stores at reservation borders, selling goods of all descriptions at deep discounts and drawing customers from surrounding areas. We do not believe that principles of federal Indian law, whether stated in terms of pre-emption, tribal self-government, or otherwise, authorize Indian tribes thus to market an exemption from state taxation to persons who would normally do their business elsewhere.[17]

Besides constraining the tribes in their efforts to generate revenue from cigarette sales, the Court has sided with the states in sanctioning increasingly onerous record-keeping burdens on tribes to support and facilitate the collection of the state's cigarette taxes.[18] It is important to note that the Court has reaffirmed the doctrine of tribal sovereign immunity from suit. In the cigarette taxing cases, the Court has made it clear that while states may tax reservation-based sales to non-Indians, they may not sue the tribe to collect unpaid taxes. In short, the Court recognizes that there "is a difference between the right to demand compliance with state laws and the means available to enforce them."[19]

More recently, however, the Court has expressed deep ambivalence about the continued relevance of tribal sovereign immunity, particularly as Indian tribes become more active and influential participants in the nation's economy. In *Kiowa Tribe of Oklahoma* v. *Manufacturing Technologies, Inc.* (1998), the Court affirmed the tribe's immunity from suits on contracts, even those negotiated off the reservation.[20] The Court's reticence in so holding is quite evident in the following passage:

> There are reasons to doubt the wisdom of perpetuating the doctrine [of tribal sovereign immunity]. At one time, the doctrine of tribal immunity from suit might have been thought necessary to protect nascent tribal governments from encroachments by States. In our interdependent and mobile society, however, tribal immunity extends beyond what is needed to safeguard tribal self-governance. This is evident when tribes take part in the Nation's commerce. Tribal enterprises now include ski resorts, gambling, and sales of cigarettes to non-Indians. In this economic context, immunity can harm those who are unaware that they are dealing with a tribe, who do not know of tribal immunity, or who have no choice in the matter, as in the case of tort victims. These considerations might suggest a need to abrogate tribal immunity, at least as an overarching rule.[21]

Given the fragility of tribal sovereign authority, and the relatively modest (though important) gains tribes have made in improving their local economies, it is remarkable that the Court would see a need to jettison this important doctrine. Equally remarkable is the notion that pervasive national ignorance of tribal sovereign status and rights could be a basis for limiting or eliminating long-recognized tribal rights. In the context of *state* sovereign immunity, the Court has gone in entirely the opposite direction and found their immunity safeguarded within the Constitution itself. In *Seminole Tribe of Florida* v. *Florida* (1996), for example, the Court struck down as unconstitutional a provision of the

Indian Gaming Regulatory Act that allowed tribes to sue states in federal court for failing to negotiate a gaming compact arrangement. The Court read the Eleventh Amendment as embracing a doctrine of state sovereign immunity and ruled that Congress did not have the authority to subject states to such lawsuits without their consent.[22]

In the Court's collective imagination, tribal sovereign immunity seems to represent "surplus power" in much the same way Congress saw "surplus lands" in Indian Country in the late nineteenth century. Congress has nibbled at tribal sovereign immunity over the years and, at times, has entertained bills stripping tribes of all immunity. In 1998, for example, Senator Slade Gorton (Republican, Washington) introduced a bill, euphemistically named the American Indian Equal Justice Act, which would have done precisely that. The bill went nowhere, thanks to the efforts of senators like Daniel Inouye (Democrat, Hawaii), who zeroed in on the true purpose behind the bill: "Let us also be clear that what some would seek from this body, is not an alternative means of collecting state taxes, but rather action by the federal government to assure that commercial activities conducted on Indian lands are rendered incapable of competing in [the] free market place."[23]

Many Indian tribes and states have managed to resolve their legal and economic differences through negotiated settlement agreements, including agreements on vexatious tax policies.[24] In other parts of the country, however, the conflicts appear intractable and even devolve into physical confrontation. In July 2003, Rhode Island state police officers entered the Narragansett Indian tribe's lands in a dramatic show of force to shut down the tribe's newly opened smokeshop because it was selling unstamped and untaxed cigarettes. In a scene reminiscent of the violent clashes over civil rights, state police equipped with full riot gear and German shepherds arrested several tribal members, including the tribal chairman, for acting in violation of state law. A flurry of lawsuits followed contesting the state's right to collect and enforce the cigarette taxes in this manner. In May 2005, a federal appeals court panel of three judges upheld the state's taxing authority but ruled that the tribe's sovereign immunity shielded it from the state's criminal law enforcement measures. The full or "en banc" federal appeals court (all five judges) revisited the enforcement issue in December 2005. In May 2006, a sharply divided appeals court upheld the state's enforcement measures, basing their decision largely on language contained in a 1978 land claims agreement between the parties that was subsequently ratified by Congress. The majority recited the well-established principle that only clear and unequivocal acts can strip away a tribe's sovereign immunity but quickly added that any such limitations "need not use magic words" to accomplish the deed. The tribe had agreed to allow "all laws of the State" to apply "in full force and effect on the settlement lands," and therefore "surrendered any right to operate the settlement lands as an autonomous enclave." Furthermore, said the majority, "It is plainly not the case, as the Tribe would have it, that an Indian tribe can render any conceivable act on Indian lands (say, drug trafficking) impervious to state regulation by the simple expedient of labelling it 'tribal.'" The two dissenting judges castigated the majority for its misreading and misapplication of basic principles of federal Indian law, particularly the rules respecting tribal sovereign immunity. A proper reading of the land claims agreement and the resulting settlement act, according to these judges, would extend the state's authority only to individuals acting inside Narragansett tribal lands, but not to the tribe itself. In any event, tribal and federal law were both available to constrain any breaches of law beyond the state's reach, including the majority's unsupported concerns about drug trafficking, which neither party had even raised with the court. Both dissenting judges listed alternative measures by which the state could have lawfully enforced its cigarette taxes without resorting to the "confrontational alternative of a *Rambo-like raid*, totally invasive of those core tribal [sovereignty] interests" (emphasis added).[25]

Tax enforcement practices against Indian tribes are also a volatile subject in New York, where the state, the tribes and private businesses remain at loggerheads on the issue of cigarette taxation policy. The state won a unanimous decision from the United States Supreme Court in 1994 upholding the state's right to tax all tribal cigarette sales except those made to tribal members.[26] Efforts to enforce the state tax met with strong opposition from the state's Indian tribes and their supporters, and at times, the demonstrations were violent. While the legislature has amended the tax laws in this area several times, most recently in April 2005 with an effective date of March 1, 2006, the administration of former governor George Pataki refused to enforce it. In May 2006, an association of private convenience stores filed a lawsuit to compel the governor and the state's tax commissioner to begin enforcing the tax on sales made by Indian tribes to non-Indians. The association asserted that the policy of nonenforcement costs the state's treasury over $450 million in lost tax revenue and represents over $1 billion in lost retail sales by the convenience stores.[27]

The economic squeeze on Indian tribes over cigarette sales comes not just from the courts. In February 2006, the attorneys general of thirty-three states announced that Philip Morris, the nation's largest tobacco company, had agreed to halt cigarette shipments to suppliers who conduct their business via the Internet or through mail order deliveries. The states were equally successful in getting cooperation from major credit card companies and private shipping companies to help dry up the cigarette business conducted "off premises." Concerns with sales to underage smokers and lost sales tax revenues motivated the states to revise their legal strategy and go right to the source of the product.[28] In the absence of a negotiated agreement on taxation and revenue sharing between the states and the tribes, Internet and mail order sales made by Indian tribes could be deemed illegal under these new enforcement schemes, depriving tribes not only of their product supply but of the substantial revenues they represent.

The New York experience suggests that both the state and Indian tribes risk losing substantial revenue sources in contesting their respective rights to tax activities within Indian Country. Part of the problem clearly is the legal framework within which tribes and the states face off on these volatile matters of economic policy. The Supreme Court has produced a body of rules that are entirely too stingy to the tribal (and federal) interests in economic sovereign authority and entirely too deferential to the state interests in capturing tax revenue generated from activities inside Indian Country. Not surprisingly, people have looked to Congress to design a more balanced and respectful framework that would address the interests of the two embattled sovereigns and those of private industry. In a private memo to his fellow Supreme Court justices in the *Colville* case (1980), Justice William Brennan expressed frustration with Congress's lack of engagement on these important issues. Justice Brennan wrote:

> However much we would like some clarification from Congress in this area, we have received none in recent years. I find the suggestion that until we do we should resolve doubtful cases against the Indians extraordinary. Rather, I would think, we must attempt to fill in the interstices in existing laws and treaties as best we can. That process inevitably involves appropriate reference to broad federal policies and notions of Indian sovereignty, however amorphous. I do not read *McClanahan, Mescalero* and *Moe* to seal off evolution of the sovereignty doctrine at some arbitrary point in the past or to deprive it of any effect in new situations. Accordingly, I do not intend to alter my position on the cigarette tax.[29]

While Congress has thus far elected to leave states and tribes to find their own way through the morass of the modern-day cigarette wars, it responded very differently to another form of tribal economic development that clashed with state policies—reservation-based gambling.

Sometimes hailed as the "new white buffalo" in Indian Country,[30] tribal gambling has revolutionized the daily lives of many tribes and tribal members and provoked an outpouring of public commentary, legislative activity and, of course, litigation. Tribal gambling represents the intertwining of two subjects that have long been riddled with national ambivalence—the nature and scope of tribal sovereignty and the morality of gambling.[31] There is little ambivalence, however, about the fact that gambling in some parts of Indian Country is big business.

According to recent estimates, Indian gambling today is a $20 billion industry, representing nearly one-fourth of the gross gambling revenue generated in the United States.[32] Approximately 225 of the 562 federally recognized Indian tribes operate some form of gambling facility, from small bingo halls to state-of-the-art casinos, scattered over thirty states. The revenue generated from these tribal operations, however, is distributed in radically uneven ways. Revenue data from 2003 show that tribes in California and Connecticut alone represented about 40 percent of the total Indian gambling revenue; adding the "gambling tribes" from Wisconsin, Minnesota and Arizona pushed that number to over 61 percent, with the tribes in the remaining twenty-five states splitting the rest.[33]

The real estate mantra of "location, location, location" applies equally well to explain the distribution of gambling revenues in Indian Country. The Mashantucket Pequot and Mohegan tribes in southeastern Connecticut benefit tremendously from their location in one of the most densely populated corridors of the nation. The state of Connecticut benefits as well; each year, the two tribes turn over 25 percent of their gross revenues to the state, which in 2003 represented an infusion of about $400 million into Connecticut's coffers.[34]

Such staggering numbers have given rise to new mythologies about Indian people—that all Indians are rich, tribal governments no longer need financial support from the federal government and "rich Indians" are not "real Indians." These strains of "rich Indian racism"[35] have provoked considerable political backlash, as noted in the *Yankee* magazine article discussed in Chapter Four. Indian gambling has certainly allowed a number of tribes to halt and even reverse the cycle of poverty within their communities, but given the uneven distribution of gambling revenues, the majority of tribes have not experienced significant changes in their overall socioeconomic conditions. As noted in the National Gambling Impact Study Commission Final Report (1999), "Indian gambling has not been a panacea for the many economic and social problems that Native Americans continue to face."[36]

The foundation for tribal gambling is tribal sovereignty. The tribal gambling industry did not arise because the federal government accorded "special rights" to a tiny segment of the American population, but because tribal governments embraced the opportunities offered by gambling to fund their government operations and to offer services and benefits to tribal citizens. Most observers agree that the modern tribal gambling industry was born in 1981, the year the Seminole tribe in Florida successfully overcame Florida's efforts to shut down their high-stakes bingo operations.[37] Ironically, in that same year, the state governors' association convened its annual meeting in Atlantic City, New Jersey. Gambling surfaced on its agenda as a possible revenue source to shore up anticipated declines in federal monies for states under President Reagan's "new federalism."[38] Congress entertained various proposals to establish a framework for Indian Country gambling but nothing gained real traction until 1987. In that year, the Supreme Court handed down its decision in *California* v. *Cabazon Band of Mission Indians*.[39]

California asserted that federal law permitted it to regulate gambling operations throughout the state, including inside Indian Country. That claim rested principally on a federal law popularly known as Public Law 280, passed in 1953 during the so-called Termination era of federal Indian policy. The Supreme Court had earlier determined that Public Law 280 permitted states to enforce their criminal laws throughout Indian Country but not their civil or regulatory laws.[40] The test focused on the state's public policy, specifically whether the state's laws prohibit the subject activity or permit it subject to some regulatory control. If the laws are in the former category, they are "criminal" laws and, thus, enforceable in Indian Country under the authority of Public Law 280. In *Cabazon,* the Court held the tribe's gambling activities were of the sort generally permitted in California and the relevant laws were therefore "regulatory" laws not enforceable in Indian Country under federal law. Furthermore, the *Cabazon* opinion, authored by Justice Byron White (also the author of the decision in the 1980 *Colville* cigarette tax case), found the tribes' investment in its gambling facilities to be sufficiently distinct from the smokeshops of earlier cases to tip the "balance of interests" on the side of the tribe:

> [The tribes] have built modern facilities which provide recreational opportunities and ancillary services to their patrons, who do not simply drive onto the reservations, make purchases and depart, but spend extended periods of time there enjoying the services the Tribes provide. . . . The tribal bingo enterprises are similar to the resort complex, featuring hunting and fishing, that the Mescalero Apache Tribe operates on its reservation through the "concerted and sustained" management of reservation land and wildlife resources.[41]

California, with a host of other states trailing, brought the battle across the street to Capitol Hill to lobby Congress for legislation tempering the stunning results in the *Cabazon* case. Congress obliged by passing the Indian Gaming Regulatory Act (IGRA) in October 1988.[42] The law created a tripartite scheme to regulate gambling in Indian Country. Traditional tribal games of chance were classified as Class One games falling solely under the tribe's regulatory authority. Bingo and related games fall under Class Two and are regulated by a newly created federal body, the National Indian Gaming Commission. Adopting *Cabazon*'s "public policy" rationale, the federal law limits tribes to gambling activities not prohibited by state or federal law. All other games, including the more lucrative casino operations, fall under Class Three and require that states and tribes negotiate compacts that may cover the range of subjects prescribed by federal law (e.g., regulatory control of gaming operations, revenue sharing and criminal law enforcement). Again, tribes are limited to gambling activities that are not prohibited by state or federal law. IGRA also restricts the uses to which tribal gambling revenues may be applied, including funding for tribal governmental operations, providing services to tribal members and stimulating economic development. Tribes are also allowed to make direct per capita payments to tribal members (which are subject to federal income tax), though only one-quarter of the gambling tribes actually do so. Gambling revenue supports a host of tribal programs and services for members and the broader tribal community including health care, education, housing, elder care and instruction in native languages.

IGRA ensures that state public policy is respected when it comes to tribal gambling operations in Indian Country. In requiring state-tribal compacts for the more lucrative casino operations, IGRA allows states to have a substantial say in determining whether and under what terms tribal casino operations will be allowed. Anticipating state resistance to the whole idea of gambling in tribal lands, Congress insisted that states negotiate in good faith, and it afforded tribes the "hammer" of taking states to federal court if resistance did occur. In 1996, the Supreme Court removed the "hammer" on grounds that Congress lacked the constitutional authority to strip states of their sovereign immunity in these circumstances.[43] States may, of course, waive their immunity (as some have), and the federal government, on the tribe's behalf, may force states into court in order to hash out gambling conflicts in Indian Country. Otherwise, in cases where a state asserts its sovereign immunity, tribes may request that the secretary of the interior issue the procedures under which gambling operations, including Class Three games, may be conducted in Indian Country.[44] In September 2005, the Northern Arapaho tribe of Wyoming became the first tribe authorized under the secretary's procedures to operate Class Three gambling without a compact. Wyoming's resistance to compact negotiations, which the federal courts found to be unfounded and evidence of bad faith, proved quite costly as the interior secretary approved the tribe's Class Three gambling proposal without requiring that any payments be made to or regulatory authority shared with the state.[45] That experience is not likely to be replicated, however, because in 2007 a federal appeals court struck down the Secretary of Interior's procedures sanctioning Class Three gambling when states raise the sovereign immunity defense.[46]

States have, at times, exploited the compact process in an effort to get tribes to compromise other rights or powers in return for the state's concurrence in a gambling compact. For example, former Wisconsin governor Tommy Thompson attempted (unsuccessfully) to secure significant concessions from several gambling tribes on their treaty-based hunting and fishing rights and to enlarge the state's taxing authority on cigarettes and motor fuels sold in Indian Country as prerequisites to the gambling compacts.[47] Other states have looked to Indian gambling compacts as major revenue sources to help patch up deficits in state budgets.[48] While states are not allowed to tax casino operations (or even negotiate for the right to tax such operations), they are permitted to negotiate for a share of revenue to offset their regulatory costs in support of tribal gambling. Additionally, the federal government allows tribal payments to states beyond their regulatory costs if the tribes realize benefits beyond those contemplated by IGRA. Tribes in Connecticut and California, for example, make payments far in excess of the state's regulatory costs in exchange for having the monopoly on conducting Class Three gambling operations within those states.[49]

AS WITH MANY stories from Indian Country, the one relating to tribal efforts to revitalize their local economies is a mix of good and bad news. The concept of "economic development" triggers a multitude of meanings for people but Indian tribes approach the matter with the singular purpose best articulated by the noted legal scholar Philip "Sam" Deloria (Standing Rock Sioux) years ago: "Indians do not want to be poor anymore."[50] The good news is that tribal efforts on the ground show real, measurable progress in checking and, in some areas, reversing the pernicious cycle of poverty that has long pervaded their communities. Invariably these results show up in areas where tribal systems of governance operate in close harmony with traditional tribal values. The increasing prevalence of tribal-state negotiated agreements on a broad range of issues—such as tax policy, law enforcement and natural resources management— also fosters greater confidence in tribal operations and allows the tribes to direct their valuable resources toward services or programs instead of costly, and often unsatisfactory, litigation.[51]

The bad news, of course, is that there is much more work to be done. Attacking the lingering social, health and educational deficits in Indian Country is made inordinately more complicated by a legal system and legal rules that often frustrate rather than facilitate tribal governmental efforts. The legacy of prior federal policies also hampers economic progress, as tribes must make do with significantly diminished land bases, largely unfulfilled access to vital water supplies and persistent legal challenges by state and non-Indian actors who often wish that Indians would simply disappear. Tribal leaders are keenly aware of the moral implications of building tribal economies selling toxic products, such as cigarettes, and operating gambling facilities. For most tribal communities, however, those choices are grounded in economic pragmatism, not moral acceptance, and reflect the limited economic opportunities available to most tribal governments today.

PART THREE

ACCOMMODATING THE
FIRST SOVEREIGNS

7

INDIVIDUAL RIGHTS AND TRIBAL COMMUNAL INTERESTS

SECURING THE TRIBES' legal position within the nation's constitutional landscape is made difficult by our American legal tradition's focus on individual rights and interests. Tracing back to European origins, this legal tradition views the individual as the principal bearer of rights who is entitled to equal treatment before the law. Constraints on the individual's liberty imposed through law are permitted under the theory that individuals—united in common cause, purpose and outlook on the world—consent to those restrictions in the interests of the broader good. In this sense, then, the dignity of the individual serves as grounding for the legitimacy of government systems created and recognized by a collective of individuals.

Indian people and tribes bring starkly different experiences and values into this philosophical and legal mix. Tribal systems of self-governance historically tend to give much greater prominence and priority to broader communal interests than to individual interests. Federal laws like the Indian Civil Rights Act of 1968 and the Indian Child Welfare Act of 1978 both walk a fine line in balancing the tribes' communal interests as sovereign governments with individual rights of personal autonomy. In 1924, Congress bestowed (some would say imposed) American citizenship on all Indian people born in the United States who were not already citizens.[1] As a result, members of federally recognized Indian tribes exercise rights of citizenship in three distinct political entities—their own tribe, their state of domicile and the United States government. It is important to note that just before Congress's unilateral citizenship act the Supreme Court had already held that Indians remained subject to Congress's plenary authority even after they became United States citizens. In *United States* v. *Nice* (1916), the Court stated, "[United States] Citizenship is not incompatible with tribal existence or continued guardianship, and so may be conferred without completely emancipating the Indians or placing them beyond the reach of congressional regulations adapted for their protection."[2] Nonmembers living within tribal communities increasingly participate in the political life of the reservations but, strictly speaking, they are not tribal citizens.[3] As we've seen in Part One, the modern Supreme Court has often pointed to this political reality as the basis for stripping tribes of legal authority over nonmembers.

The clash of political philosophies and overlapping citizenship—at least in the case of Indian citizens—gives rise to a number of interesting legal challenges in Indian Country. As domestic dual citizens, American Indian members of federally recognized tribes are heirs to the American legal tradition respecting individual autonomy as well as their own tribal systems that attach significantly higher weight to communal tribal interests. While recognizing that neither legal system functions in any absolute sense, there is clearly a tension between the two systems that complicates the administration of justice in Indian Country. This chapter brings the tension to the surface to examine how the nation's three sovereigns engage with, mediate and resolve individual rights of personal autonomy and the tribe's communal interests as America's first sovereigns.

As a preliminary matter, it should be noted that the tension between the American (which embraces the federal and state sovereigns) and tribal legal traditions has at least two important dimensions. The first has to do with legal recognition of group rights generally, especially when the group is distinguished along racial or ethnic lines. The second dimension relates to the relevance of "consent theory" as the philosophical footing of legitimate government in today's political settings.

The nation's atrocious record on the misuse of legal racial classifications to discriminate against certain racial minority groups has caused the modern Supreme Court to move with great reluctance toward sanctioning any racially based legal classifications, even those with such benevolent aims as achieving racial and ethnic diversity in American higher education.[4] On the one hand, the Court reminds us that "one of the principal reasons race is treated as a forbidden classification is that it demeans the dignity and worth of a person to be judged by ancestry instead of by his or her own merit and essential qualities."[5] On the other hand, the Court has acknowledged that in our society, "race unfortunately still matters."[6] The Supreme Court has isolated the field of federal Indian law from challenges grounded in racial discrimination on the theory that federal classifications among and distinctive treatment of Indians and tribes are in fact political, not racial, classifications.[7] This technical distinction has not prevented private citizens and elected officials from waging war against tribal sovereignty as an affront to principles of equal treatment before the law. The hostility against tribes' having any sort of "special rights" is often rooted in patent racism against Indian people. But in truth, the situation is usually more complex than that. Nontribal Americans and even many tribal members have far greater exposure to, knowledge of and experience with the prevailing legal tradition of individual rights than they do with the legal recognition of tribes as politically sovereign bodies. To the extent this collective ignorance negatively affects the development of tribal sovereign rights, it is (or should be) a cause for great concern among political, educational and policy leaders at all levels of government. As legal scholar Frank Pommersheim once noted, education for all Americans on tribal sovereignty should really begin in the third grade.[8] Otherwise, successive generations will replay the same conflicts rooted in the tensions now being addressed.

On the matter of "consent theory," the Court is ambivalent in its use of this concept as a tool to prescribe the nature and scope of legitimate governmental authority, especially tribal sovereign authority. In *Merrion* v. *Jicarilla Apache Tribe* (1982), a case upholding the tribe's taxing authority over non-Indian companies operating on tribal trust lands, a solid majority of the Court rejected "consent theory" as a limiting principle of tribal sovereignty. The Court stated, "Whatever place consent may have in contractual matters and in the creation of democratic governments, it has little if any role in measuring the validity of an exercise of legitimate sovereign authority. Requiring the consent of the entrant deposits in the hands of the excludable non-Indian the source of the tribe's power, when the power instead derives from sovereignty itself. Only the Federal Government may limit a tribe's exercise of its sovereign authority."[9] Years later, in *Duro* v. *Reina* (1990), the Court majority went in the other direction to embrace consent theory and hold that tribes lacked criminal jurisdiction over nonmember Indian offenders. According to the Court, "Tribal authority over members, who are also [American] citizens, is not subject to these objections. Retained criminal jurisdiction over members is accepted by our precedents and justified by the voluntary character of tribal membership and the concomitant right of participation in a tribal government, the *authority of which rests on consent*" (emphasis added).[10] Two dissenting justices pointed out that the Court had never applied such limits on other sovereigns: "If such were the case, a State could not prosecute nonresidents, and this country could not prosecute aliens who violate our laws. The commission of a crime on the reservation is all the 'consent' that is necessary to allow the tribe to exercise criminal jurisdiction over the nonmember Indian."[11]

More broadly, the Court's appeal to "popular sovereignty" imposes the Western legal theory of "consent of the governed" in a way that both legitimates the tribes' governance power in the eyes of the federal government and constrains them when it comes to exercising authority over nonmembers. As one legal commentator notes, "Even if Indigenous people strive to harness and deploy political power in post-colonial states they do so in the language and the terms provided for them by the constitutional forms and political culture imposed on them during the colonial past. To be citizens on a par with others is to be *de facto* whites, to engage in a process not of their making, and so to have indigenous voices silenced and replaced by voices borrowed from the other."[12]

The Court's tendency to review exercises of tribal power through the lens of Western-based legal principles and ideals reveals another pressure point on tribal sovereignty that tribes and their leaders must anticipate and be prepared to answer. This trend is likely to continue under the leadership of the new chief justice, John G. Roberts, Jr. As White House counsel during the Reagan years, Roberts's views on individual rights of equality created a blind spot that prevented him from seeing or understanding how earlier federal laws could drastically undermine the entire framework for tribal sovereignty. In 1983, for example, he was asked to respond to a proposed policy statement that called on Congress to repudiate House Concurrent Resolution 108. This 1950s resolution embodied the Termination era–philosophy that was designed to abolish all traces of tribal sovereignty and make all Indians fully subject to state law, like other American citizens. The resolution, in pertinent part, provided: "It is the policy of Congress, as rapidly as possible, to make the Indians within the territorial limits of the United States subject to the same laws and entitled to the same privileges and responsibilities as are applicable to other citizens of the United States, and to end their status as wards of the United States, and to grant them all the rights and privileges pertaining to American citizenship." In his response memo to his superiors, Roberts expressed great astonishment at tribal opposition to the "equality" principles enshrined in a resolution that, in his view, "reads like motherhood and apple pie." Roberts said he was advised "that Indians oppose the notions of 'equality' embodied in H. Con. Res. 108 as departures from their 'special' status, and that renunciation of

H. Con. Res. 108 (itself having no legal effect) has great symbolic value."[13]

In his 2005 confirmation hearings for the high court position, Judge (now Chief Justice) Roberts gave indications that he still harbored gross misunderstandings of tribal sovereignty and Indian rights generally, filtering these legal doctrines through the lens of rights designed to advance the condition of individuals, not discrete groups. For example, in response to Senator Kennedy's questions on equal opportunity and affirmative action, Judge Roberts opened with a reference to *Rice* v. *Cayetano* (2000)[14] where he said, "In the *Rice* v. *Cayetano* case, for example, before the Supreme Court, I argued in favor of affirmative action for native Hawaiians."[15] Senator Kennedy accurately reminded the nominee that *Cayetano* in fact had nothing to do with affirmative action. Instead, the case involved a legal challenge to a state election scheme for the leadership of the Office of Hawaiian Affairs (OHA), a state entity charged with improving the conditions of Native Hawaiians. Only individuals who met the state definition of "Native Hawaiian" were entitled to vote for OHA's leaders. The Supreme Court struck down this election scheme under the Fifteenth Amendment, which forbids discrimination in federal or state elections "on account of race, color, or previous condition of servitude." The fact that nominee, now chief justice, Roberts would conflate legal doctrines that advance the condition of individual citizens with those that are designed to advance the condition of discrete groups, such as Indian tribes, illustrates the serious challenges faced by tribes and their advocates in overcoming the pervasive illiteracy about tribal sovereignty that exists among the nation's most influential rulemakers.

AGAINST THIS BACKDROP of conflicting legal and philosophical traditions, we turn to consider situations arising on the ground in Indian Country that illustrate the tensions noted above and provide insight into the legal responses of the various sovereigns. Not surprisingly, some of these situations involve issues of general national significance, in which lawmakers have struggled to define the proper role of government, including government regulation of such highly sensitive personal matters as abortion, marriage between same-sex persons and child custody decisions. In these situations, the tribe's communal interests in preserving its sovereign and cultural integrity may actually be quite solicitous of the individual rights at stake and, at other times, may be in direct competition or in conflict with those interests. In other instances, the tensions between individual rights and tribal communal interests arise in contexts that more directly implicate the tribe's sovereign prerogatives to maintain its cultural integrity through regulation of group membership and its management of access to and use of various forms of cultural resources and knowledge.

BEGINNINGS: RIGHT TO LIFE AND ABORTION IN INDIAN COUNTRY

In March 2006, South Dakota governor Mike Rounds signed into law the nation's most restrictive abortion law with the stated objective of ultimately having the newly reconstituted Supreme Court reverse its controversial 1973 abortion rights decision in *Roe* v. *Wade*.[16] The South Dakota Women's Health and Human Life Protection Act of 2006 defined human life as beginning at the time of conception, and mandated that state constitutional rights of due process apply equally to born and unborn human beings, and that under the state constitution, "A pregnant mother and her unborn child each possess a natural and inalienable right to life." The law imposed criminal sanctions at the felony level against all persons who aid or facilitate an abortion with the sole exception of licensed physicians working to prevent the death of the pregnant mother. Securing an abortion in South Dakota is already difficult, because there is only one health clinic offering the procedure in the entire state. The problem is even more acute for Indian women nationally who rely on health services provided through the federal Indian Health Service. Federal law prohibits the use of federal money to perform abortion services except in cases where the mother's life would be endangered if the fetus were carried to term or in cases where the pregnancy results from rape or incest.[17]

Shortly afterward, and in response to the governor's action, Cecelia Fire Thunder, the Oglala Sioux tribe's first woman president, announced that her tribe would open its own abortion clinic on the Pine Ridge Indian Reservation to preserve the rights of all women who elected to terminate their pregnancy. Fire Thunder, a former nurse and employee of the state health department, was born and raised at Pine Ridge and later participated in the federal government's Indian Relocation program, which, she says, "put us in cities [with the hope] we would disappear."[18] She viewed the tribal initiative as an exercise of tribal sovereign rights and support for women's rights generally. She noted that "ultimately, this is a much bigger issue than just abortion. The women of America should be outraged that policies and decisions about their bodies are being made by male politicians and clergy. It's time for women to reclaim their bodies."[19]

Subsequent developments at the state and tribal level helped to dissipate this potential clash of state and tribal policies on individual rights. In November 2006, South Dakota citizens rejected the state abortion ban at a voter referendum on the new law.[20] Furthermore, Oglala Sioux tribal members voted Fire Thunder out of office, reportedly because of her views on the abortion issue, although citizens in the two counties that make up the Oglala Sioux Reservation voted against the abortion ban by substantial majorities.[21]

Notwithstanding these developments, the tribe's proposed action in response to the South Dakota abortion ban presents a fascinating case study in governmental respect for individual rights, with the tribal governmental response in the abortion context actually more solicitous of individual privacy rights than the surrounding state government. The tribe's proposed action also raised a number of interesting and challenging legal questions. For example, it is unclear whether the Oglalas' *tribal* law even supports a woman's right to abort her fetus. The Oglala Sioux tribe's Law and Order Code has a specific provision on "unborn children" stating: "A child conceived, but not born, is to be deemed an existing person so far as may be necessary for its interests and welfare to be protected in the event of its subsequent birth." Then president Fire Thunder maintained that historically, tribal women had access to traditional medicine to aid in terminating pregnancies: "You didn't have people passing laws to control a woman's body."[22] Additionally, while Indian tribes are bound by the provisions of the Indian Civil Rights Act (ICRA), including guarantees of equal protection and due process of law to all "persons," the tribal courts are not bound by federal court interpretations of those statutory terms.[23] In other words, the principle of tribal sovereignty provides tribes with flexibility to interpret the imposed ICRA rights in accordance with tribal values and traditions, with results that may be consonant with or in tension with federal (or state) court interpretations of those rights. How much tension the nation's constitutional system is prepared to tolerate or accept is always open to question, but the potential for divergent rulings is ever present given the unique and persistent cultural values that inform tribal decision-making. As legal scholar Frank Pommersheim reminds us, "Tribal courts do not exist solely to reproduce or replicate the dominant canon appearing in state and federal courts. If they did, the process of colonization would be complete and the unique legal cultures of the tribes fully extirpated."[24]

A number of states have already enacted abortion bans comparable to South Dakota's in a concerted effort to present the newly constituted Supreme Court with the opportunity to reverse its landmark ruling in *Roe* v. *Wade*. In the recent *Gonzales* v. *Carhart* (2007)[25] case, the Court upheld for the first time a governmental ban on a particular abortion procedure, a signal to some observers that *Roe*'s days may be numbered. At a minimum, these events suggest that the ground rules for government intervention into the private lives of citizens in the volatile abortion context are very much in flux. Counterinitiatives like that of the Oglala Sioux would then set up a compelling test of our national commitment to tribal sovereignty as well as our belief in cultural and legal pluralism.

We should also note that initiatives like that of the Oglala Sioux raise a host of other unanswered legal issues. For example, it is unclear whether physicians working at a tribal clinic would remain subject to state criminal sanctions if they provided abortions in violation of state law, especially if they were licensed by the state. Typically, state criminal law cannot apply in Indian Country absent express congressional approval. The Supreme Court has upheld exclusive state authority to prosecute reservation-based crimes involving only non-Indians in circumstances that do not directly implicate important tribal interests.[26] That authority alone may not be sufficient to permit state law to reach the activities of a tribal health clinic employee, even a state-licensed non-Indian physician performing an abortion on behalf of a non-Indian patient, where the activities are legally sanctioned by the tribe and consistent with prevailing national constitutional protections. The rules get even murkier if the tribe licenses the physician or if tribal members are involved either as the treating physician, the patient or even the father of the fetus. In each instance, a reviewing court would be required to examine closely the individual rights of personal autonomy, particularly the legal source and content of those rights, along with the tribe's interest in maintaining its sovereign prerogatives within Indian Country.

Setting limits on governmental authority to regulate women's bodies comes up in another equally controversial area of social, legal and health policy. Women who consume alcohol or illicit drugs during pregnancy can endanger the normal development of their fetus. In Indian Country, the incidence of children born with Fetal Alcohol Spectrum Disorder (FASD) is conservatively estimated to be three times the rate for the total population.[27] Children born with disabilities falling under FASD suffer brain damage that can cause lifelong cognitive and behavioral impairments. Most tribes lack the resources to deal effectively with this serious problem, which was elevated to national prominence following publication of the late Indian scholar Michael Dorris's book, *The Broken Cord* (1989), chronicling his family's efforts to raise a child with Fetal Alcohol Syndrome. At least one tribe reportedly employed incarceration of a pregnant woman as a drastic intervention measure,[28] while other tribes—and several states—have rewritten their criminal laws to punish prenatal injury as a form of child abuse. Health experts reject such drastic measures to address this problem and are concerned that women would simply avoid seeking prenatal care (if it's even available) if they are at risk for criminal sanctions. From the standpoint of federal Indian law, incarceration or any other court-ordered restraint on a pregnant woman's liberty would fall under the habeas corpus provisions of the Indian Civil Rights Act, allowing her to enter federal court to challenge the legality of her "detention by order of an Indian tribe." Contrary to assertions in Dorris's book, it is simply incorrect that "Indian governments can do whatever they want."[29]

RELATIONSHIPS: TWO-SPIRIT PEOPLE AND THE MARRIAGE DEBATE

The national debates on the right of same-sex couples to marry have spilled over into Indian Country as gay and lesbian tribal members demand that tribes recognize their rights to marry as expressions of individual autonomy and traditional tribal cultural values.

In September 2003, an Oklahoma hospital refused Dawn McKinley's request to be with her partner, Kathy Reynolds, who was hospitalized and treated for a serious back injury. McKinley was not considered a family member under state law. To avoid a recurrence of this problem, the two women, enrolled members of the Cherokee Nation in Oklahoma, obtained a marriage application from their tribe and were married in May 2004 by a tribally sanctioned religious official. At the time, Cherokee marriage law defined marriage as a union between a "provider" and a "companion." In June 2004, the Cherokee Tribal Council voted unanimously to amend the tribe's marriage act to expressly prohibit marriage

between persons of the same sex. The minutes of that council meeting reflect that several members objected to same-sex marriage as
being contrary to Christian values and teachings. At the same time,
one council member viewed the proposed legislation as overly in-
trusive of individual rights but ultimately voted in favor of it based
on feedback from his constituents.

Lawsuits filed against the couple in tribal courts have thus far
prevented them from registering their marriage certificate with the
Cherokee Nation, the final step in validating their marriage. On
two occasions, the Cherokee Nation's highest court, the Judicial
Appeals Tribunal (JAT—now called the Supreme Court), dismissed
the suits on grounds that the individuals filing the actions lacked
"standing," or in other words, a sufficiently strong legal interest in
the matter to bring the claim. The Cherokee Nation requires persons to demonstrate a specific particularized harm or actual injury
in order to bring claims in Cherokee courts. The latest suit, filed by
several members of the Cherokee Tribal Council, was thrown out
in December 2005. The JAT ruled that the council members' concern for the reputation of the Cherokee Nation and their assertion
that same-sex marriages were inconsistent with Cherokee culture
were insufficient grounds to support standing. The court did not
have occasion to rule on the substantive questions regarding same-
sex marriage as a matter of tribal law, though it did receive a detailed affidavit from anthropologist Brian J. Gilley, who maintained
that Cherokee culture and traditional law recognized marriages
involving "two-spirit" people.[30] In a recent book on the subject, Gilley suggests that for many tribes, two-spirit people were regarded as
a distinct third gender, neither man nor woman. For example, the
Zuni tribe recognized the genders of men, women and *lhamana*. According to Gilley, "Lhamana was the third gender occupied by a
male-bodied person. The lhamana dressed as women and per-
formed women's crafts such as weaving and potting, but also had the
physical strength to fulfil certain male-oriented pursuits such as
hunting big game and cutting firewood."[31]

In the Cherokee setting, it is unclear whether Reynolds and

McKinley will ever be allowed to finalize their marriage (a third suit is now pending). Likewise, it is uncertain whether the Cherokee Supreme Court would uphold the amendment to the Cherokee marriage act if it were challenged on constitutional grounds. The recently amended Cherokee Constitution guarantees all persons that "equal protection shall be afforded under the laws of the Cherokee Nation."[32]

The Navajo Nation also recently turned its attention to the subject of same-sex marriage. In June 2005, the tribal council voted to override the president's veto of the Dine Marriage Act of 2005, a law that expressly prohibits same-sex marriage. As in the Cherokee case, there was intense debate among tribal members about whether traditional Navajo law recognized the legal right of "two-spirited ones" to participate in Navajo marriages. A petition drive among tribal members invoked both traditional customary law and tribal constitutional law in support of same-sex marriage. One provision of the tribe's Bill of Rights provides that "equality of rights under the law shall not be denied or abridged by the Navajo Nation on account of sex." Since the ban on same-sex marriage applies equally to men and women, a reviewing Navajo court could well rule that the law does not discriminate on the basis of sex. Unlike the Cherokee Nation, however, the Navajo Nation recognizes an expansive concept of standing.[33] These legal principles suggest that there are both substantive and procedural grounds for tribal members to test the legality of the same-sex marriage ban in the Navajo Nation's courts.

In the event the Cherokee, the Navajo or any other tribal nation ultimately rules in favor of same-sex marriages as a matter of tribal law, there is no assurance that other sovereigns within the United States would respect those determinations. Congress included Indian tribes in the Defense of Marriage Act (DOMA), a federal law that essentially allows states, territories, possessions of the United States and Indian tribes to ignore another jurisdiction's rulings or public acts on the subject of same-sex marriage.[34] The Supreme Court has yet to review the federal

DOMA but at least one lower federal court has affirmed its constitutionality.[35]

THE NEXT GENERATION: INDIAN CHILDREN AS TRIBAL RESOURCES

In 1978, Congress enacted the Indian Child Welfare Act (ICWA) in an effort to stem the abuse of state legal practices that contributed to the "wholesale removal of Indian children from their homes."[36] The federal law declares that "there is no resource that is more vital to the continued existence and integrity of Indian tribes than their children and that the United States has a direct interest, as trustee, in protecting Indian children who are members of or are eligible for membership in an Indian tribe."[37] Congress considered testimony indicating that by the mid-1970s, about one-third of "all Indian children had been separated from their families and placed in adoptive families, foster care, or institutions."[38] Witnesses voiced concerns about the negative impact such practices had on individual Indian children and on the broader tribal community. Calvin Isaac, tribal leader of the Mississippi band of Choctaw Indians, spoke for much of Indian Country when he articulated the following:

> Culturally, the chances of Indian survival are significantly reduced if our children, the only real means for the transmission of the tribal heritage, are to be raised in non-Indian homes and denied exposure to the ways of their People. Furthermore, these practices seriously undercut the tribes' ability to continue as self-governing communities. Probably in no area is it more important that tribal sovereignty be respected than in an area as socially and culturally determinative as family relationships.[39]

The state practices leading to widespread and often unfounded removal of Indian children stemmed regularly from cultural ignorance or even blatant racism about Indian families and their child-rearing capacities. State child welfare officials often ignored the extensive tribal kinship systems in which relatives actively participated in raising children as departures from the preferred model of the nuclear family. Such practices ruptured family and cultural ties between Indian children and their families just as effectively as the 1830s removal policies ruptured the ties between tribes and their ancestral homelands. Sadly, the United States' experience in removing the next generation of Indian children and placing them in non-Indian homes or institutions paralleled similar (or worse) practices in other nations, such as Canada and Australia, in their treatment of indigenous children.[40]

Congress responded with a law that recognized tribal governments as the first-line jurisdictional authorities to manage Indian child welfare cases and established a system of placement preferences that even states are required to follow when dealing with any Indian child custody proceeding. These twin features of the ICWA—allocation of tribal jurisdictional authority and substantive placement directives—were designed to restore meaningful tribal sovereign authority over these important legal matters and to maintain the stability of Indian families. Indeed, one court succinctly linked these twin objectives in noting that ICWA "expresses the presumption that it is in an Indian child's best interests to be placed in an Indian home in conformance with [the act's] placement preferences."[41]

Both the jurisdictional allocations and the substantive placement directives create the potential for tension between individual rights or preferences in child welfare matters and the tribe's communal interests in preserving its sovereign and cultural integrity. The Supreme Court, in the only ICWA case it has reviewed to date, recognized this tension in the context of the act's jurisdictional framework. In *Mississippi Band of Choctaw Indians* v. *Holyfield* (1989),[42] the Court held that the tribal courts had exclusive jurisdiction over adoption proceedings involving children born to two Choctaw Indian parents, both of whom were tribal members domiciled on the Choctaw Reservation. In *Holyfield,* the Choctaw parents left the reservation to give birth to twins and voluntarily surrendered their parental rights in favor of the Holyfields, a non-Indian adoptive family, through the Mississippi state courts. Within a month of the twins' birth, the state court entered a final decree of adoption in favor of the Holyfields. About two months later, after learning about the state court adoption proceedings, the Choctaw tribe petitioned the Mississippi state court to vacate (or annul) its adoption decree on grounds that the ICWA accorded exclusive jurisdiction to the tribal courts in these matters. The state court rejected the tribe's petition, noting that at no time were the infants ever physically present on the Choctaw Reservation. The Choctaw tribe lost its appeal to the Mississippi Supreme Court but succeeded in getting the case before the United States Supreme Court.

The Supreme Court ruled in the tribe's favor and held the adoption decree invalid since the state courts had no legal authority over the proceedings. The Court noted that the ICWA assigns to tribal governments the exclusive jurisdiction for child custody proceedings involving Indian children who reside in or are "domiciled" within the reservation.[43] The Court held that for purposes of the ICWA, the children's domicile was the same as their parents'—the Choctaw Reservation—and therefore, under ICWA's express terms, only the tribe had jurisdiction to enter an adoption decree.

The Supreme Court recognized the tension between its ruling and the expectations and preferences of both the biological and adoptive parents. Nonetheless, the Court insisted that even the individual preferences of Indian families must conform to ICWA and its broader purposes: "Tribal jurisdiction under [the act] was not meant to be defeated by the actions of individual members of the tribe, for Congress was concerned not solely about the interests of Indian children and families, but also about the impact on the tribes themselves of the large numbers of Indian children adopted by non-Indians."[44] Furthermore, the Court added, "Permitting individual members of the tribe to avoid tribal exclusive jurisdiction by the simple expedient of giving birth off the reservation would, to a large extent, nullify the purpose the ICWA was intended to accomplish."[45] The Court recognized that the children had by then lived in the Holyfields' home for over three years, but it properly acknowledged that its role was not to decide the ultimate placement issue but to determine which governmental body was the proper *decision maker* under the ICWA. That governmental body was the Choctaw tribe itself. In the ensuing tribal court proceedings, the Choctaw tribal judge confirmed adoption rights in favor of the Holyfield family after finding it was in the children's best interests to remain in the only home they had known.[46]

The *Holyfield* decision is most significant for affirming the tribes' communal interests in maintaining cultural and social connections with Indian children and for recognizing those instances where the tribe's governmental authority to make related child welfare decisions is not only primary but exclusive. The tribe's exclusive jurisdiction applies to all Indian children who meet ICWA's definition of "Indian child" whether or not they are members of the tribe exercising jurisdiction.[47] In a vast number of other cases, however, the *Holyfield* holding does not apply, because the Indian child resides with a parent outside Indian Country. In those cases, tribes must rely on state courts to play their respective roles under ICWA in the proper administration of child custody matters. Generally, under ICWA, at the request of either parent, or the Indian custodian or the tribe itself, state courts must transfer an Indian child custody proceeding to the tribe's jurisdiction unless either parent objects or there is "good cause" to justify keeping the matter in state courts. A voluminous body of law has developed around this particular jurisdictional rule. The most controversial development to arise in the past two decades is the recognition of a doctrine known as the "existing Indian family" rule. Essentially, states recognizing this doctrine find that ICWA does not apply where the child involved has no demonstrable social and cultural links to an existing Indian family. The doctrine has attracted criticism for effectively substituting the state court's judgment about what it means to be "Indian" for purposes of the federal law. Most states that have actively considered the doctrine have rejected it as being out of line with overriding federal standards and policy but at least eight state jurisdictions have embraced the rule.[48]

ICWA's substantive placement directives, like its jurisdictional provisions, can also create tensions between individual rights (including those of the child) and the tribe's communal rights and interests. In making placements for adoption, for example, the federal law mandates that in the absence of good cause to the contrary, state courts must give preference to members of the child's extended Indian family, other members of the child's tribe or other Indian families.[49] The Bureau of Indian Affairs has developed guidelines for courts to find "good cause" to depart from the mandated placement preferences, which, according to some state courts, are definitive on the matter and displace even the universally applied "best interests of the child" standard that governs child custody matters in state courts.[50] The general history of ICWA litigation in the state courts suggests that most state court judges recognize, but struggle to achieve, the congressionally mandated optimum outcome of placing Indian children within Indian homes in their own tribal communities.[51] Part of the struggle, as noted above, is rooted in cultural and social ignorance about or overt hostility toward Indian societies. But another source of the struggle lies in the state courts' traditional adherence to and deeper familiarity with principles respecting individual rights and preferences, including those of children. Those individual rights and preferences are enshrined in national legislation like the Multiethnic Placement Act of 1994 that encourages interracial and interethnic adoption by explicitly forbidding discrimination in foster care and adoption placements on the basis of race, color or national origin.[52] Significantly, Congress wrote an exemption for child placements made under the ICWA. In other words, government actors are required to support the crossing of racial and ethnic boundaries in making child placement decisions if that will serve the child's best interest. In the case of Indian children, however, the presumption is that the child's best interests are served by maintaining his or her actual or even potential cultural and social links with his or her Indian tribe. Individuals who are ignorant about, unfamiliar with or hostile to the principle of tribal sovereignty are quite likely to react to such placement decisions as being antithetical to the nation's traditional respect for individual choice and discretion in the sensitive area of child custody. Divorced from the context of federal-tribal governmental relationships, the Indian child welfare cases in state courts may appear on the social radar as instances in which group rights unfairly trump individual rights and preferences. These scenarios again illustrate the urgent need for broad-scale recognition and education to enhance (or create) national literacy on Indian tribal sovereignty and the tribes' fundamental interests in preserving links to their next generation of members and leaders. An interesting and surprising twist to this story is the fact that many states, and now the federal government, are actively promoting child welfare programs that seek to bring relatives outside the nuclear family to serve as foster care placements for children who would otherwise be placed outside the family. These programs, ironically enough, are known as "kinship care programs."[53]

POLITICAL OUTSIDERS: PERSONAL IDENTITY AND TRIBAL MEMBERSHIP

The courts have long recognized the power of Indian tribes to set and enforce membership criteria for purposes of tribal law. In the landmark case of *Santa Clara Pueblo* v. *Martinez* (1978), the Supreme Court noted that "a tribe's right to define its own membership for tribal purposes has long been recognized as central to its existence as an independent political community."[54] As noted in Chapter Two, Julia Martinez challenged in federal court her own tribe's membership ordinance on equal protection grounds but was redirected by the Supreme Court to her tribe's court system. The Court in *Martinez* recognized that allowing an outside court to review such "delicate matters" would intrude on the tribe's sovereign prerogative to "maintain itself as a culturally and politically distinct entity."[55] In effect, the Court recognized the fine line

Congress attempted to walk in the Indian Civil Rights Act (1968) when it imposed Bill of Rights–style legal protections for individuals who come within the tribes' jurisdiction while respecting the tribes' traditions and unique place within the constitutional framework. According to the Court, tribes "remain quasi-sovereign nations which, by government structure, culture, and source of sovereignty are in many ways foreign to the constitutional institutions of the federal and state governments."[56]

Battles over tribal membership have a long history and, like the controversy in the *Martinez* case itself, often can be traced to the heavy hand of federal governmental intervention into the tribe's internal affairs. For instance, following the Civil War, the federal government required many of the major tribes in Oklahoma that had sided with the Confederacy to absorb as tribal citizens "persons of African descent" who were former slaves or freedmen living among the tribes.[57] In subsequent years, several of these tribes amended their constitutions and membership rules to limit membership to those persons who could prove tribal ancestry through blood relations with historical tribal members. The Cherokee Nation amended its constitution in 1975 but recognized membership broadly to include all persons who descended from "citizens" listed on the federal Dawes Commission Rolls used to allot tribal lands to individual members. The "Cherokee Freedmen" were expressly included in these historical membership rolls. In March 2006, the Cherokee Nation's highest court affirmed the tribal citizenship rights of the Cherokee Freedmen's descendants against an attempt by the tribal council to use ordinary legislation to limit membership to individuals who were "Cherokee by blood."[58] A year later, however, a majority of the Cherokee Nation approved an amendment to the Cherokee Constitution that limited membership to individuals who were bloodline descendants of Cherokee tribal members. The Freedmen's descendants, who no longer qualify for tribal membership, have taken their case to the federal government. The tribe maintains that it is merely exercising its inherent sovereign authority to determine the criteria for membership, a position backed up by federal law. The Freedmen's descendants, however, and some of their supporters in the United States Congress, see the influence of racial politics in the Cherokees' membership dispute and they want Congress to use the power of the purse as leverage to restore their membership in the tribe.[59]

In recent years, a number of membership disputes have developed in the wake of tribal success in gambling activities. Tribal enrollment offices face intense pressure from individuals seeking to attain (or in some instances, regain) membership status that, among other things, establishes their eligibility for a range of tribal benefits, including a share of the tribe's gambling revenues. Most of these disputes are contested in tribal courts as required by *Martinez*. Other individuals have tried, usually without success, to enter the federal courts through the side or back doors by naming federal officials as defendants. In one such suit, *Lewis* v. *Norton* (2005), the federal appeals court expressed sympathy for the plaintiffs' arguments but ultimately ruled that their claim could not "survive the double jurisdictional whammy of [tribal] sovereign immunity and lack of federal court jurisdiction to intervene in tribal membership disputes."[60] In *Lewis*, the plaintiffs expressly demanded to be recognized as tribal members in order to claim some share of the tribe's lucrative casino revenues. The court acknowledged that the tribal government's nonaction on the plaintiffs' membership application was "deeply troubling on the level of fundamental substantive justice," but it felt obliged to honor the longstanding principle of tribal sovereign immunity developed "before the gaming boom created a new and economically valuable premium on tribal membership."[61]

TELLING THE INDIAN STORY: MANAGING ACCESS AND USE OF CULTURAL RESOURCES AND KNOWLEDGE

Tribal efforts to maintain their cultural integrity often must rely on legal rules and procedures generated by the tribes themselves or embraced from outside sources. The management of group membership, as shown in the preceding section, has become an increasingly complex and volatile issue for tribes, particularly as the benefits of tribal membership have become more attractive in an economic and political sense. In a similar vein, tribal efforts to manage other aspects of their cultural heritage face equally daunting challenges, particularly in situations in which the tribe's cultural heritage is wrongfully appropriated for personal or commercial gain. Here, we are talking about cultural resources through which tribes and their members reproduce and transmit significant traditional values, beliefs and expressions and thereby re-create and reaffirm their distinctive cultural heritage. We've already seen how land and various other natural features are intimately connected with tribal peoples' sense of personal and group identity and, therefore, can serve as important cultural resources. In many instances, tribal members generate the items or practices that over time may comprise significant parts of the tribe's cultural storehouse. These may include tangible items such as carvings, masks, musical instruments or totem poles as well as intangible items such as songs, artistic designs, symbols and names, including the tribal name.[62] Cultural resources may also embrace traditional knowledge about plant and animal life and, in particular, uses and applications of those resources that can alleviate human suffering. These various forms or expressions of cultural heritage are often the binding ties to group and individual claims to a shared tribal identity and serve as the cornerstone for the perpetuation of a distinctive tribal voice. In short, managing the access and use of this cultural heritage is indispensable for tribes working to preserve their sovereign prerogatives to tell their own stories to succeeding tribal generations and to the world.

The threats to tribal cultural heritage most often involve various kinds of wrongful appropriation that take place outside tribal lands and are thus outside the reach of the tribe's sovereign authority. This means that Indian tribes and their members must rely on state or federal law to secure protection against such wrongful acts. When the cultural resources at issue involve such intangible items as songs, artistic designs, symbols or even the tribe's name, or some unique form of traditional knowledge, the instinctive legal reaction is to resort to protections contained in standard intellectual property law such as copyright, patent and trademark law. The appeal to standard intellectual property law to protect traditional forms of cultural heritage is often problematic and unworkable in a practical sense. The principal reason is that intellectual property law tends to operate around the axis of *individual* achievement and accomplishment. The law's operating assumption is that there is an identifiable author, composer, inventor, artist or designer whose ingenuity and personal investment, alone or sometimes in association with others, has led to the production of a work, a process or a design that may be eligible for protection under the various intellectual property laws. The legal protections, at their core, reward the creator (or a licensee) with a time-limited monopoly to profit from the creation and impose sanctions on all others who attempt to exploit the protected creation without legal authority. Many facets of a tribe's cultural heritage simply do not fit this paradigm, often because there is no identifiable creator of a particular work or the work was not produced or created for the purpose of economic gain. These legal impediments, coupled with the pervasive legacy of the "dying race" thesis and general lack of respect for Indian culture, has fueled the perception among members of the dominant society that tribal cultural heritage exists as part of the public domain and is freely available for use and exploitation. Take, for example, the widespread use of tribal names in the marketing of various products or services—the Jeep Cherokee, Apache helicopters, Winnebago recreational vehicles, Pequot hedge funds, Comanche bicycles, Dodge Dakotas, Mazda Navajo. In most instances, the appropriation of tribal names for commercial purposes occurred without the tribe's involvement or consent. Exceptions do exist, of course; the Apache tribe apparently welcomed and even conveyed blessings upon the Apache helicopter used by the United States military.[63] The irony (or perversity) of intellectual property law in the typical case is to recognize rights of trademark protection in favor of businesses or individuals who elected to trade on the tribe's name, leaving the tribe with little or no practical legal recourse for the wrongful appropriation.

There are some federal laws that attempt to provide a measure of protection against unlawful appropriation of tribal cultural heritage. The federal Indian Arts and Crafts Act,[64] dating back to 1935 and re-enacted in 1990, makes it illegal for anyone to sell a good in a way that falsely suggests the product was made by Indians. The market for genuine Indian-made articles such as jewelry, pottery, paintings, woven items and blankets is substantial. The market ranges from $400 million to $800 million annually with "rip-off" artists and producers draining between 10 and 20 percent of that market every year.[65] The central problem with this otherwise sound federal law is that it is seldom used. In 2005, a federal appeals court expressed astonishment at the paucity of activity under this law:

> Although the Indian Arts and Crafts Act dates back to 1935, this is—amazingly—the first reported appellate case under it. Until 1990, the only sanction for violating the false-advertising provision was criminal; and there were no prosecutions—zero. In 1990, Congress authorized government and private civil suits in which hefty damages can be awarded. There have been some suits under the amended statute, but none until this one that got beyond the district court level [citations omitted].[66]

On the other hand, another 1990 federal law, the Native American Graves Protection and Repatriation Act (NAGPRA), has had substantial impact on the treatment and disposition of tribal cultural resources that are associated with burial practices, including human remains of deceased tribal ancestors and other significant tribal religious or ceremonial activities. NAGPRA was written in response to yet another sad chapter in the United States' history with Indian tribes, in which the remains of deceased tribal members and other items found in tribal burial grounds were treated with profound disrespect and callousness.[67] The notorious Indian crania studies of the nineteenth century involved the desecration of grave sites and decapitation of thousands of Indian remains in an effort by some government-sponsored researchers to "prove" that Indians were intellectually inferior to whites and to confirm their fate as a dying race. In other instances, the grave robbing was done for economic gain or simply to satisfy the grotesque fascination or outright hostility some people held for dead Indians. For instance, historian Alvin Josephy describes how Kamiakin's remains were desecrated after his death in 1878:

> After his death, white men who knew who he was opened his grave and twisted his head off the decomposing body. Since white men had similarly decapitated the corpses of King Philip of New England, Osceola the Seminole, and Black Hawk the Sauk—and were later to do the same to the remains of old Joseph in the Wallowa Valley—Kamiakin was in good company.[68]

Also in the latter category comes the story of the Skull and Bones secret society at Yale University, whose members reportedly dug up the grave of the legendary Apache leader Geronimo at Fort Sill, Oklahoma, and brought back his skull to the society's campus home known as the "Tomb." In the mid-1980s, the San Carlos Apache tribe received information from an anonymous source indicating that Skull and Bones members, including Prescott Bush—a 1917 Yale graduate and grandfather of the United States president, George W. Bush—stationed at Fort Sill during the war years, had dug up the remains of the famous leader and brought his skull to New Haven. Until recently, this report was thrown into the basket of unproven college pranks gone badly. Recently, however, the *Yale Alumni Magazine* announced that a researcher had stumbled upon a letter written in 1918 by a Skull and Bones member that provides the first contemporaneous reference to the grave robbing. The letter states: "The skull of the worthy Geronimo, the Terrible, exhumed from its tomb at Fort Sill by your club & the K-t [Knight] Haffner, is now safe inside the T [Tomb]—together with his well worn femurs, bit and saddle horn."[69] The letter lends some weight to the story, but at a minimum, it reflects white society's attitude of disdain toward Indians and Indian remains that was so prevalent in this era.

NAGPRA tackles head-on this historic disdain toward Indian burial remains and related cultural items in two significant ways. First, it provides significant protection for Indian remains and related cultural items that are uncovered in the present day on federal or tribal lands. Indian burial remains found on private lands are typically handled under various state laws.[70] Second, for Indian remains and related cultural items already removed from burial sites and housed in institutions that receive federal money, the statute requires those institutions to inventory their collections, identify items that fall within NAGPRA's coverage and engage with tribes who can show a clear affiliation with the remains and cultural items on terms for the return of those cultural resources.[71]

The statute attempts to mediate a significant tension that exists between the tribe's communal interests in the respectful treatment of deceased ancestors and related cultural items and the scientists' individual interests in the study of those same resources. While many tribal leaders and legal scholars fail to see those interests as commensurable, the statute does provide a window of opportunity for scientists to conduct limited study of remains or cultural items in certain circumstances. In lawsuits brought under NAGPRA, the scientific community has argued that their statutory rights are actually grounded in constitutional norms that safeguard their individual rights of intellectual inquiry and access to information that make possible the exercise of rights to free speech.[72]

THE PRECEDING DISCUSSION highlights instances in which the tribe's communal interests in asserting and maintaining its sovereign prerogatives cut against the grain of our predominant legal philosophy and tradition anchored in respect for the rights of individual citizens. The resulting tensions often cause lawmakers and policy leaders to question the legitimacy of tribal sovereignty as both a legal and a moral concept. As a practical matter, the tension arising on the ground in Indian Country surfaces in the form of somewhat familiar claims that "government" is somehow dictating choices, or otherwise intruding unnecessarily or unlawfully into the affairs of private citizens. When that government is the Indian tribe, it invariably invites skepticism and, sometimes, outright hostility about why the law favors one group over another or why a particular group of citizens ought to be empowered to impose limits on other individuals. Compounding the problem is the fact that most American citizens see tribes as distinct racial groups, not as recognized governments. In these instances, we often see the inertia and force of equality principles being used as a sword to cut back on tribal authority, especially over nonmembers. The tradition of individual rights and equality under the law thus functions as a serious obstacle to accommodating Indian tribes as the nation's first sovereigns. As suggested above, a key step in softening these tensions would be to engage in broad-based action to enhance (or establish) greater national literacy about tribal sovereignty. Without such measures, and the requisite patience to allow them to make a meaningful impact in our communities, Indian tribes as political bodies will continue to exist precariously in the framework of our constitutional democracy.

8

A QUESTION OF
INSTITUTIONAL FIT

IN THE PREVIOUS chapter, we saw how the clash of legal and philosophical traditions between tribal and Western cultures creates tensions for tribal governments in the administration of justice within Indian Country. This tension complicates and often frustrates the efforts of legal actors working to secure the legal status of Indian tribal governments within our constitutional democracy.

In this chapter, we highlight another set of factors that influence and often complicate efforts to accommodate tribal governments as the nation's first sovereigns. Here, we focus attention on the rules of engagement by which the federal, state and tribal governments relate to one another and influence their respective internal workings. Scholars often highlight the fact that sovereignty is an inherently relational concept. In other words, governmental bodies claiming rights of sovereignty do not exercise such rights in a vacuum but in relation with other governmental bodies. A necessary consequence of this reality is that governments find it necessary to establish rules of engagement with other governments. At the international level, for example, foreign governments often come together through treaties or conventions to establish a framework of rules to govern matters of common concern, including commerce, national security, human rights and stewardship of natural resources. At the domestic level, federations like the United States often employ a national constitution to distribute political power between the national (or federal) government and the myriad local (or state) governments and to establish limits on each government's power in the lives of its citizens. As noted in earlier chapters, Indian tribes are recognized in federal law as distinct political bodies, able to dip into their own bucket of inherent sovereignty to regulate their members and activities within their territories. But Indian tribes are not "foreign nations" nor were they participants in the convention that led to the adoption of our national Constitution. As a result, their legal status is not easily accommodated within the rules of engagement typically observed by "truly" foreign nations or those rules governing federal-state relations under the rubric of the American Constitution. This question of institutional fit continues to frustrate tribal efforts to achieve a measure of security and permanence within our constitutional democracy.

Historically, United States–tribal relations swung like a pendulum, beginning with treatment of Indian tribes in the manner of foreign nations, followed by a period during which Congress treated tribes as domestic bodies subject to virtually unchecked plenary federal power, and finally settling into an ill-defined and precarious government-to-government political relationship. Along the way, the rules of engagement shifted from treaty-making between the two sovereigns to unilateral federal legislation in Indian affairs. In the modern era, there have been modest but important efforts to conduct intergovernmental relations along the lines of negotiated agreements between the federal government and tribes. The bilateral agreement on enforcement of the Endangered Species Act in Indian Country, discussed in Chapter Five, is a noteworthy example of these modern efforts.

In the early period of the nation's history, the United States adopted the rules of engagement practiced by earlier European colonizing powers, employing treaties as the principal mode for conducting relations with Indian tribes. As we've noted earlier, Article I of the federal Constitution deals with legislative powers and assigns to Congress the power "to regulate Commerce with foreign Nations, and among the several States, and with the Indian Tribes." The treaty-making power is actually covered in Article II, which deals with the powers of the executive branch. Section 2 of this article states the president "shall have Power, by and with the Advice and Consent of the Senate, to make Treaties, provided two-thirds of the Senators present concur." The nation's first elected leaders took these general constitutional provisions for their initial test runs in order to work out the ground rules by which federal relations with Indian tribes would be conducted. President George Washington insisted that the federal government follow the same formalities for ratifying treaties with Indian tribes as were observed for those with foreign nations. As historian Francis Paul Prucha explains, "The Senate, after some debate, accepted the president's view. Thus was the precedent established that Indian treaties—like those with foreign nations—be formally approved by the Senate before they took effect."[1]

It was not long before prominent American leaders began questioning the appropriateness of treaty-making with Indian tribes. The reasons underlying this skepticism were expressed in terms of political theory and racism toward Indian people. For example, in 1817, General (later president) Andrew Jackson wrote to President James Monroe counseling against the use of treaties with Indian tribes:

> I have long viewed treaties with the Indians as an absurdity not to be reconciled to the principles of our Government. The Indians are the subjects of the United States, inhabiting its territory and acknowledging its sovereignty. Then is it not absurd for the sovereign to negotiate by treaty with the subject? I have always thought that Congress had as much right to regulate by acts of legislation all Indian concerns as they had of Territories. There is only

this difference: that the inhabitants of Territories are citizens of the United States and entitled to the rights thereof; the Indians are subjects and entitled to their protection and fostering care. The proper guardian of this protection and fostering care is the legislature of the Union. I would therefore contend that the Legislature of the Union have the right to prescribe their bounds at pleasure and provide for their wants; and whenever the safety, interest or defence of the country should render it necessary for the Government of the United States to occupy and possess any part of the territory used by them for hunting, that they have the right to take it and dispose of it.[2]

Jackson also expressed concern that treaty-making would only delay the government's civilizing project among Indian people. Again, he wrote to the nation's leaders:

As long as they are permitted to roam over vast limits in pursuit of game, so long will they retain their savage manners and customs. . . . Circumscribe their bounds, put into their hands the utensils of husbandry, yield them protection, and enforce obedience to those just laws provided for their benefit, and in a short time they will be civilized. . . . There can be no doubt but that in this way more justice will be extended to the nations than by the farce which has been introduced of holding treaties with them.[3]

Over the course of the following decades, Jackson's prescriptions became hallmarks of United States Indian policy. The reservation system, the allotment policies, the regime of federal laws prohibiting Indian traditional religious practices and use of native languages and the overarching federal objective of imposing the model of the yeoman farmer on tribal communities became part and parcel of the government's civilizing plan for Indian people. Respect for the sovereign integrity of Indian tribes, as reflected in the practice of treaty-making, was in short supply during these years. Not surprisingly, Congress unilaterally ended the practice of treaty-making in 1871 by writing a law of dubious constitutional validity but which nonetheless communicated a significant demotion in the legal status of Indian tribes. The law was unceremoniously tacked on to an ordinary appropriation bill and provided the following: "That hereafter no Indian nation or tribe within the territory of the United States shall be acknowledged or recognized as an independent nation, tribe, or power with whom the United States may contract by treaty." This was a time during which the federal government's antitribalism efforts went into overdrive. In short order, Congress ushered in the policies leading to the dismantling of tribal communal lands, the prohibition of tribal cultural practices and the arrival of an enormous population of non-Indian settlers in Indian Country who would also serve as role models of honest, hard-working, patriotic Christian American citizens. The end of treaty-making with Indian tribes meant that the full Congress, not just the Senate, would oversee the process of converting former Indian lands into national lands available for white homesteaders, and it ensured that the formality of tribal consent would no longer impede that objective. Tribes were in little position to challenge this shift in federal Indian policy, since the balance of military and economic power tilted heavily in favor of the United States and tribal populations were approaching their lowest levels in history.[4] Moreover, there was ever-growing sentiment among national leaders that treaties had simply outlived whatever usefulness they had had. In 1873, the federal commissioner of Indian affairs characterized treaties as "a mere form to amuse and quiet savages, a half-compassionate, half-contemptuous humouring of unruly children."[5] Still, the inertia of treaty-making led Congress to continue to conduct much of its business with Indian tribes through the mechanism of negotiated agreements. The Supreme Court views these agreements in the same light as treaties: "Once ratified by Act of Congress, the provisions of the agreements become law, and like treaties, the supreme law of the land."[6]

Congress's 1871 legislation ending the practice of treaty-making expressly preserved the obligations and rights that were embraced within existing treaties with Indian tribes. The resulting paradox is that this particular federal law both recognized and significantly diminished the integrity of inherent tribal sovereignty. Additionally, by unilaterally altering the rules of engagement between the federal government and Indian tribes, Congress claimed a prerogative to legislate in Indian affairs in a manner that was disconnected both from the literal language of the Constitution and from long-standing federal practice. Beyond moving away from treaty-making, Congress began to assert power to regulate the affairs "*of* the Indian Tribes" instead of "*with* the Indian Tribes" as contemplated in the Constitution. For instance, in 1885, Congress enacted a criminal code, the Major Crimes Act, that applied to Indians committing certain offenses in Indian Country. Tribal members from the Hoopa Valley Reservation challenged the constitutionality of that law as going beyond Congress's constitutional authority.

In *United States* v. *Kagama* (1886), the United States Supreme Court partially agreed with the tribal defendants.[7] The Court rejected the government's efforts to characterize its criminal code for Indian tribes as an exercise of its constitutional power to regulate "commerce" with Indian tribes, concluding that this would be a "very strained construction of this clause." In essence, the Court ruled that the only constitutional provision expressly enumerating Congress's powers in Indian affairs did not authorize that body to write a law governing the internal affairs of Indian tribes. Nonetheless, the Court upheld the law as an appropriate exercise of Congress's guardianship authority over Indian people and tribes. The Court essentially gave Congress a blank check to legislate in Indian affairs when it declared Congress free from the constraints of the Constitution in this particular context. The Court turned a blind eye and deaf ear to constitutional principles and tradition that viewed federal power as a limited authority that operates lawfully and legitimately only within the safe harbor of enumerated constitutional provisions and a rather circumscribed universe of implied powers that are ancillary to the enumerated powers. The basis for this virtually unlimited federal power, according to the *Kagama* Court, was the dependent status of Indian tribes: "These Indian tribes are the wards of the nation. They are communities dependent on the United States. Dependent largely for their daily food. Dependent for their political rights." The Court even found a way to integrate and diminish the legal significance of treaty-making between the national government and Indian tribes: "From their very weakness and helplessness, so largely due to the course of dealing with the Federal Government with them and the treaties in which it has been promised, there arises the duty of protection, and with it the power." In the Court's eyes, treaties served as mere testimonials of the tribes' weakened legal status, not as legally binding covenants pledging intergovernmental cooperation between sovereign bodies.

Paradoxically, the Court continued to hand down decisions during this era of "federal plenary power" that recognized the continued sovereign authority of Indian tribes, though usually with accompanying references to Congress's overarching power in Indian affairs. In *Talton* v. *Mayes* (1896), for example, the Court confirmed that tribal powers of self-government, long recognized through treaties and other federal laws, did not originate from the federal Constitution, since they predated the adoption of that document. As a result, Indian tribes were not subject to the Constitution's constraints, though they were "subject to its general provisions and the paramount authority of Congress."[8] The Court nowhere defined the "general provisions" that might apply or the source of law that supported Congress's "paramount authority" over Indian tribes. The modern Court has done no better in articulating the legal basis for Congress's assertion of vast power over Indian tribes. In fact, in 1973, the Court made this startling admission: "The source of federal authority over Indian matters has been the subject of some confusion, but it is now generally recognized that the power derives from federal responsibility for regulating commerce with Indian tribes and for treaty making."[9] The Court offered no explanation for its reliance on the treaty-making power when Congress unilaterally ended that practice over a century earlier. In 1983, the Court muddied the waters again when it stated, "When Congress acts with respect to the Indian tribes, it generally does so pursuant to its authority under the Indian Commerce Clause, or by virtue of its superior position over the tribes."[10] Finally, in 1989, the Court simply conflated its plenary power doctrine with the language of the Constitution in order to give Congress's "at will" power in Indian affairs some colorable constitutional integrity. In *Cotton Petroleum Corp.* v. *New Mexico* (1989), the Court stated: "The central function of the Indian Commerce Clause is to provide Congress with plenary power to legislate in the field of Indian affairs."[11]

In 2004, Justice Clarence Thomas took the unprecedented step of directly and emphatically challenging Congress's claim to plenary power in Indian affairs. In his concurring opinion in *United States* v. *Lara* (2004), Justice Thomas wrote: "I cannot agree that the Indian Commerce Clause 'provide[s] Congress with plenary power to legislate in the field of Indian affairs.' At one time, the implausibility of this assertion at least troubled the Court, and I would be willing to revisit the question."[12] He also questioned the constitutionality of Congress's 1871 law ending the practice of treaty-making with Indian tribes as infringing on the constitutional powers of the executive branch. At the core of Justice Thomas's concerns was his view that federal Indian law would remain trapped in a maze of confused and contradictory principles until the Court definitively reconciled two opposing assumptions: the view that Congress possesses plenary power in Indian affairs and the view that Indian tribes possess inherent sovereignty. Clarifying these legal principles would also shed light on the appropriate and lawful rules of engagement governing relations between the federal government and Indian tribes. Justice Thomas expressed his concerns in the following language:

> The Court should admit that it has failed in its quest to find a source of congressional power to adjust tribal

sovereignty. Such an acknowledgment might allow the Court to ask the logically antecedent question *whether* Congress (as opposed to the President) has this power. A cogent answer would serve as the foundation for the analysis of the sovereignty issues posed by this case. We might find that the Federal Government cannot regulate the tribes through ordinary domestic legislation and simultaneously maintain that the tribes are sovereigns in any meaningful sense. But until we begin to analyze these questions honestly and rigorously, the confusion that I have identified will continue to haunt our cases.[13]

Justice Thomas put his finger on one of the fundamental questions arising in federal Indian law: Where and how do Indian tribes fit within the architecture of American constitutional democracy? To the casual observer, it may seem baffling that federal Indian law has still not supplied a clear answer to this basic question after more than two centuries of intergovernmental relations among the federal government, the Indian tribes and the states. Some of the reasons for that legal deficit can be extracted from the legal and political encounters discussed in the preceding chapters. At the risk of gross simplification, I will collapse those reasons into two large categories: (1) federal Indian law's incorporation of a preferred creation story about nation building and national identity; and (2) the persistence of racism.

A PREFERRED CREATION STORY ABOUT NATION BUILDING

Many of the legal opinions recounted earlier contain stories of Indian people that share striking qualities with the celebrated photographs of Edward Curtis. From 1906 and for nearly a quarter century thereafter, Curtis worked tirelessly to capture images of Indian people that reflected the dominant culture's popular conceptions of the "noble savages." The widespread belief that Indians were a dying race created both a fascination with them as a people and a sense of urgency for Curtis's massive project. Curtis's interests focused principally on the "real Indians," those individuals occupying the lower, primitive rungs on the hierarchical steps leading up to the upper, civilized levels. While some aspects of Curtis's work undoubtedly serve as an important resource for tribes, the project taken as a whole presents Indians as passive, unchanging and, most significantly, melancholy. As Curtis scholar Mick Gidley notes, "Most of the faces encountered in the collection are unsmiling, even grave, and wear expressions usually taken to betoken thoughtfulness, concern, and above all, resignation. This is not just a matter of the preponderance of expressions commonly associated with stillness as against the smile as the key expression thought to indicate change and animation."[14]

Perpetuating the idea of Indians as a savage, primitive and dying race was a critical and necessary element in the grand story of America's nation-building mythology. A fundamental tenet of that mythology was the idea that Western legal systems, philosophy, religion and social structures represented the height of civilization that was preordained to grow and dominate in the lands formerly occupied by infidels. Admitting that Indians had equal claims to lands, governance structures and an enduring way of life was simply incompatible with this worldview. In short, as the late anthropologist and writer Michael Dorris (Modoc) once noted, "Indian peoples were perceived not as they were but as they *had* to be, from a European point of view."[15] Like the frontiers they occupied, Indians and their way of life would inevitably and irrevocably be transformed under the taming, civilizing influences of the dominant white society. Historian Robert F. Berkhofer, Jr., summarizes the grand narrative of American nation building and identity in these words:

> The quest for American cultural identity, the role of the United States in history, faith in the future greatness of the nation, and the fate of the Indian and the frontier in general were all seen as connected by the White Americans of

the period. What reconciled the ambivalent images of nature, the Indian, and the frontier was an ideology of social progress that postulated the inevitable evolution of the frontier from savagery to civilization. American nature was beautiful for its wildness, its great expanse, and its unspoiled picturesqueness, but it was equally or even more beautiful in the eyes of many Whites for what it promised to become—a land of farms and a treasure house of resources for exploitation. Regardless of whether the Indian was savage or noble, he would inevitably be replaced by White civilization and its benefits. The transition from wild, savage nature to a cultivated, domesticated garden in the American West was believed to be as certain as the westward movement of progress had been in European history.[16]

The celebrated Chief Justice John Marshall offered his own creation story about America's nation building that contained all the central elements memorialized by Curtis and described by Berkhofer—noble but savage (and dying) Indians, a diminishing frontier and the emerging dominance of the civilized white race. In *Johnson* v. *McIntosh* (1823), the chief justice noted the following:

The tribes of Indians inhabiting this country were fierce savages, whose occupation was war, and whose subsistence was drawn chiefly from the forest. To leave them in possession of their country, was to leave the country a wilderness; to govern them as a distinct people, was impossible, because they were as brave and as high spirited as they were fierce, and were ready to repel by arms every attempt on their independence. . . . Frequent and bloody wars, in which the whites were not always the aggressors, unavoidably ensued. European policy, numbers, and skill, prevailed. As the white population advanced, that of the Indians necessarily receded. The country in the immediate neighbourhood of agriculturalists became unfit for them. The game fled into thicker and more unbroken forests, and the Indians followed.[17]

As author of the leading Supreme Court opinion laying out the legal justification by which Indians became guests in their own ancestral homelands, the chief justice could ill afford to offer an account of Indian society that conflicted with the prevailing mythology. To cast whites as the "agriculturalists," for example, it was necessary to omit references to the longstanding and persistent agricultural practices of most tribes throughout the country, including areas east of the Appalachians.[18] It was also important to draw stark lines of distinction between savage and civilized, infidel and Christian, even though those lines were blurred by Marshall's time through intermarriage between Indians and whites and generations of intercultural trade relations. Clearly, Marshall was not setting out to write a history of Indian-white relations up to the early nineteenth century but rather supplying a legal rationale to support past, present and future transactions involving Indian lands. Marshall forthrightly expressed his ambivalence about the discovery doctrine and its assumptions about Indian inferiority but seemed unwilling or unable to write his way around it. At one point, Marshall stated, "However extravagant the pretension of converting the discovery of an inhabited country into conquest may appear; if the principle has been asserted in the first instance, and afterwards sustained; if a country has been acquired and held under it; if the property of the great mass of the community originates in it, it becomes the law of the land, and cannot be questioned."[19]

Daniel Webster argued the case in *Johnson* on behalf of the land speculators whose claims traced to early transactions with Indian tribes. For purposes of this important precedent-setting case, Webster had to spin a tale that was at odds with the nation's emerging creation story. Webster's argument was premised on presenting Indian tribes as true sovereigns with full ownership rights to their territories that could only be divested through formalized agreements. This argument ran counter to most of Webster's contemporary writings and orations about the nation's history and destiny. Indeed, one historian noted that Webster "more than any other figure was responsible for creating the triumphantly mythic story of the nation's history that sees its beginning at Plymouth Rock."[20] In 1820, for example, Webster celebrated the bicentennial of the Pilgrims' arrival on the *Mayflower* with the following remarks:

> Two thousand miles westward from the rock where their fathers landed, may now be found the sons of the Pilgrims, cultivating smiling fields, rearing towns and villages, and cherishing, we trust, the patrimonial blessings of wise institutions, of liberty, and religion. The world has seen nothing like this. Regions large enough to be empires, and which, half a century ago, were known only as remote and unexplored wildernesses, are now teeming with population, and prosperous in all the great concerns of life; in good governments, the means of subsistence, and social happiness. It may be safely asserted, that there are now more than a million of people, descendants of New England ancestors, living, free and happy, in regions which scarce sixty years ago were tracts of unpenetrated forests. Nor do rivers, or mountains, or seas resist the progress of industry and enterprise. Ere long, the sons of the Pilgrims will be on the shores of the Pacific.[21]

Indian people and their sovereign governments are entirely missing in action in Webster's soaring orations and writings, surfacing only, as in the *Johnson* arguments, on occasions that advance the interests of white settlers.

This is not to suggest that the preferred national creation story went unchallenged by Indian people. For example, William Apess, a Pequot Indian and Christian convert, produced a series of blistering commentaries and orations written and delivered during the late 1820s and 1830s, many of them in direct response to Webster.[22]

Apess's rhetorical strategy was to counter white society's claims to moral superiority and commitment to equality and turn the arguments against their proponents. In one of his best-known essays, aptly titled *An Indian's Looking-Glass for the White Man* (1833), Apess offered the following series of indictments:

> Now let me ask you, white man, if it is a disgrace for to eat, drink, and sleep with the image of God, or sit, walk and talk with them. Or have you the folly to think that the white man, being one in fifteen or sixteen, are the only beloved images of God? Assemble all nations together in your imagination, and then let the whites be seated among them, and then let us look for the whites, and I doubt not it would be hard finding them; for to the rest of the nations, they are still but a handful. Now suppose these skins were put together, and each skin had its national crimes written upon it—which skin do you think would have the greatest? I will ask one question more. Can you charge the Indians with robbing a nation almost of their whole continent, and murdering their women and children, and then depriving the remainder of their lawful rights, that nature and God require them to have? And to cap the climax, rob another nation to till their grounds and welter out their days under the lash with hunger and fatigue under the scorching rays of a burning sun? I should look at all the skins, and I know that when I cast my eye upon that white skin, and if I saw those crimes written upon it, I should enter my protest against it immediately and cleave to that which is more honourable. And I can tell you that I am satisfied with the manner of my creation, fully—whether others are or not.[23]

Ultimately, for Apess, the point of challenging the preferred national creation story was to expose the evils of colonial practices and attitudes—"It was indeed nothing more than the spirit of avarice and usurpation of power that has brought people in all ages to hate and devour each other"—and propose an alternative pathway toward peaceful and respectful coexistence: "You and I have to rejoice that we have not to answer for our fathers' crimes, neither shall we do right to charge them one to another. We can only regret it, and flee from it, and from henceforth, let peace and righteousness be written upon our hearts and hands forever."[24]

Evidence of the emerging preferred national creation story from this period survives beyond recorded essays, speeches and legal opinions. In the Rotunda of the nation's Capitol building, visitors today can see bas-relief depictions of the national narrative carved out in four sculptures above the four directional entrances. These sculptures were done between 1825 and 1828, sandwiched in between the foundational cases that make up the Marshall Trilogy of Indian law cases. Art historian Vivien Green Fryd gives us this synopsis of the four sculptures: "In rendering episodes of discovery, conquest, and colonization in the New World, these Rotunda reliefs emphasize through dress and physiognomy the differences between the European emigrants and the continent's original occupants, providing an excuse for the latter's subjugation by what the general public believed was a superior, civilized culture. The four sculptures resonate with ideological meanings and reflect changes taking place in federal Indian policy that were occurring in Washington while the artists worked."[25] Among the changes in federal Indian policy then occurring was the formulation of the removal policy that led to the forcible expulsion of thousands of southeastern tribal members from their homelands in order to create distance between Indians and white settlers. Life imitated art in a federal policy that embraced the prevailing belief that the savage and the civilized races could never coexist.

As we've shown in earlier chapters, the modern Supreme Court must often turn to the history of Indian-white relations in order to resolve many of the contemporary disputes arising in Indian Country. When it does so, the Court invariably confronts some version of the preferred national creation story embodied in an earlier federal policy or legal opinion. Such cases as *Montana* v. *United States* (1981) teach us that tribal sovereignty and treaty rights can be severely eroded when the Court embraces the preferred national narrative. *Montana* effectively endorsed the historical premises that Indian tribes were expected to fade away into oblivion, thereby eliminating any possibility that non-Indian reservation residents would ever come under the jurisdictional authority of tribal governments. It is difficult to predict how the Court will react when confronted with a choice on how to interpret historical precedents. This leads to criticism that the Court has abandoned foundational principles respecting the integrity of tribal sovereignty and instead relies on its own subjective judgment on the conditions that "ought to exist" in Indian Country in light of historical expectations about Indian people.[26] Indeed, a private memo from Justice Antonin Scalia written in 1990 in the *Duro* v. *Reina* case reveals that the Court has engaged in precisely that kind of analysis. The memo was addressed to Justice William Brennan to explain Scalia's decision to jump ship and join the majority in ruling against the tribe's jurisdiction to prosecute nonmember Indians. I discovered this memo while reviewing the papers of Justice Thurgood Marshall at the Library of Congress. Since it provides rare insight into the actual thought processes of a sitting justice on the Supreme Court, it is worth reproducing at length:

> Dear Bill:
>
> When you asked me to take on the dissent in this case, I replied that I hoped to be persuaded by the majority, but that if I was not I would be happy to write. I am sorry to say that after a lot of work on the subject I have decided that—if only because I cannot come up with anything better—I ought to go along with Tony's opinion. I owe you at least a brief explanation:
>
> My initial reaction to the case was based on my certainty that when the arrangements governing Indians were established in the 19th century . . . the inhabitants of

Indian territory were regarded as consisting of two classes, Indians and non-Indians—and that there would have been no thought of providing for an Indian from another tribe to be treated like a non-Indian for tribal jurisdictional purposes. I am still persuaded of that, but efforts to craft an opinion have also persuaded me of the reality that our opinions in this field have not posited an original state of affairs that can subsequently be altered only by explicit legislation, but have rather sought to discern what the current state of affairs ought to be by taking into account all legislation, and the congressional "expectations" that it reflects, down to the present day. I would not have taken that approach as an original matter, but it seems too deeply imbedded in our jurisprudence to be changed at this stage. And if one takes that approach, I think Tony [Kennedy] has the better of the argument.[27]

While refreshing in its candor, the memo serves as disturbing confirmation that the preferred national creation story is not a mere abstraction but a real, influential and often determinative force in the modern Court's Indian law cases. The judicial impulse to give effect to this story poses significant problems for Indian tribes and their supporters in seeking to enhance the security of tribes within the framework of America's constitutional democracy. Furthermore, Justice Scalia's memo confirms that the modern Court has not hesitated to insert itself as the principal voice in ordering relations among the tribes, the states and the federal government and in prescribing limits on the scope of tribal sovereignty. The former role is constitutionally assigned to Congress, not to the Supreme Court. Furthermore, it's not at all clear that any branch of the federal government is authorized unilaterally to write prescriptions that modify the scope of inherent tribal sovereignty. Equally problematic is the fact that federal courts—including the Supreme Court—are limited in their exercise of common law rulemaking authority to instances in which a federal statute or constitutional provision requires their interpretive assistance.[28] For instance, in *Holyfield,* the Court properly supplied its own definition of the term "domicile" under the Indian Child Welfare Act to fill an interpretive gap left by Congress. Still, the Court limited its role to providing a definition that was consistent with Congress's overarching policy objectives in that particular law. The courts are on much shakier legal ground when they assert authority to fill gaps in federal law in the absence of clearly applicable statutes or constitutional provisions. This was the situation in such cases as *Oliphant* and *Duro.* Frank Pommersheim has described the Court's rulings in those cases as an exercise in "judicial plenary power."[29] In effect, the decisions violate the rules of engagement contemplated in the Constitution, according to which Congress, not the Supreme Court, is supposed to function as the principal voice in regulating relations with the Indian tribes. If tribes are to be prohibited from prosecuting persons other than tribal members, then it should be up to Congress to work out those arrangements with the tribes. Congress stepped back into its proper lead role when it enacted its "*Duro*-fix" legislation restoring tribal criminal authority over nonmember Indian defendants.

At times, the challenge for Indian tribes is even more fundamental; it is simply to be acknowledged as political entities in accordance with the literal language of the Constitution. Even here we can find notable occasions on which Indian tribes are simply erased from the picture, airbrushed out of the Constitution like the unwanted items in an Edward Curtis photograph. For example, former chief justice William Rehnquist's book, *The Supreme Court: How It Was, How It Is* (1987), gives readers a general overview of the Court's inner workings using a number of major precedents to help explain the process for interpreting the Constitution. Indian law cases rarely figure in the general published writings of the justices, or for that matter, in books written by constitutional law scholars, and Justice Rehnquist's book is no exception. After describing the commerce clause power as "probably the most important" of Congress's enumerated powers, Justice Rehnquist gives the reader an edited version of the constitutional provision "to regulate commerce with foreign Nations, and among the several States."[30] The edited language from the commerce clause omits the last clause, "and with the Indian Tribes." The reader, unfamiliar with the Constitution's actual language, is given the impression that this is precisely what the commerce clause says. After all, the author is the chief justice of the United States Supreme Court, who ought to know what he's talking about. In the catalogue of great insults and offenses directed against Indian tribes, this event probably would not generate much concern from the average person. Then again, when we're talking about the power of enduring symbols—and the preferred national creation story is surely a symbol of the triumph of civilization in America—the chief justice's omission of "Indian Tribes" from the edited commerce clause serves as a powerful and disturbing symbolic act (whether deliberate or not) that represents the broader erasure of Indian tribes and their concerns from the popular imagination.

THE PERSISTENCE OF RACISM

In Part One, we examined the strains of racism contained in many of the Court's major Indian law cases as well as the policies coming from both the legislative and executive branches throughout the nineteenth and twentieth centuries. These strains of racism are evident in many of the Court's modern Indian law cases, although they typically appear (with some notable exceptions) in more nuanced forms. Along with Professor Robert Williams, Jr., I find it helpful to use the definition of racism developed by Albert Memmi, a prominent scholar of decolonization efforts following World War II. Memmi defines racism as "the generalized and final assignments of values to real or imagined differences, to the accuser's benefit and at his victim's expense, in order to justify the former's own privileges or aggression."[31]

By this measure, the preferred national creation story itself is properly considered racist, a candidate for William Apess's list of "national crimes" written upon the white skins at his imagined assembly of nations.

Professor Williams's recent book, *Like a Loaded Weapon: The Rehnquist Court, Indian Rights, and the Legal History of Racism in America* (2005), documents the persistence of racist thinking and beliefs that pervade federal Indian law and policy. Like a modern-day William Apess, Williams's purpose is to highlight these racist elements and thereby expose the law's underlying assumptions about the inherent inferiority of Indian people. Without such efforts to acknowledge and tackle head-on the legacy of racism, Indian tribes will continue to work with tainted legal doctrines and will never achieve secure accommodation within America's constitutional democracy. It is the legal equivalent of being required to build a structure with rotten timber and crooked nails on a bed of sand.

On occasion, Congress has demonstrated a willingness to confront directly and honestly the legacy of racism that contributed to errant and destructive federal Indian policies. The legislative history behind the Indian Child Welfare Act is perhaps one of the most notable examples of this. Likewise, various presidents from Richard Nixon to Bill Clinton have acknowledged the destructive force of federal Indian law over the course of the nation's history.

The Supreme Court has had a more difficult time confronting the legacy of racism contained in federal Indian policy and, especially, in its own Indian law cases. On those rare occasions when a justice managed to confront the legacy of racism while still commanding a majority opinion, another justice was provoked to offer a more tempered analysis. For example, in *United States* v. *Sioux Nation of Indians*, Justice Harry Blackmun opened the majority opinion's lengthy historical analysis with this statement: "This case concerns the Black Hills of South Dakota, the Great Sioux Reservation, and a colorful, and in many respects tragic, chapter in the history of the Nation's West."[32] Justice Blackmun then proceeded to catalogue the history of the federal government's fraudulent, abusive and destructive practices inflicted upon members of the Sioux Nation, including the withholding of treaty-based rations in the dead of winter, all in efforts to secure the tribe's surrender of their sacred Black Hills. Justice Byron White responded critically to Justice Blackmun's draft opinion for casting the federal government's actions in such a negative light. In a private memo to Justice Blackmun, Justice White wrote the following:

> Dear Harry,
>
> Regretfully, for the reasons I shall state, I am reluctant to join all of your opinion. In the first place, I have found the case a much closer one on the merits than your opinion makes it out to be. Also, the validity of the Indian Claims Commission finding that the government acted unfairly and dishonorably is not before us, and I do not entirely share the atmosphere of your draft that often casts the conduct of the government in such an unfavorable light. I would also prefer in stating the historical facts to stand on the record rather than to rely on accounts by historians and other writers whose accuracy and objectivity have not been put to the test.
>
> I agree with your Part II and with the general conclusion stated in Part V that when judged by currently prevailing Fifth Amendment standards, the Court of Claims was correct in concluding that the government actions at issue here effected a taking for which compensation was and is due.
>
> I shall file a statement to this effect.[33]

Justice White did indeed write a brief concurring opinion simply stating his agreement with portions of the majority opinion, but he left out his criticism about the "atmosphere" created by Justice Blackmun's opinion. Then associate justice William Rehnquist, on the other hand, went public with his criticisms in a published dissenting opinion that Williams calls the "most racist" and "Indianophobic" legal opinion of the twentieth century.[34] The last portion of his dissenting opinion attacked the majority for relying on certain historical sources that Justice Rehnquist characterized as "revisionist," apparently because they took up the Indians' side. According to Justice Rehnquist, the majority's historical sources failed to acknowledge that despite the government's "less-than-admirable tactics" in the settlement of the West, it was clear that "the Indians did not lack their share of villainy either."[35] Justice Rehnquist quoted at length from other, evidently more reliable, historians, such as Samuel Morison, who offered this commentary on the Plains Indians: "They lived only for the day, recognized no rights to property, robbed or killed anyone if they thought they could get away with it, inflicted cruelty without a qualm, and endured torture without flinching."[36] Justice Blackmun shot right back to defend the majority's historical accounts and, in a pointed jab at Justice Rehnquist, said: "The dissenting opinion does not identify a single author, non-revisionist, neorevisionist, or otherwise, who takes the view of the history of the cession of the Black Hills that the dissent prefers to adopt, largely, one assumes, as an article of faith."[37]

Unfortunately, there is no justice on the current Supreme Court who has shown the courage of convictions like Justice Blackmun in the Indian law cases, nor has any justice assumed the sort of intellectual leadership in the field that justices like William Brennan and Thurgood Marshall (and later, Blackmun) offered for many years. Justice Thomas's bold statements in the *Lara* case certainly opened the windows to change in challenging the Court's deadened acceptance of federal plenary power, but in truth, his focus is less on preserving the integrity of Indian sovereignty than on finding other ways to constrain the national power.

Federal Indian law's incorporation of a preferred national creation story and the persistence of racism have also encouraged bad habits among the lower courts in frustrating tribal efforts to secure better accommodation within our constitutional structure. This is particularly true in situations where other courts—state or federal—are called upon by tribal courts to help carry out the laws

and orders produced by tribal governments. Sovereigns often develop rules of engagement that call for mutual cooperation in a
number of different circumstances. For example, foreign nations
will often draw up extradition agreements providing for the surrender of persons trying to escape the laws of another country. Within
the United States, Article IV of the Constitution spells out terms for
intergovernmental cooperation among the states by requiring each
state to accord "Full Faith and Credit" to the laws of another state.
In a number of instances, Congress has also passed statutes that impose the same requirements on states and Indian tribes, including
enforcement of Indian child welfare determinations and protective
orders to relieve victims of domestic violence. The signature feature
of a "full faith and credit" requirement is the mandatory nature of
intergovernmental cooperation. In other words, assuming there were
no jurisdictional problems in the proceedings of the sovereign generating the order or decree, the other sovereign is required to give effect to such laws. Thus, an adoption decree properly entered by a
tribal court must be respected by all other tribes and by the states.

Another form of intergovernmental cooperation is called "comity," derived from the Latin *comis,* which means friendly or
courteous. Unlike full faith and credit, the comity doctrine is a voluntary system of cooperation among different sovereigns relying on
mutual trust and good faith. The doctrine traces to international
law practices by which foreign nations determine whether and under what circumstances they will recognize judgments and other
orders from a different sovereign. This is the doctrine that generally
prevails in the United States by which states and federal courts determine whether they will cooperate with tribes in the enforcement
of a tribe's judgments and orders. For example, assume that a person succeeds in getting a tribal court judgment for money damages
against a defendant who is properly within the tribe's jurisdiction.
If the only assets available to satisfy the judgment are located outside the reservation—a common occurrence—then the person
holding the judgment will have to secure the cooperation of a state
court judge, or in some instances, a federal court judge, to assist in

collecting on the judgment. There is no federal law that explicitly imposes a mandatory full faith and credit requirement in such instances, and therefore the courts rely on the doctrine of comity to determine whether to recognize and enforce the tribal court's judgment.

A major difference between these two forms of intergovernmental cooperation is that a court bound only by comity rules can inquire not only into whether the other court had proper jurisdiction over the case and its parties, but also as to the basic standards of fairness observed by the other court in its proceedings. In the hands of some federal courts, such open-ended inspections leave tribal courts vulnerable to rulings that not only refuse to enforce the judgment of a particular tribal court but seriously endanger the authority of *all* tribal courts by ruling that certain controversies, usually involving non-Indians, are entirely outside a tribal court's jurisdiction.[38] The groundwork for such invasive judicial action, of course, was laid by the Supreme Court when it authorized federal courts to conduct far-reaching reviews of tribal jurisdiction, even in the absence of a congressional statute that might legitimate such conduct.[39] As a result, rules designed to facilitate intergovernmental cooperation can sometimes lead instead to further erosion of the tribe's sovereign authority. As summarized by the noted Indian law scholar and tribal court justice Robert Clinton, "The federal courts, therefore, building on the lead recently offered by the United States Supreme Court, are excusing their neocolonialism over Indian tribes through comity, thereby totally perverting the comity doctrine, which is designed to facilitate, rather than frustrate, interjurisdictional judicial cooperation."[40] This is yet another area where Congress could seize the initiative to develop clear rules by which tribal judgments can be enforced across jurisdictional boundaries.

TAKEN TOGETHER, the review in this and the preceding chapter shows that there are a number of significant ideological and institutional forces that frustrate efforts to secure the role of

Indian tribes within our constitutional democracy. The significant point to take away from all this is that none of these barriers are really insurmountable. For example, tribal governments and their courts have shown great capacity to accommodate both their own communal interests and the individual interests of parties appearing before them. Given the peculiar vulnerability of tribal governments, it's arguable that tribes must be even more solicitous of these respective interests than their state or federal counterparts. After all, neither of these other sovereigns has to worry that another reviewing governmental body will decide to slash a significant chunk of their sovereign powers away in a preemptive strike to avert some perceived greater danger. The danger of that occurring will persist so long as the preferred national creation story and our legacy of racism continue to roam freely in the minds and hearts of federal and state rulemakers. It is certainly within their capacity to reject the power of both forces and decide, as William Apess urged long ago, to "let peace and righteousness be written upon our hearts and hands forever."

PART FOUR

FOUNDATIONS FOR
RESPECTFUL COEXISTENCE

9

AVOIDING MISTAKES
OF THE PAST

*Let us put our heads together and see what kind of life we can
make for our children.*

—Sitting Bull

THERE ARE AT LEAST three important reservoirs of knowledge and tradition that today's advocates of tribal sovereignty can
draw upon to advance modern efforts to clarify, support and
strengthen the role of tribal governments within our constitutional
democracy. These reservoirs include the rich body of historical Indian knowledge and practice governing relations among different
societies and nations, a reconsideration of first efforts to integrate
Indian tribes into the fabric of the American constitutional system as envisioned by the Marshall Court and finally international
law's growing concern for indigenous rights to meaningful self-
determination. These elements, along with the political will to put
them to practical use, can help lay a firmer foundation for productive and respectful relations among tribes, the states and the federal
government.

First Sovereigns and Indigenous Traditions
of Political Coexistence

The Haudenosaunee or tribes of the Iroquois Confederacy developed one of the earliest and still influential models for governance and intergovernmental relations this side of the Atlantic. The *Gayaneshakgowa* or Great Law of Peace united the Six Nations under a principle that recognizes the distinct nationhood of each tribe while affording them strength in confederation. Onondaga leader and noted historian Oren Lyons provides this summary of the Great Law:

> It is the earliest surviving governmental tradition in the world that we know of based on the principle of peace; it was a system that provided for peaceful succession of leadership; it served as a kind of early United Nations; and it installed in government the idea of accountability to future life and responsibility to the seventh generation to come. All these were prevalent among the Haudenosaunee before the arrival of the white man, according to the oral history of the elders of that society.[1]

The Great Law of Peace embodied principles of respect for the distinctive cultures and traditions of different nations, indigenous and European. This principle of respect was the underpinning for another Haudenosaunee expression of traditional diplomacy, the *Kaswentha* or Two-Row Wampum. Haudenosaunee leaders often commemorated important events, particularly the establishment of formal political relations, through the use of ceremonial wampum belts constructed of differently colored shells. The *Kaswentha* is perhaps one of the most significant examples of this traditional practice of diplomacy, since it served not only to commemorate historical events but as the embodiment of Haudenosaunee political philosophy regarding the proper model of peaceful coexistence for different nations sharing the same territory. Mohawk political scientist Taiaiake Alfred offers this analysis of the *Kaswentha*:

> The Kanien'kehaka [or Mohawk] *Kaswentha* (Two-Row Wampum) principle embodies this notion of power in the context of relations between nations. Instead of subjugating one to the other, the Kanien'kehaka who opened their territory to Dutch traders in the early seventeenth century negotiated an original and lasting peace based on coexistence of power in a context of respect for the autonomy and distinctive nature of each partner. The metaphor for this relationship—two vessels, each possessing its own integrity, travelling the river of time together—was conveyed visually on a wampum belt of two parallel purple lines (representing power) on a background of white beads (representing peace). In this respectful (co-equal) friendship and alliance, any interference with the other partner's autonomy, freedom, or powers was expressly forbidden. So long as these principles were respected, the relationship would be peaceful, harmonious, and just.[2]

This indigenous philosophy for peaceful coexistence in shared territories derives its moral force from the right of nations or "peoples" to persist in their differences from each other while also acknowledging relationships of mutual dependence. Indeed, this is one of the core justifications for tribal claims to inherent sovereignty, the fact of their historic existence as distinct cultural and social systems, and their tradition of forging alliances with other nations in ways that protected their political and cultural autonomy. In the words of political philosopher Will Kymlicka, "Indigenous peoples do not just constitute distinct cultures, but they form entirely distinct forms of culture, distinct 'civilizations.'"[3] This is not to suggest that tribal cultures are immune to the forces of change brought on by contact with other societies and through changed environmental conditions (e.g., loss of major food sources, displacement from ancestral homelands). Like all cultures of the world, tribal cultures are dynamic and subject to some revision by their members. At the same time, tribes have endured extensive periods of coerced changes imposed through federal Indian policy. The resulting adaptations among tribes and individuals can unleash an endless cycle of debates about Indian identity, especially when measured against some filter of "cultural authenticity," or worse, some stereotyped notion of what a "real Indian" is. As we've seen above, these adaptations can have significant consequences for both tribes and individuals when particular legal rights, benefits or restrictions are tied to one's status as an "Indian" for purposes of federal and tribal law. The point here is not to resolve that controversy but to underscore the historical prerogative that tribes have exercised to manage cultural change within their communities and to create a meaningful "context of choice" to help members make intelligent decisions about their lives, and their place in the world.[4]

In terms of framing relations among different nations, the principles underlying the *Kaswentha* parallel those underlying federalism, which suggests that at least on paper, a federation of nations could easily accommodate and accord protection to distinct tribal nations. According to Alfred, "To accommodate indigenous notions of nationhood and cease its interference in indigenous communities, the state need only refer to the federal principle."[5]

Not surprisingly, some of America's founding fathers took great interest in the Haudenosaunee's Great Law of Peace and its principles for building confederations of nations while respecting the autonomy of each constituent member. As early as 1751, Benjamin Franklin wrote approvingly, in the language of the day, of the Iroquois' system of confederation as a model worth replicating among the new colonies: "It would be a very strange thing if six nations of ignorant savages should be capable of forming a scheme for such a union, and be able to execute it in such a manner as that it has subsisted for ages, and appears indissoluble; and yet that a like union should be impracticable for ten or a dozen English colonies, to whom it is more necessary, and must be more advantageous."[6] Likewise, in 1787, John Adams published his *Defence of the Constitutions of Government of the United States*, a significant and influential study of world governments, including those of American Indians. Adams recommended that the political leaders of the day give attention to the Indians' government structures, especially their notion of a separation of political powers and a legislative structure that was so democratic, the "real sovereignty resided in the body of the people."[7] References like these have subsequently fueled scholarly debate on the extent to which Indian political philosophy and organization influenced the American constitutional design.[8] What is most significant for our purposes is to note that historical Indian political theory offers an important framework and example for establishing relations of peaceful coexistence among distinct national societies living in shared territories. As Robert Williams has pointed out, "The language of American Indian multicultural constitutionalism employed a vocabulary so unlike anything brought by Europeans to America or implemented by them once they got here and acquired power over the continent."[9]

The widespread Indian practice of sharing and smoking a pipe of peace at significant tribal events gives further insight into tribal understandings for building lasting relationships across cultural and political boundaries. The smoking of the sacred pipe was an important feature of treaty-making that, at least from the tribal perspective, gave the proceedings a solemn and sacred dimension and served as sacred testimony to the promises exchanged between the treaty parties. It is quite significant, therefore, to note that Kamiakin, the nineteenth-century Yakama leader, refused an offer of tobacco for his pipe from Governor Isaac Stevens and his men, an indication of Kamiakin's distrust for both the federal treaty negotiators and the integrity of that particular treaty process.

In the tradition of the Lakota people, the smoking of the sacred pipe of peace was an indispensable part of the ritual for "making relatives." This ritual was yet another means of establishing relations for peaceful coexistence among different people or nations. Black

Elk, the well-known Sioux holy man, offered this description of the "threefold peace" established through the ritual of making relatives:

> The first peace, which is the most important, is that which comes within the souls of men when they realize their relationship, their oneness, with the universe and all its Powers, and when they realize that at the center of the universe dwells *Wakan Tanka*, and that this center is really everywhere, it is within each of us. This is the real Peace, and the others are but reflections of this. The second peace is that which is made between men. But above all you should understand that there can never be peace between nations until there is first known that true peace which, as I have often said, is within the souls of men.[10]

These are limited, but important, examples from the storehouse of Indian tradition, philosophy and practice illustrating indigenous perspectives on establishing relations of peaceful coexistence among different nations. Underlying these perspectives is a morality of respect for cultural differences among the parties. Accommodating these differences was made possible through negotiation and through mutual commitments to confer regularly as a way to renew the bonds of association. The mutual obligation for regular conferences was designed both to strengthen the bonds of association and to impress upon younger generations the continuing obligations of the nation. The Creek leader Stumpee underscored his people's understanding of their treaty obligations in these words from the mid–eighteenth century:

> We are sensible that these treaties are binding not only upon those who signed them but upon our whole people and their posterity. Yet it would be well that they are renewed and confirmed in our days, that the young men may be witnesses to them and transmit a knowledge of them to their children.[11]

POLITICAL COEXISTENCE AND THE MARSHALL COURT

Chief Justice John Marshall's opinion in *Worcester* v. *Georgia*,[12] the third in his trilogy of Indian law cases, offers a strong validation of tribal sovereignty and an understanding of how the framers attempted to accommodate tribes within the nation's constitutional structure. The differences in tone, analysis and result in *Worcester* compared to Marshall's opinion in *Johnson* v. *McIntosh*[13] are quite remarkable despite the fact that the opinions were written within a decade of each other. Certainly, one explanation for the differences, at least superficially, is that the cases involved different substantive issues—*Johnson* was a property rights case while *Worcester* raised questions about the legitimacy of political power. *Johnson* looked backward to resolve historical land transactions involving Indian tribes that would produce minimal disruption to land titles long considered settled, while *Worcester* looked forward to spell out the rules of government interaction involving tribes, the states and the federal government. Perhaps most significantly, however, *Worcester* was written against the backdrop of aggressive state action in Indian affairs, an area the Constitution committed exclusively to the national government. Checking Georgia's aggression into Cherokee country was important not only to protect the tribe's sovereign and territorial integrity, but also to preserve the still-fragile distribution of power contemplated in the constitutional order. In short, Marshall's forceful *Worcester* opinion in favor of the tribe was an effort to prevent Georgia's end-run around the Constitution and the related threat to the stability of the young union of states.

One of the most significant aspects of Chief Justice Marshall's *Worcester* opinion is its heavy reliance on international law to help interpret the Constitution and, by extension, the proper role of Indian tribes within our constitutional structure. Marshall's opinion makes clear that the Constitution contemplates two sets of bilateral relations, one bilateral relationship between the national government and the several states, and another between the national government and Indian tribes. The states, in ratifying the

Constitution, agreed to hand over to the national government exclusive authority to manage relations with Indian tribes. In turn, the Constitution authorizes the national government to engage in treaty-making, a process that was well understood to include foreign nations and Indian tribes. Marshall carefully laid out the connections between the Constitution's language and the well-established treaty practices of the day for dealing with Indian tribes:

> The very term "nation," so generally applied to them, means "a people distinct from others." The constitution, by declaring treaties already made, as well as those to be made, to be the supreme law of the land, has adopted and sanctioned the previous treaties with the Indian nations, and consequently admits their rank among those powers who are capable of making treaties. The words "treaty" and "nation" are words of our own language, selected in our diplomatic and legislative proceedings, by ourselves, having each a definite and well understood meaning. We have applied them to Indians, as we have applied them to the other nations of the earth. They are applied to all in the same sense.[14]

Marshall canvassed the various treaties involving the Cherokee Nation, particularly the provisions whereby the tribe acknowledged being under the protection of other nations, initially the British, and later the United States. According to Marshall, these provisions were designed to protect tribes against unlawful acts committed by non-Indian outsiders who might encroach on Indian lands or otherwise stir up trouble in Indian Country: "The Indians perceived in this protection only what was beneficial to themselves—an engagement to punish aggressions on them. It involved, practically, no claim to their lands, no dominion over their persons. It merely bound the nation to the British crown, as a dependent ally, claiming the protection of a powerful friend and neighbour, and receiving the advantages of that protection, without involving a surrender of their national character."[15]

Chief Justice Marshall linked this interpretation of the treaty language with the prevailing theories of international law and practice. According to Marshall:

> These articles [of protection] are associated with others, recognizing their title to self government. The very fact of repeated treaties with them recognizes it; and the settled doctrine of the law of nations is, that a weaker power does not surrender its independence—its right to self government, by associating with a stronger, and taking its protection. A weak state, in order to provide for its safety, may place itself under the protection of one more powerful, without stripping itself of the right of government, and ceasing to be a state. Examples of this kind are not wanting in Europe. "Tributary and feudatory states," says Vattel, "do not thereby cease to be sovereign and independent states, so long as self government and sovereign and independent authority are left in the administration of the state." At the present day, more than one state may be considered as holding its right of self government under the guarantee and protection of one or more allies.
>
> The Cherokee nation, then, is a distinct community, occupying its own territory, with boundaries accurately described, in which the laws of Georgia can have no force, and which the citizens of Georgia have no right to enter, but with the assent of the Cherokees themselves, or in conformity with treaties, and with the acts of congress. The whole intercourse between the United States and this nation, is, by our constitution and laws, vested in the government of the United States.[16]

The Court referenced the work of the Swiss scholar Emmerich de Vattel, perhaps the leading international law scholar of the day and an influential voice in the nation-building efforts of the founding fathers.[17] Indeed, the lens of international law enabled the Marshall Court to present a comprehensible vision for how Indian tribes "fit" within the new nation's constitutional framework. As sovereign nations existing before the formation of the United States, who were not participants in the Constitutional Convention that produced the current Constitution, Indian tribes are literally outside the scope of the Constitution's coverage—and the Supreme Court has so held.[18] Instead, the Constitution provides for treaty-making between the national government and the various tribes as the principal means to engage in nation-to-nation relations. This arrangement comes closest to the forms of government relations developed and practiced by Indian tribes themselves, as discussed in the examples above. Marshall's interpretation of the "protectorate" treaty clauses also supplies the proper understanding of the trust relationship between tribes and the federal government. At its core, the trust doctrine gives life to the treaty promises that safeguard the integrity of the tribes' political and territorial interests. It was decidedly not an unrestricted license for the federal government to remake Indian society in its own image, a perverted legal version of "Great Father" knows best.

Of course, we know that in relatively short order, federal Indian law shifted away from the framework outlined in Marshall's *Worcester* opinion. Demand for Indian land and resources, fed by the growing sense of entitlement that would later flourish under the banner of manifest destiny, and a pretty toxic brew of racism toward Indians and their "primitive" ways of life, eventually turned Marshall's system of bilateral relations with tribes into one of unilateral legislation by Congress. To this day, the Court has still not provided a defensible argument supporting this dramatic shift in law and policy. The modern Court's statement that the Indian commerce clause functions to give Congress "plenary power" in Indian affairs is a gross perversion of what the framers actually intended, which was simply to clarify that as between the states and the federal government, only the latter was empowered to engage in relations with Indian tribes. In short, the plenary power doctrine stands as the most potent reminder of America's rejection of respectful, bilateral relations with Indian tribes, and its abandonment of the fundamental principle that our national government is one of limited powers.

THE EMERGING FORCE OF INTERNATIONAL LAW AND INDIGENOUS PEOPLES' RIGHTS

Chief Justice Marshall's *Worcester* opinion was remarkable for a number of reasons, not the least of which was the Court's courageous defense of tribal rights in the face of overwhelming opposition from the other two branches of the federal government. The opinion was also noteworthy for its treatment of tribes as political bodies worthy of protection under principles of international law. At the time, and until very recently, international law reflected a fairly narrow conception of the political bodies—or "states"—that qualified as proper subjects of international law. Essentially, as international law scholar James Anaya reports, qualifying states had to resemble European models that featured a "political and social organization whose dominant defining characteristics are exclusivity of territorial domain and hierarchical, centralized authority."[19] Under Marshall's analysis, the Cherokee Nation qualified as a "state" for international law purposes, but it's not clear how smaller or less organized tribes would have fared under these rules.

In any event, both federal Indian law and international law turned quite sour for indigenous peoples, as both sets of rules became key instruments of colonization and suppression for "different peoples" who stood in the way of civilization and progress. Noticeable change occurred after World War II, particularly following the decolonization movement by which former European colonies were liberated and eventually joined the "family of nations." During this same period, the rise of human rights as a concern of international law caused significant reconsideration of the former principles of noninterference in the affairs of other sovereign nations. The range of human rights concerns embraced both individual and group interests. As a result, international law increasingly provided occasions for nations to peer over the fences of their neighbors (even those across the seas) and, in exceptional situations, take action against nations found to be in violation of international conventions or agreements. Indigenous peoples benefited from these developments as international law became "reformulated into a force in aid of indigenous peoples' own designs and aspirations."[20] To be sure, human rights principles do not carry the entire load for indigenous peoples, since their claims typically include recognition of their right of self-determination with governmental authority over people and activities within their ancestral homelands. Their host nations, understandably enough, resist recognizing a competing governmental body or, worse, one that might (hypothetically) insist on seceding from the nation and taking with it valuable lands and resources. This helps explain why many nations—including the United States—have developed an allergic reaction to the notion that indigenous people are *peoples* entitled to the right of self-determination under international law.

As with developments in federal Indian law, international law has walked a tortured path in trying to find the proper institutional "fit" for indigenous peoples and their aspirations for self-determination. To date, there is only one formally binding international convention that specifically applies to indigenous peoples, the International Labour Organisation's (ILO) Convention No. 169, known as the Indigenous and Tribal Peoples Convention, 1989. That document's introductory passage recognizes "the aspirations of these peoples to exercise control over their own institutions, ways of life and economic development and to maintain and develop their identities, languages and religions, within the framework of the States in which they live." The framers had to include tempering language on the meaning of "peoples" to assuage concerns among nation-states that recognizing indigenous people as "peoples" might set them on a path to demand full rights of statehood. Despite such careful dancing with words, the convention has been ratified by fewer than twenty nations. Not surprisingly, the United States is not among the signatory nations.

On September 13, 2007, the United Nations General Assembly formally adopted the Declaration on the Rights of Indigenous People following decades of drafting and debate within that body's subordinate committees. The third article of the draft declaration expressly states that indigenous peoples have the right of self-determination. The fourth article goes further than ILO Convention No. 169 in providing that indigenous peoples have the right to "maintain and strengthen their distinct political, economic, social and cultural characteristics, as well as their legal systems, while retaining their rights to participate fully, *if they so choose,* in the political, economic, social and cultural life of the State" (emphasis added). While Convention No. 169 assumes the dominance of the state, envisioning pockets of sovereignty within which indigenous peoples can operate with some latitude, the declaration makes cooperation with the state a matter of negotiation between the state and indigenous peoples. As a practical matter, few indigenous communities and no American Indian tribes are demanding their own state. At the same time, there is some evidence that nation-states are moving away from their politics of paranoia and now understand the concept of self-determination for indigenous peoples as a call for "belated state-building," or in other words, "a process 'through which indigenous peoples are able to join with all the other peoples that make up the State on mutually-agreed upon and just terms, after many years of isolation and exclusion. This process does not require the assimilation of individuals, as citizens like all others, but the recognition and incorporation of distinct peoples in the fabric of the State, on agreed terms.'"[21]

The declaration does not have the binding force of a convention or treaty, but it nonetheless represents the strongest affirmation by the international community that indigenous peoples have rights to self-determination within their ancestral homelands. Equally significant, the declaration's call for negotiated terms for coexistence echoes the long traditions of Indian political philosophy as reflected in the *Kaswentha* and the rituals for "making relatives." Unfortunately for American Indian tribes, the United States was one of only four nations (Australia, Canada and New Zealand were the others) to vote against the Declaration.

Appeals to international law and its regime of human rights protections will create opportunities and challenges both for Indian tribes and for the United States. Indian tribes, already operating within the strictures of the Indian Civil Rights Act, may eventually find their local actions subject to further scrutiny under the lens of international human rights rules. While it's unlikely that aggrieved individuals would be able to enter an international forum to seek redress for tribal actions, they would be able to buttress their existing claims within tribal or federal courts with arguments couched in the terms of international human rights law. The United States, on the other hand, recently received its first formal citation from a modern international body in response to alleged violations of the rights of Indian people under international law. In March 2006, the Committee for the Elimination of Racial Discrimination (CERD), the body charged with monitoring compliance with the International Convention on the Elimination of All Forms of Racial Discrimination, took the United States to task for allegedly denying the Western Shoshone their full rights to land, natural resources and their traditional way of life. While the government has yet to file its response, the CERD's action signals that international law may yet prove useful to Indian tribes in getting the United States to the bargaining table to work out better, more respectful terms for peaceful coexistence. This move parallels the Supreme Court's recent, and perhaps growing, interest in embracing principles of international law to help resolve domestic issues.[22] While acknowledging the Court's historical reluctance to move into this area, former Supreme Court justice Sandra Day O'Connor confirmed the Court's growing interest in international law in these terms:

I suspect that with time, we will rely increasingly on international and foreign law in resolving what now appear to be domestic issues, as we both appreciate more fully the ways in which domestic issues have international dimension, and recognize the rich resources available to us in the decisions of foreign courts. Doing so may not only enrich our own country's decisions; it will create that all important good impression. When U. S. courts are seen to be cognizant of other judicial systems, our ability to act as a rule-of-law model for other nations will be enhanced.[23]

In a similar way, a return to negotiated arrangements between Indian tribes and the United States would go a long way toward re-establishing the United States' historical commitment to the rule of law in Indian affairs. The practice of negotiated arrangements is more in line with the rich historical tradition of Indian diplomacy between nations, is consistent with the Marshall Court's vision for structuring enduring relations among the three domestic sovereigns and is in accord with the emerging pronouncements of international law when it comes to respecting the rights of indigenous peoples around the world.

10

CONVENTIONS ON TRIBAL SOVEREIGNTY

ON THE MORNING of September 11, 2001, tribal leaders from across the country joined attorneys and members of Congress in Washington, D.C., to discuss the need for a unified and comprehensive strategy to protect and enhance the sovereign authority of Indian tribes. The gathering was in response to two Supreme Court cases, *Atkinson Trading Company* v. *Shirley* and *Nevada* v. *Hicks,* decided earlier that same year. The decisions triggered immense concern throughout Indian Country about the Court's continued erosion of tribal sovereign rights that began in the late 1970s. For some of those gathered, the scene must have felt like a replay of the national tribal meetings following the Court's triad of Indian law decisions in 1978 (*Oliphant, Wheeler* and *Martinez*) and the 1990 *Duro* decision. Tribalism was under assault again and required an organized and principled response from the tribal community. The leadership present included representatives from the National Congress of American Indians (NCAI), the oldest tribal political advocacy organization in the country, the Native American Rights Fund, the pre-eminent nonprofit law firm dedicated to protecting the rights of tribes and Indian people, elected tribal leaders from a broad swath of Indian Country and, finally, some of the most distinguished Indian law specialists in the country.

Obviously, no one could have imagined the events that would occur shortly after the meeting began. Senator Daniel Inouye (Democrat, Hawaii), a long-time supporter of tribal sovereignty issues, was called out of the meeting and returned shortly thereafter to inform the group about the attacks upon the World Trade Center towers. A summary report of the September 11 Tribal Leaders Forum noted how the meeting "was changed decidedly as the participants grieved and offered prayers for the victims and their families." Since the tribal leaders were detained in their location, they agreed to continue their discussions on a strategic plan to stop the erosion of tribal sovereignty, mindful of the unfolding national crisis and "the heightened sense of loss caused by the day's terrible events."

The tribal leaders ultimately agreed to pursue a multiprong strategy they called the Tribal Sovereignty Protection Initiative (TSPI). The principal features of this initiative included the development of draft congressional legislation, the creation of an advisory forum for tribal advocates working on Indian law cases that might come before the Supreme Court and the organization of a broad-based educational campaign designed to inform public officials and the general public on the importance of tribal sovereignty.

By summer 2002, the legislative drafting committee had produced a Concept Paper and a draft congressional bill that basically urged Congress to step up to the plate and restore a sense of order and direction in the field. The Concept Paper "calls upon Congress, as trustee for Indian tribes, to address the situation by asserting its primary constitutional authority in Indian affairs and setting forth clear guidelines for jurisdiction in Indian country." While there has also been action on the other prongs of the TSPI, I will focus attention on the draft legislation, since it most directly relates to the legal and political issues discussed throughout this book.

The draft bill is tentatively styled the Tribal Sovereignty and Economic Enhancement Act. Its introductory passages point directly at the Supreme Court's recent Indian law decisions as the corrosive agent that has caused confusion and a steady erosion of tribal rights. In relevant part, the bill characterizes the central problem in the following language:

> Recent opinions of the United States Supreme Court have left unclear the respective powers of tribal and state governments within Indian country. Many of these opinions have: contradicted Congress' statutory policies and the Executive branch's conforming practices of recognizing tribal governance authority; created confusion regarding the respective powers of tribes and states within Indian country; and interfered with tribal efforts in such areas as raising tax revenues, regulating land use practices, ensuring law and order, and generally governing Indian country in a stable and efficient manner.

The bill proceeds to lay out a jurisdictional framework that, if enacted into law, would dramatically change the legal landscape in Indian Country. This review will highlight three of the most significant changes that would occur under the proposed legislation.

First and foremost, the proposed legislation would restore the tribe's full territorial inherent sovereignty except for those powers expressly negotiated away by treaty or legislated away by Congress. This is accomplished through language by which Congress "affirms and declares" the precise scope of inherent tribal powers. The drafters' intent here is to make clear that the source of the tribe's authority is inherent, not delegated federal power. Congress used similar language in its *Duro*-fix legislation that was upheld by the Supreme Court in *United States* v. *Lara* (2004). Notwithstanding the result in *Lara*, there is still a possibility that the newly constituted Court could revisit Justice Kennedy's oft-repeated concerns about the constitutional limits on Congress's power to subject American citizens to criminal trials in tribunals that do not provide the full array of constitutional rights. The Court's recent decision in *Hamdan* v. *Rumsfeld* striking down the use of military commissions in the nation's war on terrorists does not directly speak to this issue, but it does reflect the Court's broad concern that in criminal trials, citizens must be provided at a minimum "all the judicial guarantees recognized as indispensable by civilized peoples."[1] The proposed legislation would largely eliminate the current "checkerboard" jurisdictional scheme that has plagued the administration of justice in Indian Country for decades. The tribe's civil, criminal and regulatory jurisdiction would extend throughout the tribe's territory, trust and fee lands alike, and would reach all persons—members and nonmembers alike. The breathtaking sweep of these provisions is brought home when one considers that the legislation would effectively overrule the decisions in *Oliphant, Montana, Brendale, Strate, Hicks* and *Atkinson*. Just as significantly, the bill eliminates any further use of *Oliphant*'s destructive "implicit divestiture" doctrine by specifying that inherent tribal powers may only be divested through treaties or acts of Congress, which "expressly and clearly" limit the tribe's powers. The bill also clarifies the tribe's "long-arm" jurisdictional authority to reach nonresidents who have "sufficient minimum contacts" with the tribe's territory to meet the requirements of due process. This would confirm the exercise of tribal jurisdiction in cases such as the Lummi tribal member's action against the nonresident pharmaceutical company that allegedly sold harmful prescription drugs within the reservation, as discussed in Part One.

Second, the proposed legislation substantially rebuilds the Marshall Court's "impenetrable barrier" to state authority in Indian Country. At the tribe's request, the United States would be required immediately to reassume on the tribe's behalf governance powers that Congress had earlier shifted to states through Public Law 280 and similar jurisdictional acts. The state could support extending its laws into Indian Country only if it could point to a treaty, act of Congress or bilateral tribal-state agreement that "expressly and clearly" grants the state such authority. Under these rules, any revenue-sharing agreements negotiated as part of a tribal-state Class Three gambling compact would still be valid, since they are expressly authorized through an act of Congress.

However, these rules would likely prohibit states from enforcing cigarette and motor fuels taxes on all purchases made in Indian Country except those covered by a valid tribal-state taxation agreement. Once current agreements expire, however, it is unlikely that a tribe would be under any obligation to renew the revenue-sharing agreements, since the draft bill removes the state's authority to extend these particular taxing laws in Indian Country.

Taken together, these first two changes would bring Indian law much closer to the Marshall Court's description of the respective powers of tribes and states in Indian Country: "[The federal laws] manifestly consider the several Indian nations as distinct political communities, having territorial boundaries, within which their authority is exclusive, and having a right to all the lands within those boundaries, which is not only acknowledged, but guarantied by the United States."[2]

Finally, the proposed legislation rewrites the rules for review of tribal court decisions in federal court. Under current federal law, a person alleging a violation of the Indian Civil Rights Act (ICRA) can only bring that claim into tribal court. ICRA provides a limited exception for persons challenging the legality of their detention who are permitted to bring those claims into federal court under the writ of habeas corpus. Additionally, persons—usually only non-Indian claimants—who challenge the tribe's jurisdiction can bring those claims into federal district court under the rules laid out in *National Farmers Union Insurance Co.* v. *Crow Tribe* and *Iowa Mutual Ins. Co.* v. *LaPlante* (1987). Under the proposed legislation, any person can seek federal court review of certain tribal court decisions from the federal court of appeals within whose circuit the tribe is located. The areas subject to federal review include ICRA claims, interpretations of other federal laws and questions about the tribe's jurisdiction. ICRA claims are subject to certain exceptions and conditions for review. For example, matters relating to tribal elections, tribal enrollment or "other matters internal to the tribe" are not permitted to be taken into federal court. Thus, membership disputes of the sort involved in *Santa Clara Pueblo* v. *Martinez* (1978) would remain within the tribal court's exclusive jurisdiction. The bill is not entirely clear on what "other matters internal to the tribe" means or which court is expressly authorized to make these determinations. Federal courts are admonished to review ICRA claims with sensitivity to the "unique political, cultural and economic needs of tribal governments" and in light of Congress's policy to promote tribal self-determination.

The proposed bill has been circulated throughout Indian Country and has been the subject of extensive discussion at regular meetings of the NCAI. At least one set of revisions was formally acted upon and supported by the NCAI at the request of the Pueblo tribes in New Mexico. The requested revisions added tribal governmental actions based on traditional and customary governance practices to the list of items not reviewable in federal court.

To date, this proposed legislation has not been introduced in Congress. Tribal leaders have not reached consensus on all aspects of the bill or on an alternative strategy to sever portions of the bill and introduce them on a piecemeal basis. This is not surprising given the enormous sweep of the bill and the need to anticipate the range of likely challenges from states, private parties and, indeed, the federal government itself. There is widespread consensus that the field of federal Indian law is in dire need of direction and clarification; even members of the Supreme Court agree they've made a mess of this area. While the proposed legislation is very much a work in progress, it already stands as one of the most ambitious, comprehensive and meaningful efforts to restore significant protections to tribal sovereignty and to provide a substantial measure of clarity to a field that sorely needs it.

There are lingering concerns, however, with the proposed legislation, and I turn to address just a few of the more significant ones. First, in calling on Congress to assert its primary constitutional authority, the authors of the Concept Paper expressly note that there is nothing in the proposed bill "that would limit Congress' existing broad authority over Indian affairs." The clear target of the proposed legislation is the Supreme Court's body of federal

Indian law that has steadily eroded tribal powers and simultaneously enlarged the scope of state power in Indian Country. In all likelihood, the Concept Paper simply reflects the political realities facing tribes. In asking Congress, in effect, to take on the Supreme Court, most of the states and some pretty powerful corporate interests on behalf of a politically marginal group of citizens, it would seem foolhardy in the same stroke to demand that Congress unilaterally renounce its "existing broad authority in Indian affairs."

Yet, when we add the perspective of history, we know that Congress has often abused its "broad authority" in Indian affairs. Congress wrote the Removal Bills that authorized the executive branch to "negotiate" terms for massive tribal relocation. Congress unilaterally ended the practice of treaty-making with tribes and, shortly thereafter, authored the Allotment Acts that devastated tribal landholdings, altered the demographic profile of reservation residents and outlawed the Indian way of life in Indian Country. Congress wrote the Termination era legislation that unilaterally severed its trust obligations with Indian tribes and left tribes and their members vulnerable to exploitation by state powers. These acts have all been upheld by the Court under a "plenary power" doctrine invented out of whole cloth in the late nineteenth century to support the federal government's radical assimilation project among Indian people. In the same way that the Supreme Court must be held morally accountable for its recent Indian law jurisprudence, Congress must be held morally accountable for these devastating breaches of trust, policy and constitutional law. To be sure, Congress does possess constitutional authority to "regulate Commerce with the Indian tribes," but there is nothing in that language, in the notes of the Constitutional Convention or in the first decisions that came out of the Supreme Court to support an interpretation that Congress possesses unbridled, absolute power in Indian affairs. And yet, that is how Congress has behaved for a large part of this nation's history, largely with the blessings of the Supreme Court.

An appeal to Congress's true "primary constitutional authority in Indian affairs" on issues as fundamental as the nature of tribal sovereign authority would actually require that Congress establish a framework within which the national government and tribes (and the states, if Congress chose to include them) would engage in negotiations over the allocation and exercise of political power within Indian Country. In short, it would require a return to treaty-making, the only constitutionally sanctioned mechanism by which the federal government is empowered to engage in relations with Indian tribes. It would not necessarily entail a return to the individual tribe-specific practices of treaty-making from the nineteenth century. Taking a page from practices in international law, the framework could take the form of a convention—a "master treaty"—in which many of the same provisions outlined in the proposed legislation could be included. After all, the proposed legislation is essentially a "belated state-building" project involving the considered attention of all three sovereign bodies sharing the common territory embraced within the United States.

A call for conventions on tribal sovereignty does not elevate form over substance. It directly addresses one of the most significant problems Indian tribes have faced for two centuries: the unbridled exercise of federal political power over Indian tribes built on a value and belief system that considers Indian people inherently inferior to white Euro-Americans. It is true that the recently prevailing winds from Capitol Hill have blown favorably in the tribes' direction since the mid-1970s and Congress has shown no real appetite for diminishing the scope of tribal authority. Still, except for the notable *Duro*-fix legislation, Congress has largely stood by while the Supreme Court used its newly created implicit divestiture doctrine to impose an evolving constellation of constraints on the tribes' sovereign powers.

A second set of concerns with the proposed legislation is that in giving tribes an option to exercise "the full authority, powers, and jurisdiction affirmed in this section," it manages to create an awkward and potentially unmanageable two-tier system of inherent tribal powers. Here's the current language: "In addition to exercising the inherent authority, powers, and jurisdiction *recognized under existing law*, Indian tribes shall have the option of exercising the *full authority, powers, and jurisdiction affirmed in this section*" (emphasis added). The apparent intent behind this language is to recognize that different tribes may not want or need to exercise the full panoply of inherent sovereign rights in order to govern their tribal communities effectively. For example, in reservations where the non-Indian population dramatically exceeds that of the tribal members, tribes may not want to assume criminal jurisdiction for reservation-based non-Indian crimes even if federal law supported it. Or the tribe may want to limit its jurisdiction to prosecute non-Indians only when the victims are tribal members. Even that would create a hefty caseload for most tribes. Recent statistics from the United States Department of Justice show that American Indians experience a per capita rate of violence twice that of the general population. Moreover, 60 percent of American Indian victims of violent crime report the offender as white, and among American Indian victims of rape, four out of five victims describe the perpetrator as white.[3] Under current federal Indian law, of course, tribes have absolutely no criminal authority over non-Indian offenders. In preserving the "old law" for those tribes electing not to exercise the "full authority" affirmed in the legislation, the proposed legislation creates unnecessary confusion about the precise scope of inherent tribal authority in critically important areas of the law. Additionally, the bill creates an opening for federal courts to continue creating common law under "existing law" that could frustrate the overall aim of the project. It would seem far simpler to endorse the "full territorial authority" model for inherent tribal jurisdiction, explicitly toss out the "existing law," and then leave it to individual tribes to work out terms for sharing their jurisdictional authority with state and federal governments.

In addition, the proposed legislation should more explicitly distinguish between the precise scope of inherent tribal powers and the "bureaucratic forms" that each tribe may adopt in order to implement those powers on the ground. Tribes with smaller land bases and populations will invariably structure their governmental forms in different ways. This is certainly true for the states as well. For example, in the creation of their judicial systems, many of the smaller states elect not to have an intermediate court of appeals. All appeals flow directly from the trial courts to the state's supreme court. Similarly, while all state legislatures (except Nebraska's) have a two-house legislature, the legislative sessions operate differently. In fact, the legislatures of six states meet only every other year.[4] Neither of these state bureaucratic forms affects the overall scope of state sovereignty authority; the same should be true of Indian tribes.

Third, the proposed bill opts to permit aggrieved parties to seek federal court review of tribal court opinions with the exceptions and conditions discussed above. This provision is likely to be controversial in many tribal communities, since it preserves a measure of federal oversight into Indian tribal court decision-making. Granted, the federal oversight would come from the higher-placed federal appellate courts and not the local federal district court, but the provision will almost certainly leave a sour taste in the mouths of most tribal jurists. In the context of ICRA claims, it's probably too late in the day to revisit the question of whether Congress actually possessed the constitutional authority unilaterally to pass an act that is so invasive of tribal sovereignty. Opening up the federal courts to even broader review of ICRA claims would seem to compound the insult to tribal sovereignty. On the other hand, it is undeniable that the modern Court's concern for individual civil rights rooted in the Constitution has contributed greatly to the massive erosion of the tribes' inherent sovereign authority. Permitting limited federal court review of tribal court ICRA claims and general jurisdictional questions may be one of those necessary compromises tribes will have to make, particularly if in return, federal law restores the tribe's full territorial authority over all persons and activities within Indian Country.[5]

Finally, the proposed legislation should address two matters not included in the draft bill. First, litigants seeking federal review of a tribal court's jurisdiction should still be required to exhaust all tribal court remedies before applying to federal court so that tribal courts are provided the first opportunity to rule on the scope of their inherent sovereign authority. Second, the proposed legislation should set out with clarity the rules by which judgments of tribal courts should be recognized and enforced by state and federal courts. As noted in Chapter Nine, this is an area that has frustrated tribal efforts to bring full and fair closure to claims brought in the tribal systems. This is an opportunity to resolve those problems.

IT BEARS REPEATING that the proposed legislation is an immensely significant step in redressing the erosion of tribal sovereign authority over the past few decades. The criticisms lodged here are offered in the spirit of helping to redress that problem. The call for conventions on tribal sovereignty, as opposed to unilateral congressional legislation, is an effort to reconstruct the framework through which tribes, the federal government and the states negotiate the distribution of power in our constitutional democracy. It is a call for belated state-building in which tribes are no longer regarded as political outsiders or separatists but as full and necessary partners in the national discussion on sovereign authority. That process can help establish a firmer foundation for respectful coexistence among the nation's three sovereigns and further secure the role of Indian tribes within our nation's constitutional democracy.

CONCLUSION

AT OUR LAW school's orientation for entering students, I use an exercise in which I ask students to describe in a few short sentences their first encounter with justice. We then discuss how law can be used to advance or to impede the pursuit of justice.

In the course of this exercise, I share with students the story of my first experience with justice. It goes something like this: I was six years old during the late summer of 1965. My family had joined all the other local families in evacuating our homes on Louisiana's Gulf Coast to escape the wrath of Hurricane Betsy. When the flood waters finally receded, we were allowed to return to our communities to see what was left of our homes and possessions. As we drove slowly down the gravel road to our house in Dulac, I remember seeing piles and piles of ruined furniture and appliances stacked alongside the roadway. We passed through the white communities, the black communities and, finally, my Indian community in Dulac, and the scenes were exactly the same wherever we looked. Even as a young child, I remember feeling a perverse sense of satisfaction that everyone in our town had been affected in much the same way—white, black and Indian. I felt that this was justice because for once, it wasn't just the Indians who were left out or hurt.

I grew up as a member of the Houma Indian tribe of Louisiana, the largest tribe in the state. Absent a history of treaty-making with the United States and distrustful of our oral history, the federal government elects not to recognize our people as a tribal political body with powers of self-governance. Segregation by race was the order of the day in my community. For decades, the state operated three separate school systems—white, black and Indian. I attended the Dulac Indian School until 1969, when the state finally completed the process of integrating its schools under pressure from a federal court decree. Most of us grew up speaking an archaic form of French and worshipped in the Catholic Church, the legacy of Louisiana's strong French heritage and the result of intermarriage between French immigrants and tribal members. At the Indian school, we were punished for speaking French. And in the Catholic Church, tribal members continued to sit in the "Indian section" and received communion only after the white parishioners, old habits that endured even years after the church stopped enforcing the practice.

These formative experiences influenced how I interpreted the aftermath of Hurricane Betsy. They explain why I experienced the devastation of that storm as my first encounter with justice. It was as if nature were giving us an opportunity to start over, to rebuild our coastal communities without the stain of racism and discrimination. We didn't seize the opportunity. We rebuilt our separate school systems and continued to live under the code of color. The tragic images from 2005 in the aftermath of Hurricanes Katrina and Rita, two storms that also devastated many Houma tribal communities, show that we still have a long way to go.

The history of federal Indian law reveals similar instances of missed opportunities and seriously misguided turns. The recently proposed Tribal Sovereignty Protection Initiative is only the latest opportunity, but surely one of the most promising, to build an enduring and principled framework for respectful coexistence among the nation's three sovereigns. With due regard for the effort it would require, that initiative could be reframed in the context of a convention or master treaty to signify the importance of proceeding in the spirit of negotiation and consensus. As the United States looks to restore its international stature as a nation committed to the rule of law, the opportunity to move in this direction should not be missed. It should not take a natural—or man-made—disaster to cause us to seize the opportunity and make things right.

NOTES

PREFACE AND ACKNOWLEDGMENTS

1. Indian Self-Determination and Education Assistance Act of 1975, Pub. L. 93–638, 88 Stat. 2203 (1975) codified at 25 U.S.C. 450.

INTRODUCTION

1. Alvin M. Josephy, Jr., *The Nez Perce Indians and the Opening of the Northwest* (New Haven: Yale University Press, 1965), 319.
2. See Treaty with the Yakima, 1855, 12 Stat. 951, June 9, 1855. Article 5 of the treaty provides: "And it is distinctly understood and agreed that at the time of the conclusion of this treaty Kamaiakun is the duly elected and authorized head chief of the confederated tribes and bands aforesaid, styled the Yakama Nation, and is recognized as such by them and by the commissioners on the part of the United States holding this treaty."
3. Washington State Historical Society, http://washingtononline.org/treatytrail/context/bios/kamiakin-yakima.htm.
4. *The Papers of John Marshall,* Volume XI, Charles F. Hobson, ed. (Chapel Hill: University of North Carolina Press, 1990), 179 n.2 (citing Story, ed., Miscellaneous Writings, 457, 462–63).
5. Ibid., 178–79.
6. Frederick E. Hoxie, *A Final Promise: The Campaign to Assimilate the Indians, 1880–1920* (Cambridge University Press, 1989), 102. Professor Hoxie reminds us that the memorialization of the Indian on this date included the distribution by the United States mint of the Indian-head nickel. See also Lucy Maddox, *Citizen*

Indians: Native American Intellectuals, Race, and Reform (Ithaca, N.Y.: Cornell University Press, 2005), 39.

7. Howard Zinn, *A People's History of the United States 1492–Present* (rev. ed.) (New York: Harper Perennial, 1995), 10–11.

8. See U.S. Constitution, Article 1, Section 8, Clause 3. This clause empowers Congress "to regulate Commerce with foreign Nations, and among the several States, and with the Indian Tribes."

9. See *Cherokee Nation* v. *Georgia,* 30 U.S. 1, 17 (1831); Worcester v. Georgia, 31 U.S. 515, 557 (1832).

10. *Cherokee Nation* v. *Georgia,* 30 U.S. 1, 17 (1831).

11. *Worcester* v. *Georgia,* 31 U.S. 515, 560–61 (1832).

12. *Worcester* v. *Georgia,* 31 U.S. 515, 557 (1832) ("All these acts . . . manifestly consider the several Indian nations as distinct political communities, having territorial boundaries, within which their authority is exclusive, and having a right to all the lands within those boundaries, which is not only acknowledged, but guarantied by the United States"). See generally Nell Jessup Newton, et al., eds., *Cohen's Handbook of Federal Indian Law,* 2005 edit. (Newark, N.J.: LexisNexis Matthew Bender, 2005), 122–23 (hereinafter *Cohen Handbook*).

13. *United States* v. *Wheeler,* 435 U.S. 313, 322–23 (1978).

14. The BIA currently employs nearly eleven thousand people, almost 90 percent of them American Indian or Alaska Natives.

15. See Fergus M. Bordewich, *Killing the White Man's Indian: Reinventing Native Americans at the End of the Twentieth Century* (New York: Doubleday, 1996), quoting spokesman from the Sisseton-Wahpeton Sioux Tribe, 323.

16. See *Cohen Handbook,* 58–59.

17. Sonny Skyhawk, "A Conversation with Presidential Candidate Bill Richardson," *Indian Country Today* (Feb. 23, 2007).

18. Robert A. Williams, Jr., *Like a Loaded Weapon: The Rehnquist Court, Indian Rights, and the Legal History of Racism in America* (Minneapolis: University of Minnesota Press, 2005).

19. T. Alexander Aleinikoff, *Semblances of Sovereignty: The Constitution, the State, and American Citizenship* (Cambridge: Harvard University Press, 2002), 118.

20. John Bradley and Kathryn Seton, "Self-Determination or 'Deep Colonising': Land Claims, Colonial Authority and Indigenous Representation," in *Unfinished Constitutional Business: Rethinking Indigenous Self-Determination,* Barbara A. Hocking, ed. (Canberra, Australia: Aboriginal Studies Press, 2005), 32–46.

21. See Steven Curry, *Indigenous Sovereignty and the Democratic Project* (Hants, England: Ashgate Publishing, Ltd., 2004).

22. Ibid., 32.

23. Taiaiake Alfred, *Peace, Power, Righteousness: An Indigenous Manifesto* (Oxford, England: University Press, 1999), 56.

24. Ibid., 42.

25. *Cohen Handbook*, 9.

26. "For most of its existence, the BIA has mirrored the American public's ambiva-

lence towards the Nation's indigenous peoples by carrying out federal policies that had helped or hurt them," www.doi.gov/bureau-indian-affairs.html.

CHAPTER ONE: THE DIGNITY OF TRIBAL GOVERNMENTS

1. See *City of Albuquerque* v. *Browner,* 97 F.3d 415 (10th Cir. 1996).
2. There are also scores of Indian groups that lack formal federal recognition of tribal political status for various reasons, including federal oversight or neglect over time. In 1978, the Department of the Interior formalized an administrative process by which Indian tribes that were not federally recognized could petition the government for acknowledgment as Indian tribes in order to operate in governmental capacities. See, generally, *Cohen Handbook,* 155–61.
3. See *Cohen Handbook,* 210.
4. See Stella U. Ogunwole, *We the People: American Indians & Alaska Natives in the United States,* Census 2000 Special Reports, Censr-28 (Feb. 2006), available at http://www.census.gov/population/www/socdemo/race/indian.html. American Indian areas include reservations, off-reservation trust lands, Oklahoma tribal statistical areas, and other specially designated tribal areas.
5. Jonathan B. Taylor and Joseph P. Kalt, *American Indians on Reservations: A Databook of Socioeconomic Change Between the 1990 and 2000 Censuses* (Cambridge: Harvard Project on American Indian Economic Development, Jan. 2005), iv, available at http://www.ksg.harvard.edu/hpaied.
6. *MacArthur* v. *San Juan County,* 391 F.Supp.2d 895, 937–38 (D. Utah 2005).
7. Oliphant v. Schlie, 544 F.2d 1007, 1014 (1976).
8. See *Alvarado* v. *Warner-Lambert Company,* 30 Indian L. Rep. 6174 (May 22, 2003) Lummi Nation Tribal Court.
9. See *McDonald* v. *Means,* 309 F.3d 530 (9th Cir. 2002).
10. See *Ford Motor Company* v. *Todecheene,* 394 F.3d 1170 (9th Cir. 2005).
11. See *Means* v. *Navajo Nation,* 432 F.3d 924 (9th Cir. 2005).
12. *Worcester* v. *Georgia,* 31 U.S. 515, 557 (1832).
13. Harry L. Watson, *Liberty and Power: The Politics of Jacksonian America* (New York: Hill and Wang, 1990), 111.
14. Theda Perdue and Michael D. Green, eds., *The Cherokee Removal: A Brief History with Documents* (Boston & New York: Bedford Books of St. Martin's Press, 1995), 15.
15. In his first message to Congress, Jackson stated, "Surrounded by the whites with their arts of civilization, which by destroying the resources of the savage doom him to weakness and decay, the fate of the Mohegan, the Narragansett, and the Delaware is fast overtaking the Choctaw, the Cherokee, and the Creek. That this fate surely awaits them if they remain within the limits of the States does not admit of a doubt." See Jackson's First Annual Message to Congress, Dec. 8, 1829, quoted in H. W. Brands, *Andrew Jackson: His Life and Times* (New York: Doubleday, 2005), 435.
16. Howard Zinn, *A People's History of the United States: 1492–Present* (Revised and Updated Edition) (New York: HarperCollins Publishers, Inc., 1980, 1995), 130. Zinn notes that Harvard University bestowed an honorary degree on Lewis Cass in 1836, "at the height of Indian removal."

17. H. W. Brands, *Andrew Jackson: His Life and Times* (New York: Doubleday, 2005), 492–93.

18. *The Papers of John Marshall*, Vol. XI, Correspondence, Papers, and Selected Judicial Opinions April 1827–Dec. 1830, Charles F. Hobson, ed. (Chapel Hill: University of North Carolina Press, 2002), 378–79.

19. Ibid., 374.

20. Rennard Strickland, *Tonto's Revenge: Reflections on American Indian Culture and Policy* (Albuquerque: University of New Mexico Press 1997), 107.

21. *Williams* v. *Lee,* 358 U.S. 217, 220 (1959).

22. *McClanahan* v. *State Tax Commission of Arizona,* 411 U.S. 164, 179 (1973).

23. *McBratney* v. *United States,* 104 U.S. 621 (1882).

24. *Williams* v. *Lee,* 358 U.S. 217, 220–21 (1959).

25. *Williams* v. *Lee,* 358 U.S. 217, 223 (1959).

26. Ibid., 223 (citations omitted).

27. *White Mountain Apache Tribe* v. *Bracker,* 448 U.S. 136, 141 (1980).

28. *McClanahan* v. *State Tax Commission of Arizona,* 411 U.S. 164, 172 (1973).

29. *McClanahan* v. *State Tax Commission of Arizona,* 411 U.S. 164 (1973).

30. Ibid., 172.

31. *Cohen Handbook,* 101, citing Richard Nixon, Special Message to Congress, July 8, 1970, in *Public Papers of the President of the United States: Richard Nixon, 1970,* 564.

32. Charles Wilkinson, *Blood Struggle: The Rise of Modern Indian Nations* (New York: W.W. Norton & Co., 2005), 139–43.

33. See Peter Mathiessen, *In the Spirit of Crazy Horse* (New York: Viking Penguin, 1983), 52–55.

34. *United States* v. *Kagama,* 118 U.S. 375, 384 (1886).

35. See Carl T. Rowan, *Dream Makers, Dream Breakers: The World of Justice Thurgood Marshall* (Boston: Back Bay Books, 1993).

36. *Worcester* v. *Georgia,* 31 U.S. 515, 561 (1832).

CHAPTER TWO: 1978—A WATERSHED YEAR IN INDIAN LAW

1. See generally Francis Paul Prucha, *The Great Father: The United States Government and the American Indians* (Lincoln: University of Nebraska Press, 1986), 384.

2. 25 U.S.C. 1901–1923.

3. 42 U.S.C. 1996.

4. *Cohen Handbook,* 821.

5. B. J. Jones, *The Indian Child Welfare Act Handbook: A Legal Guide to the Custody and Adoption of Native American Children* (Chicago: American Bar Association, Section of Family Law, 1995), 2.

6. Ibid. "Native American children were rarely removed because of physical abuse; instead, their families were routinely judged unfit by non–Native American social workers and judges because of alleged neglect or emotional mistreatment. A common ground for removal was that the natural parent had left the child with

an extended relative for a prolonged period of time. To the non–Native American social worker ignorant of the traditional ways of child-rearing such behavior was unacceptable under Anglo-Saxon traditions. To Native American families, however, such methods of raising children were common-place because the notion of extended family included not only those in the nuclear family but also those related by marriage or by some other traditional bond" (3).

7. *Cohen Handbook,* 820.

8. See Allison Dussias, "Ghost Dance and Holy Ghost: The Echoes of 19th Century Christianization Policy in 20th Century Native American Free Exercise Cases," 49 *Stan. L. Rev.* 773 (1997). See also Peter Mathiessen, *In The Spirit of Crazy Horse* (New York: Viking Penguin, 1983), 17; Dorothy H. Bracey, "Criminalizing Culture: An Anthropologist Looks at Native Americans and the U.S. Legal System," in Jeffrey Ian Ross and Larry Gould, eds., *Native Americans and the Criminal Justice System* (Boulder, Colo.: Paradigm Publishers, 2006), 39–43.

9. Tom Holm, *The Great Confusion in Indian Affairs: Native Americans & Whites in the Progressive Era* (Austin: University of Texas Press, 2005), 35–38.

10. 42 U.S.C. 1996.

11. See *Cohen Handbook,* 937–44.

12. 25 C.F.R. 83, 43 Fed. Reg. 39, 361 (1978).

13. See *Cohen Handbook,* 138.

14. The process has been criticized as overly burdensome, inconsistent and costly. Since 1994, the costs for pursuing acknowledgment through the administrative process have been estimated at $1 million per petition. The process has also become heavily politicized as a result of the proliferation of gaming activities in Indian Country. See Renee Ann Cramer, *Cash, Color, and Colonialism: The Politics of Tribal Acknowledgment* (Norman: University of Oklahoma Press, 2005). See also Bruce Granville Miller, *Invisible Indigenes: The Politics of Nonrecognition* (Lincoln: University of Nebraska Press, 2003).

15. *Oliphant* v. *Schlie,* 544 F.2d 1007, 1019 (9th Cir. 1976).

16. *Oliphant* v. *Schlie,* 544 F.2d 1007, 1015 (9th Cir. 1976).

17. Philip P. Frickey, "A Common Law for Our Age of Colonialism: The Judicial Divestiture of Indian Tribal Authority over Nonmembers," 109 *Yale L. J.* 1, 36 n.178 (1999) ("Before *Oliphant,* one would have thought that the Marshall Court had specified *all* such limitations").

18. Robert A. Williams, Jr., *Like a Loaded Weapon: The Rehnquist Court, Indian Rights, and the Legal History of Racism in America* (Minneapolis: University of Minnesota Press, 2005), 107. Professor Williams's book title comes from the dissenting opinion of Justice Robert Jackson in *Korematsu* v. *United States,* 323 U.S. 214, 246 (1944). Justice Jackson wrote, "But once a judicial opinion rationalizes such an order to show that it conforms to the Constitution, or rather rationalizes the Constitution to show that the Constitution sanctions such an order, the Court for all time has validated the principle of racial discrimination. . . . The principle then lies about like a loaded weapon ready for the hand of any authority that can bring forward a plausible claim of an urgent need."

19. *Oliphant* v. *Suquamish Indian Tribe,* 435 U.S. 191, 210 (1978).

20. Ibid.

21. *Talton* v. *Mayes,* 163 U.S. 376 (1896).

22. At a practical level, the decision effectively immunizes non-Indian offenders from tribal criminal prosecution. This result is especially unfortunate in cases of sexual violence against American Indian women, where four out of five victims report their perpetrators as white offenders. Federal (or in some cases, state) officials rarely take on these cases which only enhances the offenders' sense that they can act with impunity. Steven W. Perry, U.S. Department of Justice, "American Indians and Crime: A BJS Statistical Profile, 1992–2002" (2004), 9; Amnesty International, *Maze of Injustice: The Failure to Protect Indigenous Women from Sexual Violence in the USA* (2006), available at http://www.amnestyusa.org/women/maze/report.pdf.

23. *United States* v. *Kagama,* 118 U.S. 375, 379 (1886):35.

24. *Williams* v. *Lee,* 358 U.S. 217, 223 (1959).

25. See *Montana* v. *United States,* 450 U.S. 544 (1981).

26. See Judith V. Royster, "The Legacy of Allotment," 27 *Ariz. St. L. J.* 1 (1995).

27. See *Oliphant* v. *Suquamish Indian Tribe,* 435 U.S. 191, 193 n.1 (1978).

28. Steven Curry, *Indigenous Sovereignty and the Democratic Project* (Hants, England: Ashgate Publishing, Ltd, 2004), 77.

29. *Ex Parte Crow Dog,* 109 U.S. 556, 571 (1883).

30. *Oliphant* v. *Suquamish Indian Tribe,* 435 U.S. 191, 212 (1978).

31. See Kevin K. Washburn, "American Indians, Crime, and the Law," 104 *Mich. L. Rev.* 709, 711 n. 4 (2006).

32. See Frickey, "A Common Law for Our Age of Colonialism," 79.

33. Philip P. Frickey, "(Native) American Exceptionalism in Federal Public Law," 119 *Harv. L. Rev.* 431, 434 (2005).

34. Robert J. Nordhaus, G. Emlen Hall, and Anne Alise Rudio, "Revisiting *Merrion* v. *Jicarilla Apache Tribe:* Robert Nordhaus and Sovereign Indian Control Over Natural Resources on Reservations," 43 *Natural Resources Journal* 223, 265 (2003). The comment was made during the first oral arguments in *Merrion* v. *Jicarilla Apache Tribe,* 455 U.S. 130 (1982).

35. U.S. Constitution, Amendment V; "nor shall any person be subject for the same offence to be twice put in jeopardy of life or limb."

36. Memorandum of Justice Thurgood Marshall (Jan. 16, 1978), on file with author.

37. *United States* v. *Wheeler,* 435 U.S. 313, 330–31 (1978).

38. 435 U.S. 323.

39. 435 U.S. 326.

40. Article I, Section 8, cl. 18 provides: "To make all Laws which shall be necessary and proper for carrying into Execution the foregoing Powers, and all other Powers vested by this Constitution in the Government of the United States, or in any Department or Officer thereof."

41. *McCulloch* v. *Maryland,* 17 U.S. 316, 421 (1819).

42. Laurence H. Tribe, *American Constitutional Law,* 3d ed., Vol. One (New York: Foundation Press, 2000), 802.

43. *Cohen Handbook,* 122.

44. See Frickey, "A Common Law for Our Age of Colonialism," 38. ("In short, the

Marshall Court considered tribes subservient to clear assertions of authority deemed necessary for the colonizing government to conduct the colonial process efficiently. *Oliphant* involved no conflict of this sort. . . . Instead of involving a conflict between sovereigns, *Oliphant* involved a matter of individual rights against governmental authority").

45. 25 U.S.C. 1301 et seq. Section 1302 provides, "No Indian tribe in exercising powers of self-government shall— . . . (8) deny to any person within its jurisdiction the equal protection of its laws or deprive any person of liberty or property without due process of law."

46. Brief on behalf of Santa Clara Pueblo in the United States Supreme Court, 1977 WL 189105.

47. Brief on behalf of Julia Martinez in the United States Supreme Court, 1977 WL 189106.

48. See Judith Resnik, "Dependent Sovereigns: Indian Tribes, States, and the Federal Courts," 56 *University of Chicago L. Rev.* 671, 712–21 (1989).

49. United States Dept. of Interior Circular No. 3123 (Nov. 18, 1935), cited in *Cohen Handbook*, 175.

50. Eva Marie Garroutte, *Real Indians: Identity and the Survival of Native America* (University of California Press, 2003), 42. See also Bruce Granville Miller, *Invisible Indigenes: The Politics of Nonrecognition* (Lincoln: University of Nebraska Press, 2003), 69.

51. *Talton* v. *Mayes,* 163 U.S. 376 (1896). The Court held the Cherokee Nation's authority over a tribal member in a criminal prosecution stemmed from their "local powers not created by the constitution, although subject to its general provisions and the paramount authority of congress" (382). This passage could have come straight from Blackstone's *Commentaries on the Laws of England,* in which the noted jurist declared that the applicable ancient law in "conquered" countries would remain in force—unless contrary to the law of God—until altered by the crown: "They are subject however to the control of the parliament, though . . . not bound by any acts of parliament, unless particularly named," William Blackstone, *Commentaries on the Laws of England,* 1765, Book 1 (1976), cited in *Indigenous Legal Issues: Commentary and Materials* 3d edit., Heather McRae et al., eds. (Sydney: Thomson Law Book, 2003), 104–5.

52. *Santa Clara Pueblo* v. *Martinez,* 436 U.S. 49, 62–63 (1978).

53. *Gideon* v. *Wainright,* 372 U.S. 335 (1963).

54. *Miranda* v. *Arizona,* 384 U.S. 436 (1966). In 2000, the Court confirmed that *Miranda* was a constitutional ruling and, thus, immune from alteration by subsequent congressional action. See *Dickerson* v. *United States,* 530 U.S. 428 (2000).

55. *Santa Clara Pueblo* v. *Martinez,* 436 U.S. 49, 60 (1978).

56. See *Cohen Handbook*, 956.

57. See Charles F. Wilkinson, *American Indians, Time, and the Law* (New Haven: Yale University Press, 1987), 115.

58. See *Shenandoah* v. *Halbritter,* 366 F.3d 89 (2nd Cir. 2004). ("If this danger exists in cases such as the instant one, and the presence of twenty or thirty Indian

women engaged in prayer in the courtroom and adjoining hallway when this appeal was argued is some indication of its possible existence, Congress should consider giving this Court power to act.")

59. See *Cohen Handbook,* 958–59. See also Frank Pommersheim, *Braid of Feathers: American Indian Law and Contemporary Tribal Life* (Berkeley: University of California Press, 1995).

60. David E. Wilkins, *American Indian Sovereignty and the U.S. Supreme Court: The Masking of Justice* (Austin: University of Texas Press, 1997), 215.

CHAPTER THREE: CREEPING CONSTITUTIONALISM FROM THE TEMPLE

1. Stephen E. Feraca, "Inside BIA: Or, 'We're Getting Rid of All These Honkies,'" in *The Invented Indian: Cultural Fictions and Government Policies*, James A. Clifton, ed. (New Brunswick, N.J.: Transaction Publishers, 1990), 278. The BIA currently employs nearly eleven thousand people, almost 90 percent of them American Indian or Alaska Native.

2. *Morton* v. *Mancari,* 417 U.S. 535 (1974).

3. *Morton* v. *Mancari,* 417 U.S. 535, 555 (1974).

4. *Talton* v. *Mayes,* 163 U.S. 376 (1896).

5. For a brief moment, it appeared that the Court would confine the implicit divestiture analysis to instances in which the tribal power was demonstrably inconsistent with an overriding federal interest as opposed to the broader formulation that the tribal power was inconsistent with a tribe's "dependent status." See *Washington* v. *Confederated Tribes of the Colville Indian Reservation,* 447 U.S. 134, 153–54 (1980). As shown above, both variations of the analysis are present in the *Oliphant* opinion. Subsequent cases, however, have shown a greater reliance on the "dependent status" framework to determine which tribal powers have been implicitly divested.

6. *Montana* v. *United States,* 450 U.S. 544 (1981).

7. *Montana* v. *United States,* 450 U.S. 544, 564 (1981).

8. *Montana* v. *United States,* 450 U.S. 544, 565 (1981).

9. *Montana* v. *United States,* 450 U.S. 544, 565–66 (1981).

10. *Montana* v. *United States,* 450 U.S. 544, 566 (1981).

11. *Strate* v. *A-1 Contractors,* 520 U.S. 438, 445 (1997).

12. *Atkinson Trading Company* v. *Shirley,* 532 U.S. 645, 650 (2001).

13. *Strate* v. *A-1 Contractors,* 520 U.S. 438 (1997).

14. *National Farmers Union Ins. Cos.* v. *Crow Tribe,* 471 U.S. 845 (1985).

15. *Iowa Mutual Ins. Co.* v. *LaPlante,* 480 U.S. 9 (1987).

16. *Strate* v. *A-1 Contractors,* 520 U.S. 438, 453 (1997).

17. *Strate* v. *A-1 Contractors,* 520 U.S. 438, 459 (1997).

18. *Strate* v. *A-1 Contractors,* 520 U.S. 438, 458–59 (1997).

19. *Atkinson Trading Company* v. *Shirley,* 532 U.S. 645 (2001).

20. *Merrion* v. *Jicarilla Apache Tribe,* 455 U.S. 130 (1982).

21. *Merrion* v. *Jicarilla Apache Tribe,* 455 U.S. 130, 137 (1982).

22. *Merrion* v. *Jicarilla Apache Tribe,* 455 U.S. 130, 143–44 (1982).

23. *Montana* v. *United States,* 450 U.S. 544, 565–66 (1981).

24. *Brendale* v. *Confederated Tribes and Bands of the Yakima Indian Nation,* 492 U.S. 408 (1989).

25. Brief for Respondents, Navajo Nation Department of Justice, *Atkinson Trading Company, Inc.* v. *Shirley,* 2001 WL 175274 (2001).

26. *Atkinson Trading Company* v. *Shirley,* 532 U.S. 645, 653 (2001).

27. *Atkinson Trading Company* v. *Shirley,* 532 U.S. 645, 653 n.4 (2001).

28. *Atkinson Trading Company* v. *Shirley,* 532 U.S. 645, 654 (2001).

29. *Atkinson Trading Company* v. *Shirley,* 532 U.S. 645, 656 (2001).

30. *Atkinson Trading Company* v. *Shirley,* 532 U.S. 645, 655 (2001).

31. *Atkinson Trading Company* v. *Shirley,* 532 U.S. 645, 657 n.12 (2001).

32. See *Cohen Handbook,* 231–32 n. 220.

33. *Atkinson Trading Company* v. *Shirley,* 532 U.S. 645, 658 (2001).

34. N. Bruce Duthu, "The Thurgood Marshall Papers and the Quest for a Principled Theory of Tribal Sovereignty: Fueling the Fires of Tribal/State Conflict," 21 *Vermont L. Rev.* 47, 82 (1996), quoting from Memorandum of Justice Marshall (June 25, 1981), 1 (on file with author).

35. *Atkinson Trading Company, Inc.* v. *Shirley,* Brief on Behalf of Respondents Navajo Nation Tax Commission, 2001 WL 175274 (Feb. 15, 2001).

36. Robert J. Nordhaus, G. Emlen Hall, and Anne Alise Rudio, "Revisiting *Merrion* v. *Jicarilla Apache Tribe:* Robert Nordhaus and Sovereign Indian Control Over Natural Resources on Reservations," 43 *Natural Resources J.* 223, 282 (2003).

37. Ibid., 283.

38. *Strate* v. *A-1 Contractors,* 520 U.S. 438, 442 (1997).

39. *Nevada* v. *Hicks,* 533 U.S. 353 (2001).

40. *Nevada* v. *Hicks,* 533 U.S. 353, 359–60 (2001).

41. *Nevada* v. *Hicks,* 533 U.S. 353, 361–62 (2001).

42. See *Atkinson Trading Company, Inc.* v. *Shirley,* 532 U.S. 645, 659–60 (2001) (concurring opinion of Justice Souter, joined by Justices Kennedy and Thomas).

43. *MacArthur* v. *San Juan County,* 391 F.Supp. 2d 895, 953 n.90 (D. Utah 2005).

44. *Duro* v. *Reina,* 495 U.S. 676 (1990).

45. *Duro* v. *Reina,* 495 U.S. 676, 693 (1990).

46. *Duro* v. *Reina,* 495 U.S. 676, 694 (1990).

47. Steven Curry, *Indigenous Sovereignty and the Democratic Project* (Hants, England: Ashgate Publishing Ltd., 2004), 73–74.

48. *Duro* v. *Reina,* 495 U.S. 676, 707 (1990).

49. See Steven W. Perry, *U.S. Department of Justice, American Indians and Crime: A BJS Statistical Profile, 1992–2002* (2004).

50. 18 U.S.C. 1153. This act only applies to enumerated crimes committed by Indians within Indian Country.

51. 18 U.S.C. 1152 (also known as the General Crimes Act). This act extends general federal criminal laws, including assimilated state laws, into Indian Country. See *Cohen Handbook,* 729–71.

52. States may prosecute non-Indian defendants who commit crimes against another non-Indian in Indian Country. See *United States* v. *McBratney,* 104 U.S. 621 (1882). A handful of states exercise criminal jurisdiction over Indian defendants

in Indian Country under the authority of P.L. 280, a federal law dating from 1953. This law was amended in 1968 to require tribal consent before any other states may assume jurisdiction under its provisions. See Carole Goldberg-Ambrose, *Planting Tail Feathers: Tribal Survival and Public Law 280* (American Indian Studies Center Publications, UCLA Los Angeles, 1997).

53. See Nell Jessup Newton, "Permanent Legislation to Correct *Duro v. Reina*," 17 *American Indian L. Rev.* 109 (1992).

54. Ibid., 124.

55. 25 U.S.C. 1301(2), amended by Act of Oct. 28, 1991, 105 Stat. 646.

56. *United States* v. *Lara,* 541 U.S. 193 (2004).

57. *Marbury* v. *Madison,* 5 U.S. 137 (1803).

58. *United States* v. *Lara,* 541 U.S. 193, 200 (2004).

59. *United States* v. *Lara,* 541 U.S. 193, 210 (2004).

60. *United States* v. *Lara,* 541 U.S. 193, 212 (2004).

61. *United States* v. *Lara,* 541 U.S. 193, 214 (2004).

62. *United States* v. *Lara,* 541 U.S. 193, 224 (2004).

63. *United States* v. *Lara,* 541 U.S. 193, 218 (2004).

64. *United States* v. *Lara,* 541 U.S. 193, 215 (2004).

65. *MacArthur* v. *San Juan County,* 391 F.Supp.2d 895, 934 (D. Utah 2005).

66. *Alvarado* v. *Warner-Lambert Company,* 30 Indian L. Rep. 6174, 6177 (May 22, 2003), Lummi Nation Tribal Court.

67. *Nelson* v. *Pfizer,* No. SC-CV-01-02, Paragraph 35 (Navajo Supreme Court 11/17/03), available at www.tribal-institute.org/opinions/2003.nann.0000002.htm.

68. See *Nelson* v. *Pfizer,* No. SC-CV-01-02 (Navajo Supreme Court 11/17/03), available at. www.tribal-institute.org/opinions/2003.nann.0000002.htm.

69. *McDonald* v. *Means,* 309 F.3d 530, 540 (9th Cir. 2002).

70. *Ford Motor Company* v. *Todecheene,* 394 F.3d 1170 (9th Cir. 2005).

71. *Ford Motor Company* v. *Todecheene,* 394 F.3d 1170, 1178 (9th Cir. 2005).

72. *Ford Motor Company* v. *Todecheene,* 394 F.3d 1170, 1183 (9th Cir. 2005).

73. *Ford Motor Company* v. *Todecheene,* 394 F.3d 1170, 1187 (9th Cir. 2005).

74. *Ford Motor Company* v. *Todecheene,* 394 F.3d 1170, 1188–89 (9th Cir. 2005).

75. *Means* v. *Navajo Nation,* 432 F.3d 924, 931 (9th Cir. 2005).

76. *Montana* v. *United States,* 450 U.S. 544, 559–60 n.9 (1981).

77. *Confederated Salish & Kootenai Tribes of the Flathead Reservation* v. *Namen,* 665 F.2d 951, 963–64 n.30 (9th Cir. 1982), *cert. denied,* 459 U.S. 977 (1982).

78. Simon J. Ortiz, "The Historical Matrix Towards a National Indian Literature: Cultural Authenticity in Nationalism," in *Critical Perspectives on Native American Fiction* 68, Richard F. Fleck, ed. (1993).

CHAPTER FOUR: IDENTIFYING THE CONTOURS OF INDIAN COUNTRY

1. See the Trade and Intercourse Act, codified at 25 U.S.C. 177.

2. See Laurence M. Hauptman & James D. Wherry, eds., *The Pequots in Southern New England: The Fall and Rise of an American Indian Nation* (Norman: University of Oklahoma Press, 1993).

3. Steve Kemper, "This Land Is Whose Land? A territorial dispute between Indians and 'settlers' in Connecticut," *Yankee* magazine 46–54, 120–23, 123 (Sept. 1998).

4. Milner S. Ball, "Stories of Origin and Constitutional Possibilities," 87 *Mich. L. Rev.* 2280, 2310 (1989).

5. Kemper, "This Land Is Whose Land?" 120.

6. *Documents of United States Indian Policy*, 2d edit., Francis Paul Prucha, ed. (Lincoln: University of Nebraska Press, 1990), 2. See also Colin G. Calloway, *The Scratch of a Pen: 1763 and the Transformation of North America* (New York: Oxford University Press, 2006).

7. See Department of Interior website, www.doi.gov.

8. See *Cohen Handbook,* 340–43.

9. See *Cohen Handbook,* 182–96. See also 18 U.S.C. 1151.

10. John Fleischman, "Out of the Ashes . . . The Rebirth of the Pequots," *Yankee* magazine 53 (Sept. 1998). The Old Testament passages are from the Psalms 76:5; 110:6. John Mason's account of this war is recorded in *The History of The Pequot War,* first published in 1677.

11. The sidebar also notes that the "apparent destruction" of the Pequots inspired Herman Melville to name the doomed whaling ship in *Moby-Dick* the *Pequod.*

12. *Johnson* v. *McIntosh,* 21 U.S. 543 (1823).

13. See Lindsay G. Robertson, *Conquest by Law: How the Discovery of America Dispossessed Indigenous Peoples of Their Lands* (New York: Oxford University Press, 2005).

14. *Johnson* v. *McIntosh,* 21 U.S. 543, 573 (1823).

15. *Johnson* v. *McIntosh,* 21 U.S. 543, 547 (1823).

16. *Johnson* v. *McIntosh,* 21 U.S. 543, 567 (1823).

17. *Johnson* v. *McIntosh,* 21 U.S. 543, 576 (1823).

18. *Johnson* v. *McIntosh,* 21 U.S. 543, 576–77 (1823).

19. *Johnson* v. *McIntosh,* 21 U.S. 543, 573 (1823).

20. *Johnson* v. *McIntosh,* 21 U.S. 543, 590–91 (1823).

21. *Tee-Hit-Ton* v. *United States,* 348 U.S. 272 (1955). See also *Cohen Handbook,* 1024–25.

22. *Brown* v. *Board of Education,* 347 U.S. 483 (1954).

23. *Tee-Hit-Ton* v. *United States,* 348 U.S. 272, 287–88 (1955).

24. *Tee-Hit-Ton* v. *United States,* 348 U.S. 272, 289–90 (1955).

25. *Tee-Hit-Ton* v. *United States,* 348 U.S. 272, 285 n.17 (1955). Scholars have suggested that government lawyers may have improperly "cooked the books" in exaggerating the scope of outstanding tribal property claims. See Robert A. Williams, Jr., *Like a Loaded Weapon: The Rehnquist Court, Indian Rights, and the Legal History of Racism in America* (Minneapolis: University of Minnesota Press, 2005), 236, n. 10.

26. Robert A. Williams, Jr., *Like a Loaded Weapon: The Rehnquist Court, Indian Rights, and the Legal History of Racism in America* (Minneapolis: University of Minnesota Press, 2005), 51.

27. Ibid., 57–58.

28. See *Mabo* v. *Queensland,* 107 A.L.R. 1 (1992) (Australian High Court).

29. See *Wi Parata* v. *Bishop of Wellington,* 3 JUR (N.S.) 72 (1877).

30. See *Guerin* v. *The Queen,* 2 S.C.R. 335 (Supreme Court of Canada, 1984).

31. *City of Sherrill, New York* v. *Oneida Indian Nation of New York,* 544 U.S. 197, 125 S.Ct. 1478, 1483 n. 1 (2005).

32. In *Cayuga Indian Nation of New York* v. *Pataki,* 413 F.3d 266 (2nd Cir. 2005), the federal court of appeals relied on Sherrill's "disruptive remedy" analysis to strike down an award of nearly a quarter billion dollars in favor of the tribe for past land claims violations. The dissenting judge noted that while *Sherrill* would preclude an action to eject current non-Indian residents from the disputed lands, it did not preclude a claim for money damages. In May 2006, the United States Supreme Court declined to accept the tribe's appeal.

33. *City of Sherrill, New York* v. *Oneida Indian Nation of New York,* 544 U.S. 197, 125 S.Ct. 1478, 1490 (2005).

34. See 25 U.S.C. 465.

35. *Carcieri* v. *Norton,* 398 F.3d 22 (1st Cir. 2005); *South Dakota, City of Oacoma* v. *United States Department of Interior,* 423 F.3d 790 (8th Cir. 2005); *United States* v. *Roberts,* 185 F.3d 1125 (10th Cir. 1999).

36. See *Cohen Handbook,* 77–79.

37. Frederick E. Hoxie, *A Final Promise: The Campaign to Assimilate the Indians, 1880–1920* (New York: Cambridge University Press, 1989), 156.

38. *Lone Wolf* v. *Hitchcock,* 187 U.S. 553 (1903).

39. Hoxie, *A Final Promise,* 157.

40. Ibid.

41. For an instructive and detailed account of the case, see Blue Clark, *Lone Wolf v. Hitchcock: Treaty Rights & Indian Law at the End of the Nineteenth Century* (Lincoln: University of Nebraska Press, 1994).

42. *Lone Wolf* v. *Hitchcock,* 187 U.S. 553, 565 (1903).

43. *Lone Wolf* v. *Hitchcock,* 187 U.S. 553, 564 (1903).

44. *Lone Wolf* v. *Hitchcock,* 187 U.S. 553, 566 (1903).

45. *Chae Chan Ping* v. *United States,* 130 U.S. 581, 595 (1888).

46. See Gabriel J. Chin, "Segregation's Last Stronghold: Race Discrimination and the Constitutional Law of Immigration," 46 *UCLA L. Rev.* 1, 30 (1998) (quoting 13 Cong. Rec. 1584, 2031 [1882] [statement of Rep. Deuster]).

47. Tom Holm, *The Great Confusion in Indian Affairs: Native Americans & Whites in the Progressive Era* (Austin: University of Texas Press, 2005), 25.

48. T. Alexander Aleinikoff, *Semblances of Sovereignty: The Constitution, the State, and American Citizenship* (Cambridge: Harvard University Press, 2002), 26.

49. Ibid., 26–28.

50. *Lone Wolf* v. *Hitchcock,* 187 U.S. 553, 568 (1903).

51. *United States* v. *Sioux Nation of Indians,* 448 U.S. 371 (1980).

52. *United States* v. *Sioux Nation of Indians,* 448 U.S. 371, 408–9 (1980).

53. See John P. LaVelle, "Rescuing Paha Sapa: Achieving Environmental Justice by Restoring the Great Grasslands and Returning the Sacred Black Hills to the Great Sioux Nation," *Great Plains Natural Resource Journal* 5 (2001), 42–101.

54. N. Scott Momaday, *The Man Made of Words: Essays, Stories, Passages* (New York: St. Martin's Press, 1997), 49.

55. *South Dakota* v. *Yankton Sioux Tribe,* 522 U.S. 329 (1998).

56. For a detailed analysis of the case, see Judith V. Royster, "Of Surplus Lands and Landfills: The Case of the Yankton Sioux," 43 *S.D.L. R.* 283 (1998).

57. *South Dakota* v. *Yankton Sioux Tribe,* 522 U.S. 329, 338–39 (1998).

58. *South Dakota* v. *Yankton Sioux Tribe,* 522 U.S. 329, 357 (1998).

59. See *Brendale* v. *Confederated Tribes & Bands of Yakima,* 492 U.S. 408, 464 (1989).

60. *South Dakota* v. *Yankton Sioux Tribe,* 522 U.S. 329, 335–36 (1998).

61. Patricia Nelson Limerick, *The Legacy of Conquest: The Unbroken Past of the American West* (New York: W.W. Norton, 1987), 215.

62. Ibid., 213.

63. Hoxie, *A Final Promise,* 91.

64. Barry Pritzker, *Edward S. Curtis* (Avenel, N.J.: Crescent Books, 1993), 13.

65. Gerald Hausman and Bob Kapoun, eds., *Prayer to the Great Mystery: Edward S. Curtis* (New York: St. Martin's Press, 1995), xviii–xix.

66. Gerald Vizenor, "Socioacupuncture: Mythic Reversals and the Striptease in Four Scenes," in *The American Indian and the Problem of History*, Calvin Martin, ed. (New York: Oxford University Press, 1987), 182.

67. Robert M. Cover, "Violence and the Word," 95 *Yale L.J.* 1601 (1986).

68. *United States* v. *Sandoval,* 231 U.S. 28 (1913).

69. *United States* v. *Sandoval,* 231 U.S. 28, 39 (1913).

70. *United States* v. *Sioux Nation of Indians,* 448 U.S. 371, 436–37 (1980).

71. *United States* v. *Sioux Nation of Indians,* 448 U.S. 371, 437 (1980).

72. *Brendale* v. *Confederated Tribes and Bands of the Yakima Indian Nation,* 492 U.S. 408 (1989).

73. In 1994, the tribe reverted to "Yakama," the original spelling of the tribal name.

74. *Brendale* v. *Confederated Tribes and Bands of the Yakima Indian Nation,* 492 U.S. 408, 465 (1989).

75. These letters were discovered by the author within the Papers of Justice Thurgood Marshall, Library of Congress, Washington, D.C., and discussed in my earlier article, "The Thurgood Marshall Papers and the Quest for a Principled Theory of Tribal Sovereignty: Fueling the Fires of Tribal/State Conflict," 21 *Vermont L. Rev.* 47, 92–93 (1996).

76. Robert F. Berkhofer, Jr., *The White Man's Indian: Images of the American Indian from Columbus to the Present* (New York: Vintage Books, 1978), 29.

CHAPTER FIVE: STEWARDS OF THE NATURAL WORLD

1. John R. Welch and Ramon Riley, "Reclaiming Land and Spirit in the Western Apache Homeland," *American Indian Quarterly* 25.1 (2001) 5–12, at 7.

2. Charles Wilkinson, *Messages from Frank's Landing: A Story of Salmon, Treaties, and the Indian Way* (Seattle: University of Washington Press, 2000), 101.

3. Ibid., 43.

4. Welch and Riley, "Reclaiming Land and Spirit," 5.

5. Ibid., 7.
6. Ibid.
7. N. Scott Momaday, *The Man Made of Words: Essays, Stories, Passages* (New York: St. Martin's Press, 1997), 49.
8. Winona LaDuke, Foreword to *The New Resource Wars: Native Struggles Against Multinational Corporations,* Al Gedicks, ed. (Boston: South End Press, 1993), xi.
9. *New Mexico* v. *Mescalero Apache Tribe,* 462 U.S. 324 (1983).
10. See, e.g., *El Paso Natural Gas Co.* v. *Neztsosie,* 526 U.S. 473 (1999), a case holding that only federal courts can hear claims for alleged damages resulting from nuclear incidents; *Northern States Power C.* v. *Prairie Island Mdewakanton Sioux Indian Community,* 991 F.2d 458 (8th Cir. 1993), striking down tribal ordinances that purported to regulate the transportation of nuclear wastes contrary to federal law.
11. *Hoopa Valley Tribe* v. *Bugenig,* 25 Indian L. Rep. 6137, 6138 (July 11, 1996).
12. *Roberta Bugenig* v. *Hoopa Valley Tribe,* 266 F.3d 1201 (9th Cir. 2001).
13. David H. Getches, Charles F. Wilkinson, and Robert A. Williams, Jr., *Cases and Materials on Federal Indian Law* 5th edit., (St. Paul, Minn.: West, 2005), 714–15.
14. See *Cohen Handbook,* 1159–60.
15. See *Cohen Handbook,* 780.
16. See *Cohen Handbook,* 783–802.
17. James M. Grijalva, "Where Are the Tribal Water Quality Standards and TMDLs?" 18 *Natural Resources & Environment* 63, 68 (2003).
18. See U.S. Environmental Protection Agency—Tribes, Water Quality Standards & Criteria; Indian Tribal Approvals, available at: http://epa.gov/waterscience/tribes/approvtable.htm (last updated April 17, 2006).
19. *City of Albuquerque* v. *Browner,* 97 F.3d 415 (10th Cir. 1996).
20. See Anna Fleder and Darren J. Ranco, "Tribal Environmental Sovereignty: Culturally Appropriate Protection or Paternalism," 19 J. *Nat. Resources & Envtl. L.* 35 (2004–5).
21. See City of Albuquerque Annual Information Statement (Jan. 23, 2004), 109, available at: http://cabq.gov/investor/annualstatement.html.
22. See *Cohen Handbook,* 1086, 1107. Curiously, the Supreme Court narrowly interpreted a number of early federal statutes relating to coal development to find that an Indian tribe retained an interest in the coal itself but not the pockets of coalbed methane gas contained within the resource. Coalbed methane gas is often a much more lucrative resource to develop. See *Amoco Production Co.* v. *Southern Ute Indian Tribe,* 526 U.S. 865 (1999).
23. See, e.g., *Cobell* v. *Norton,* 334 F. 3d 1128 (D.C. Cir. 2003).
24. See Intertribal Council on Utility Policy, available at http://www.intertribalcoup.org.
25. Jim Robbins, "Sale of Carbon Credits Helping Land-Rich, but Cash-Poor, Tribes," *New York Times* (May 8, 2007).
26. John M. Broader, "Forces Clash on Tribal Lands," *New York Times* (Jan. 1, 2006).
27. See Charles Wilkinson, *Blood Struggle: The Rise of Modern Indian Nations* (New York: W.W. Norton, 2005), 198.

28. Treaty with the Yakama, June 9, 1855, 12 Stat. 951.

29. The Makah tribe in northwestern Washington secured an express guarantee for their continued right to hunt whales. See Treaty with the Makah, 1855, Section 4, 12 Stat. 939.

30. *United States* v. *Winans,* 198 U.S. 371, 381 (1905).

31. *United States* v. *Winans,* 198 U.S. 371, 381 (1905).

32. Fay G. Cohen, *Treaties on Trial: The Continuing Controversy over Northwest Indian Fishing Rights* (Seattle: University of Washington Press, 1986), 54, citing the opinion of Justice Bausman, 89 Wash. 478, 481–82 (1916).

33. Wilkinson, *Messages from Frank's Landing,* 38.

34. *Washington* v. *Washington State Commercial Passenger Fishing Vessel Association,* 443 U.S. 658 (1979).

35. *Washington* v. *Washington State Commercial Passenger Fishing Vessel Association,* 443 U.S. 658, 696, n.36 (1979).

36. *Washington* v. *Washington State Commercial Passenger Fishing Vessel Association,* 443 U.S. 658, 686 (1979).

37. *United States* v. *State of Washington,* 157 F.3d 630 (9th Cir. 1998).

38. In *United States* v. *Dion,* 476 U.S. 734, 740 (1986), the Supreme Court affirmed that federal statutes enacted after a treaty may serve to abrogate treaty rights if there is clear evidence that Congress recognized the conflict between the aims of the new law and the Indian's treaty rights and elected to resolve the conflict by overriding the treaty rights.

39. See *Cohen Handbook,* 1163.

40. See *Skokomish Indian Tribe* v. *United States,* 410 F.3d 506 (9th Cir. 2005) (en banc).

41. Rex Wirth and Stefanie Wickstrom, "Competing Views: Indian Nations and Sovereignty in the Intergovernmental System of the United States," *American Indian Quarterly* 26.4 (2002), 509–25, at 519.

42. See N. Bruce Duthu, "The Thurgood Marshall Papers and the Quest for a Principled Theory of Tribal Sovereignty: Fueling the Fires of Tribal/State Conflict," 21 *Vt. L. Rev.* 47, 92 (1996), citing Second Draft, *Oregon Dep't. of Fish & Wildlife* v. *Klamath Indian Tribe* 5 (Oct. 4, 1984, White, J., dissenting from denial of cert.).

43. *Oregon Department of Fish & Wildlife* v. *Klamath Indian Tribe,* 473 U.S. 753 (1985).

44. *Winters* v. *United States,* 207 U.S. 564 (1908).

45. See Lloyd Burton, *American Indian Water Rights and the Limits of Law* (Lawrence: University of Kansas Press, 1991), 19–20.

46. Frederick E. Hoxie, *A Final Promise: The Campaign to Assimilate the Indians, 1880–1920* (New York: Cambridge University Press, 1989), 170–71.

47. Burton, *American Indian Water Rights,* 130.

48. *Winters* v. *United States,* 207 U.S. 564, 576 (1908).

49. Hoxie, *A Final Promise,* 186–87.

50. *Arizona* v. *California,* 373 U.S. 546 (1963).

51. See *Cohen Handbook,* 1176–79.

52. One study suggests that the PIA standard led to windfall amounts of water being awarded to the Wind River Reservation in Wyoming. The reservation received an allocation of one-half million acre-feet of water, "enough water for a city of 2.5 million people." See Bonnie G. Colby, John E. Thorson, and Sarah Britton, *Negotiating Tribal Water Rights: Fulfilling Promises in the Arid West* (Tucson: University of Arizona Press, 2005), xiii. The *Cohen Handbook* authors, however, maintain that "the more common result . . . is that a PIA award provides insufficient water for tribes that have few irrigable acres, but do possess other resources that, with adequate water, could provide an economic base for the reservation." See *Cohen Handbook,* 1185.

53. Contrast and compare *In re General Adjudication of All Rights to Use Water in the Gila River System and Source,* 35 P.3d 68 (Ariz. 2001), adopting a broader "reservation as homeland" approach, with *In re General Adjudication of All Rights to Use Water in the Big Horn River System,* 753 P.2d 76 (Wyo. 1988), narrowly construing treaty language as primarily establishing reservation for agricultural purposes.

54. See *Cohen Handbook,* 1181–82.

55. Draft Opinion of Justice Sandra Day O'Connor in *Wyoming* v. *United States,* No. 88–309 (June 1989) at 11, obtained from the Papers of Associate Justice Thurgood Marshall, Library of Congress, Washington, D.C. (on file with author).

56. Ibid., 17.

57. Letter from Justice Byron R. White to Justice Sandra Day O'Connor (June 6, 1989) in *Wyoming* v. *United States,* No. 88–309, obtained from the Papers of Associate Justice Thurgood Marshall, Library of Congress, Washington, D.C. (on file with author).

58. See *Cohen Handbook,* 1210–20.

59. *Lyng* v. *Northwest Indian Cemetery Protective Association,* 485 U.S. 439 (1988).

60. 42 U.S.C. 2000bb-1(a).

61. *Employment Division, Department of Human Resources of Oregon* v. *Smith,* 494 U.S. 872 (1990).

62. See *City of Boerne* v. *Flores,* 521 U.S. 507 (1997).

63. Randal C. Archibold, "Commerce and Religion Collide on a Mountainside," *New York Times* (Oct. 23, 2005).

64. *Navajo Nation* v. *United States Forest Service,* 479 F.3d 1024 (9th Cir. 2007).

65. See the trial court's discussion of the consultation process in *Navajo Nation* v. *United States Forest Service,* 408 F.Supp.2d 866 (D. Ariz. 2006).

66. See *Cohen Handbook,* 938–44.

67. *United States* v. *Navajo Nation,* 537 U.S. 488, 506 (2003).

68. *United States* v. *Navajo Nation,* 537 U.S. 488, 506 (2003).

69. *United States* v. *Mitchell,* 463 U.S. 206 (1983) (*Mitchell* II).

70. See *Cohen Handbook,* 1117–18.

71. *United States* v. *Navajo Nation,* 537 U.S. 488 (2003).

72. Oliver Wendell Holmes, Jr., *The Common Law* (New York: Dover Publications, 1991; originally published by Little, Brown, Boston, 1881), 3.

73. Edmund O. Wilson, *The Creation: An Appeal to Save Life on Earth* (New York: W. W. Norton & Company, Inc., 2006), 5.

74. William H. Rodgers, Jr., "Tribal Government Roles in Environmental Federalism," *Natural Resources and Environment* 21 (Winter 2007), 3.

CHAPTER SIX: REVITALIZING TRIBAL ECONOMIES

1. See Ambrose I. Lane, Sr., *Return of the Buffalo: The Story Behind America's Indian Gaming Explosion* (Westport, Conn.: Bergin and Garvey, 1995), 127.

2. See Joseph P. Kalt and Joseph William Singer, *Myths and Realities of Tribal Sovereignty: The Law and Economics of Indian Self-Rule* (Cambridge, Mass.: John F. Kennedy School of Government, Faculty Research Working Papers Series, March 2004), 40, available at http://www.ksg.harvard.edu/hunap (hereinafter Kalt and Singer).

3. Jonathan B. Taylor and Joseph P. Kalt, *American Indians on Reservations: A Databook of Socioeconomic Change Between The 1990 and 2000 Censuses* (Cambridge: Harvard Project on American Indian Economic Development, Jan. 2005), xi, available at http://www.ksg.harvard.edu/hpaid (hereinafter Taylor and Kalt).

4. Ibid., xii. See also Terry L. Anderson, *Sovereign Nations or Reservations? An Economic History of American Indians* (San Francisco: Pacific Research Institute, 1995).

5. See *Cohen Handbook,* 1378–79.

6. See Kalt and Singer, *Myths and Realities of Tribal Sovereignty,* 41.

7. William G. McLoughlin, *After the Trail of Tears: The Cherokees' Struggle for Sovereignty 1839–1880* (Chapel Hill: University of North Carolina Press, 1993), 264.

8. *Cherokee Tobacco* case, 78 U.S. 616 (1870).

9. *Cherokee Tobacco* case, 78 U.S. 616, 621 (1870).

10. McLoughlin, *After the Trail of Tears,* 266.

11. See *Merrion* v. *Jicarilla Apache Indian Tribe,* 455 U.S. 130 (1982).

12. *Atkinson Trading Company, Inc.* v. *Shirley,* 532 U.S. 645 (2001).

13. See *Cotton Petroleum Corporation* v. *New Mexico,* 490 U.S. 163 (1989). (Characterized by the Court as the "sequel" to its *Merrion* decision. The Court majority approved the state's severance taxes on the same oil and gas production taxed by the Jicarilla Apache tribe.) The Court's recent decision in *Wagnon* v. *Prairie Band Potawatomi Nation,* 126 S.CT. 676 (2005) approved the state's tax on non-Indian distributors of motor fuel on the basis that the transaction occurred off reservation.

14. *Oklahoma Tax Commission* v. *Chickasaw Nation,* 515 U.S. 450 (1995).

15. *White Mountain Apache Tribe* v. *Bracker,* 448 U.S. 136, 145 (1980).

16. *Washington* v. *Confederated Tribes of the Colville Indian Reservation,* 447 U.S. 134, 152–53 (1980).

17. *Washington* v. *Confederated Tribes of the Colville Indian Reservation,* 447 U.S. 134, 155 (1980).

18. See *Department of Taxation and Finance of New York* v. *Milhelm Attea & Bros., Inc.,* 512 U.S. 61 (1994).

19. *Oklahoma Tax Commission* v. *Citizen Band Potawatomi Indian Tribe of Oklahoma,* 498 U.S. 505, 514 (1991).

20. *Kiowa Tribe of Oklahoma* v. *Manufacturing Technologies, Inc.,* 523 U.S. 751, 760 (1998).

21. *Kiowa Tribe of Oklahoma* v. *Manufacturing Technologies, Inc.,* 523 U.S. 751, 758 (1998).

22. See *Seminole Tribe of Florida* v. *Florida,* 517 U.S. 44 (1996).

23. W. Dale Mason, *Indian Gaming: Tribal Sovereignty and American Politics* (Norman: University of Oklahoma Press, 2000), 257.

24. See *Cohen Handbook,* 725–26.

25. See *Narragansett Indian Tribe* v. *State of Rhode Island,* 449 F.3d 16 (1st Cir. 2006), available at 2006 WL 1413012.

26. *Department of Taxation and Finance of New York* v. *Milhelm Attea & Bros., Inc.,* 512 U.S. 61 (1994).

27. See press release of the New York Association of Convenience Stores, "Pataki Sued to Enforce New Law on Taxation of Native American Sales to Non-Native Americans" (May 2, 2006), available at http://www.nyacs.org.

28. See Associated Press, "Philip Morris to Stop Sales to Online Smoke Shops," *Indian Country Today* (Feb. 7, 2006).

29. Correspondence of Justice William Brennan to the U.S. Supreme Court Justices (Jan. 14, 1980), obtained from the Papers of Justice Thurgood Marshall, Library of Congress, Washington, D.C. (on file with author).

30. Jose J. Monsivais, "The Return of the White Buffalo: Taxation Issues Facing American Indian Tribes Conducting Gambling Enterprises on Tribal Lands," 20 *Amer. Indian L. Rev.* 399 (1995–96). For many tribes, the white buffalo symbolizes good fortune.

31. See N. Bruce Duthu, "Crow Dog and Oliphant Fistfight at the Tribal Casino: Political Power, Storytelling, and Games of Chance," 29 *Ariz. St. L.J.* 171 (1997).

32. National Indian Gaming Association Media Release, National Indian Gaming Association (NIGA) Opens to Reflect $20 Billion Industry (April 4, 2006), available at http://www.indiangaming.org; American Gaming Association, Gaming Revenue: 10-Year Trends (Aug. 2004), available at http://www.americangaming.org/Industry/factsheets/statistics. See also Eve Darian-Smith, *New Capitalists: Law, Politics, and Identity Surrounding Casino Gaming on Native American Land* (Toronto: Thomson-Wadsworth, 2004), 52–53. Darian-Smith notes that in 2000, American spending on gambling was three times the rate of spending on all other forms of entertainment combined (including sporting events, concerts, and movies).

33. Steven Andrew Light and Kathryn R. L. Rand, *Indian Gaming and Tribal Sovereignty: The Casino Compromise* (Lawrence: University Press of Kansas, 2005), 91–92.

34. Ibid., 87.

35. See Katherine A. Spilde, "Rich Indian Racism: The Uses of Indian Imagery in the Political Process," presented at the 11th International Conference on Gambling and Risk-Taking (June 20, 2000), available at http://www.indiangaming.org/library/articles/rich-indian-racism.shtml.

36. National Gambling Impact Study Commission Final Report (June 1999), available at http://govinfo.library.unt.edu/ngisc.

37. See *Seminole Tribe* v. *Butterworth*, 658 F.2d 310 (5th Cir. 1981).

38. See John Dombrink and William N. Thompson, *The Last Resort: Success and Failure in Campaigns for Casinos* (Reno: University of Nevada Press, 1990), 1–2.

39. *California* v. *Cabazon Band of Mission Indians*, 480 U.S. 202 (1987).

40. See *Bryan* v. *Itasca County*, 426 U.S. 373 (1976).

41. *California* v. *Cabazon Band of Mission Indians*, 480 U.S. 202, 219–20 (1987).

42. See 25 U.S.C. 2701–21.

43. See *Seminole Tribe of Florida* v. *Florida*, 517 U.S. 44 (1996).

44. See Cohen Handbook, 884–85.

45. See Associated Press, "Feds Reject State's Call for Casino Payment," *Indian Country Today* (Jan. 3, 2006), available at http://www.indiancountry.com.

46. *Texas* vs. *U.S.*, 497 F.3d 491 (5th Circ. 2007).

47. Light and Rand, *Indian Gaming and Tribal Sovereignty*, 58–59.

48. Ibid., 72–73.

49. Ibid., 71, 86.

50. Kenneth R. Philp, ed., *Indian Self-Rule: First-Hand Accounts of Indian-White Relations from Roosevelt to Reagan* (Salt Lake City: Howe Brothers, 1986), 321.

51. See *Government to Government: Understanding State and Tribal Governments* (National Conference of State Legislatures, 2000).

CHAPTER SEVEN: INDIVIDUAL RIGHTS AND TRIBAL COMMUNAL INTERESTS

1. The latest iteration of Indian citizenship statutes is found at 8 U.S.C. 1401(b).

2. *United States* v. *Nice*, 241 U.S. 591, 598 (1916).

3. Some tribes are beginning to examine the implications of according tribal citizenship status to nonmembers, including non-Indian residents in Indian Country. For discussion of this proposition, see Frank Pommersheim, "Democracy, Citizenship, and Indian Law Literacy: Some Initial Thoughts," *T.M. Cooley L. Rev.* 457, 465–66 (1997).

4. Contrast *Grutter* v. *Bollinger*, 539 U.S. 306, 333 (2003) with *Parents Involved in Community Schools v. Seattle School District No. 1*, 127 S.Ct. 2738 (2007).

5. *Rice* v. *Cayetano*, 528 U.S. 495, 517 (2000).

6. *Grutter* v. *Bollinger*, 539 U.S. 306, 333 (2003).

7. *Morton* v. *Mancari*, 417 U.S. 535 (1974).

8. Statements of Frank Pommersheim at the Vermont Law Review Symposium: Stewards of the Land: Indian Tribes, the Environment, and the Law (South Royalton, Vt.: Fall 1996).

9. *Merrion* v. *Jicarilla Apache Tribe*, 455 U.S. 130, 147 (1982).

10. *Duro* v. *Reina*, 495 U.S. 676, 694 (1990).

11. *Duro* v. *Reina*, 495 U.S. 676, 707 (1990).

12. Steven Curry, *Indigenous Sovereignty and the Democratic Project* (Aldershot Hants, England: Ashgate Publishing Limited, 2004), 99.

13. Memorandum of John G. Roberts, Jr., to Fred F. Fielding (Jan. 18, 1983) (on file with author). In 1988, Congress finally did expressly repudiate the Termination-era

philosophy embodied in House Concurrent Resolution 108 and "any policy of unilateral termination of Federal relations with any Indian Nation." See 25 U.S.C.
2501(f).

14. *Rice* v. *Cayetano*, 528 U.S. 495 (2000).

15. See Transcript: Day Four of Roberts Confirmation Hearings (Thursday, Sept.
15, 2005) before U.S. Senate Judiciary Committee, available at http://www
.washingtonpost.com.

16. John Holusha, "South Dakota Governor Signs Abortion Ban," *New York Times*
(March 6, 2006); *Roe* v. *Wade*, 410 U.S. 113 (1973).

17. See 42 C.F.R. 136.54 and 42 C.F.R. 50.306.

18. Rose Aguilar, "The Power of Thunder," *AlterNet* (April 4, 2006), available at
http://www.alternet.org/story/34314/.

19. Ibid.

20. Bill Harlan, "Votes Reveal Two Types of Conservatism," *Rapid City Journal*
(Nov. 9, 2006), available at http://www.rapidcityjournal.com/articles/2006/11/09/
news/top/news02.prt.

21. Ibid.

22. Aguilar, "The Power of Thunder."

23. See *Cohen Handbook*, 956.

24. Frank Pommersheim, *Braid of Feathers: American Indian Law and Contemporary
Tribal Life* (Berkeley: University of California Press, 1995), 99.

25. *Gonzales* v. *Carhart,* 127 S.Ct. 1 (April 18, 2007).

26. See *McBratney* v. *United States,* 104 U.S. 621 (1882).

27. "Fetal Alcohol Spectrum Disorders in Indian Country," Report from the Substance Abuse and Mental Health Services Administration, Fetal Alcohol Spectrum Disorders Center for Excellence (March 2004), 1, U.S. Department of
Health and Human Services, available at www.samhsa.gov.

28. Kathleen Stratton et al., eds, *Fetal Alcohol Syndrome: Diagnosis, Epidemiology,
Prevention, and Treatment* (Washington, D.C.: National Academy Press, 1996),
137.

29. Michael Dorris, *The Broken Cord: A Family's Ongoing Struggle with Fetal Alcohol
Syndrome* (New York: Harper and Row, 1989), 176.

30. Affidavit of Brian J. Gilley, Assistant Professor of Anthropology, University of
Vermont (dated 11/20/05), entitled Gender Diversity and the Cultural Crossfire,
filed with Cherokee Nation Supreme Court, Dec. 20, 2005, in Case Number
05–11, *Baker et al.* v. *McKinley et al.*

31. Brian Joseph Gilley, *Becoming Two-Spirit: Gay Identity and Social Acceptance in
Indian Country* (Lincoln: University of Nebraska Press, 2006), 8.

32. Constitution of the Cherokee Nation (as amended 1999), Article III, Section 1.

33. In *Judy* v. *White* (2004), the Navajo Nation Supreme Court noted that it is "ab-
horrent to the Dine Life Way to violate the right of a community member to
speak or to express his or her views or to challenge an injury, whether tangible or
intangible. This right is protected to such an extent that the right to speak to an
issue is not limited to the 'real party in interest.' Rather, the right belongs to the
community as a whole, and any member of that community may speak." *Judy* v.

White, No. SC-CV-35-02 (Navajo Supreme Court 08/02/2004), available at http://www.versuslaw.com.

34. See 28 U.S.C. 1738(C).

35. See *Wilson* v. *Ake,* 354 F.Supp.2d 1298 (M.D.Fla. 2005).

36. *Mississippi Band of Choctaw Indians* v. *Holyfield,* 490 U.S. 30, 33 (1989).

37. 25 U.S.C. 1901(3).

38. *Mississippi Band of Choctaw Indians* v. *Holyfield,* 490 U.S. 30, 33 (1989).

39. *Mississippi Band of Choctaw Indians* v. *Holyfield,* 490 U.S. 30, 34 (1989).

40. See Basil H. Johnston, *Indian School Days* (Norman: University of Oklahoma Press, 1989); Antonio D. Buti, *Separated: Aboriginal Childhood Separations and Guardianship Law* (Sydney, Australia: Institute of Criminology, 2004); *Bringing Them Home,* Report of the National Inquiry into the Separation of Aboriginal and Torres Strait Islander Children from Their Families (April 1997).

41. *In Re C.H.,* 997 P.2d 776, 780 (Mont. 2000).

42. *Mississippi Band of Choctaw Indians* v. *Holyfield,* 490 U.S. 30 (1989).

43. The act expressly provides for state jurisdiction if Congress has otherwise provided for it, even in cases where the Indian child lives in Indian Country. At least one federal circuit has ruled that Public Law 280 permits state courts to exercise jurisdiction in these particular child custody proceedings, without distinguishing between "voluntary" or "involuntary" proceedings. See *Doe* v. *Mann,* 415 F.3d 1038 (9th Cir. 2005).

44. *Mississippi Band of Choctaw Indians* v. *Holyfield,* 490 U.S. 30, 49 (1989).

45. *Mississippi Band of Choctaw Indians* v. *Holyfield,* 490 U.S. 30, 52 (1989).

46. See *Cohen Handbook,* 833, n. 96.

47. B. J. Jones, *The Indian Child Welfare Act Handbook: A Legal Guide to the Custody and Adoption of Native American Children* (Chicago: American Bar Association, 1995), 30.

48. See *Cohen Handbook,* 852–53, n. 245, listing the jurisdictions that have actively considered the doctrine and either endorsed it or rejected it.

49. See 25 U.S.C. 1915(a).

50. See *In the Matter of C.H.,* 997 P.2d 776 (Mont. 2000). ("[The trial court's] statement clearly reflects the court's application of a best interests of the child balancing test which, as discussed above, is inappropriate in an ICWA proceeding.")

51. See Barbara Ann Atwood, "Flashpoints under the Indian Child Welfare Act: Toward a New Understanding of State Court Resistance," 51 *Emory L.J.* 587 (2002).

52. 42 U.S.C. 1996(b).

53. See Ian Urbina, "Trying to Keep Child Care in the Family," *New York Times* (July 23, 2006).

54. *Santa Clara Pueblo* v. *Martinez,* 436 U.S. 49, 72 n. 32 (1978).

55. *Santa Clara Pueblo* v. *Martinez,* 436 U.S. 49, 72 (1978).

56. *Santa Clara Pueblo* v. *Martinez,* 436 U.S. 49, 71 (1978).

57. See *Cohen Handbook,* 304–5.

58. *Lucy Allen* v. *Cherokee Nation Tribal Council,* Judicial Appeals Tribunal of the Cherokee Nation (March 7, 2006).

59. Ben Evans, "So. Cal. Lawmaker Eyes Cutting Cherokee Funding Over Ex-Slave

Vote," SFGATE.com (April 19, 2007), reporting that the vast majority of the Cherokee Nation's budget comes from federal funding.

60. *Lewis* v. *Norton,* 424 F.3d 959, 960 (9th Cir. 2005).

61. *Lewis* v. *Norton,* 424 F.3d 959, 963 (9th Cir. 2005).

62. See *Cohen Handbook,* 1228–29.

63. Michael F. Brown, *Who Owns Native Culture?* (Cambridge, Mass.: Harvard University Press, 2003), 91.

64. 25 U.S.C. 305 et seq.

65. See *Cohen Handbook,* 1264.

66. *Native American Arts, Inc.* v. *Waldron Corporation,* 399 F.3d 871, 873 (7th Cir. 2005).

67. Kathleen S. Fine-Dare, *Grave Injustice: The American Indian Repatriation Movements and NAGPRA* (Lincoln: University of Nebraska Press, 2002).

68. Alvin M. Josephy, Jr., *The Nez Perce Indians and the Opening of the Northwest* (New Haven, Conn.: Yale University Press, 1965), 384.

69. Kathrin Day Lassila and Mark Alden Branch, "Whose Skull and Bones?" *Yale Alumni Magazine* (May/June 2006), 20–22, at 20.

70. See H. Marcus Price III, *Disputing the Dead: U.S. Law on Aboriginal Remains and Grave Goods* (Columbia: University of Missouri Press, 1991).

71. See Sherry Hutt and C. Timothy McKeown, "Control of Cultural Property as Human Rights Law," 31 *Ariz. St. L.J.* 363 (1999).

72. See *Bonnichsen* v. *United States,* 367 F.3d 864 (9th Cir. 2004). See also Allison M. Dussias, "Kennewick Man, Kinship, and the 'Dying Race': The Ninth Circuit's Assimilationist Assault on the Native American Graves Protection and Repatriation Act," 84 *Nebraska L. Rev.* 55, 110–11 (2005).

CHAPTER EIGHT: A QUESTION OF INSTITUTIONAL FIT

1. Francis Paul Prucha, *The Great Father: The United States Government and the American Indians,* abridged edition (Lincoln: University of Nebraska Press, 1984), 20.

2. H. W. Brands, *Andrew Jackson: His Life and Times* (New York: Doubleday, 2005), 319–20.

3. Ibid., 320.

4. Russell Thornton, *American Indian Holocaust and Survival: A Population History Since 1492* (Norman: University of Oklahoma Press, 1987), 91; Stephen Cornell, *The Return of the Native: American Indian Political Resurgence* (New York: Oxford University Press, 1988), 50.

5. Prucha, *The Great Father,* 164.

6. *Antoine* v. *Washington,* 420 U.S. 194, 204 (1975).

7. *United States* v. *Kagama,* 118 U.S. 375 (1886).

8. *Talton* v. *Mayes,* 163 U.S. 376 (1896).

9. *McClanahan* v. *Arizona State Tax Commission,* 411 U.S. 164, 172 n.7 (1973).

10. *Merrion* v. *Jicarilla Apache Tribe,* 455 U.S. 130, 155 n.21 (1982).

11. *Cotton Petroleum Corporation* v. *New Mexico,* 490 U.S. 163, 192 (1989).

12. *United States* v. *Lara,* 541 U.S. 193, 224 (2004).

13. *United States* v. *Lara,* 541 U.S. 193, 226 (2004).

14. Mick Gidley, *Edward S. Curtis and the North American Indian, Incorporated* (Cambridge, England: Cambridge University Press, 1998), 279.

15. Michael Dorris, "Indians on the Shelf," in *The American Indian and the Problem of History*, Calvin Martin, ed. (New York: Oxford University Press, 1987), 102.

16. Robert F. Berkhofer, Jr., *The White Man's Indian: Images of the American Indian from Columbus to the Present* (New York: Vintage Books, 1979), 92.

17. *Johnson* v. *McIntosh,* 21 U.S. 543, 590–91 (1823).

18. See Daniel K. Richter, *Facing East from Indian Country: A Native History of Early America* (Cambridge, Mass.: Harvard University Press, 2001); Michael D. Green, *The Politics of Indian Removal: Creek Government and Society in Crisis* (Lincoln: University of Nebraska Press, 1982).

19. *Johnson* v. *McIntosh,* 21 U.S. 543, 591 (1823).

20. Richter, *Facing East from Indian Country*, 243.

21. Ibid., 243–44.

22. Barry O'Connell, ed., *On Our Own Ground: The Complete Writings of William Apess, a Pequot* (Amherst: University of Massachusetts Press, 1992), xx–xxi.

23. Ibid., 157.

24. Richter, *Facing East from Indian Country*, 251.

25. Vivien Green Fryd, "Imaging the Indians in the United States Capitol during the Early Republic," in *Native Americans and the Early Republic*, Frederick E. Hoxie et al., eds. (Charlottesville: University Press of Virginia, 1999), 297.

26. See, e.g., David H. Getches, "Conquering the Cultural Frontier: The New Subjectivism of the Supreme Court in Indian Law," 84 *California L. Rev.* 1573 (1996).

27. Letter from Associate Justice Antonin Scalia to Associate Justice William Brennan (April 4, 1990) in No. 88-6546—*Duro* v. *Reina;* Papers of Justice Thurgood Marshall, Library of Congress, Washington, D.C. (on file with author).

28. Martha A. Field, "Sources of Law: The Scope of Federal Common Law," 99 *Harv. L. Rev.* 881, 899 (1986).

29. Frank Pommersheim, "'Our Federalism' in the Context of Federal Courts and Tribal Courts: An Open Letter to the Federal Courts' Teaching and Scholarly Community," 71 *Colorado L. Rev.* 123, 128 (2000).

30. William H. Rehnquist, *The Supreme Court: How It Was, How It Is* (New York: William Morrow, & Co. Inc. 1987), 116.

31. Robert A. Williams, Jr., *Like a Loaded Weapon: The Rehnquist Court, Indian Rights, and the Legal History of Racism in America* (Minneapolis, Minn.: University of Minnesota Press, 2005), 116.

32. *United States* v. *Sioux Nation of Indians,* 448 U.S. 371, 374 (1980).

33. Letter from Justice Byron R. White to Justice Harry Blackmun (June 16, 1980) in No. 79-639 *United States* v. *Sioux Nation of Indians,* from the Papers of Justice Thurgood Marshall, Library of Congress, Washington, D.C. (on file with author).

34. Williams, *Like a Loaded Weapon*, 115.

35. *United States* v. *Sioux Nation of Indians,* 448 U.S. 371, 435 (1980).
36. *United States* v. *Sioux Nation of Indians,* 448 U.S. 371, 437 (1980).
37. *United States* v. *Sioux Nation of Indians,* 448 U.S. 371, 422 n.32 (1980).
38. See Robert N. Clinton, "Comity & Colonialism: The Federal Courts' Frustration of Tribal-Federal Cooperation," 36 *Ariz. State L. J.* 1 (2004).
39. *National Farmers Union Insurance Companies* v. *Crow Tribe,* 471 U.S. 845 (1985) and *Iowa Mutual Insurance Company* v. *LaPlante,* 480 U.S. 9 (1987) are the two principal cases authorizing non-Indians to enter federal court to challenge the scope of the tribe's jurisdiction, typically only after they have "exhausted" tribal court procedures.
40. Clinton, "Comity & Colonialism," 58.

CHAPTER NINE: AVOIDING MISTAKES OF THE PAST

1. Oren R. Lyons, "The American Indian in the Past," in *Exiled in the Land of the Free: Democracy, Indian Nations, and the U.S. Constitution*, Oren R. Lyons and John C. Mohwak, eds. (Santa Fe, N.M.: Clear Light Publishers, 1992), 33.
2. Taiaiake Alfred, *Peace, Power, Righteousness: An Indigenous Manifesto* (Don Mills, Ontario: Oxford University Press, 1999), 52.
3. Will Kymlicka, "Theorizing Indigenous Rights," 49 *U. Toronto L.J.* 281, 289 (1999).
4. Will Kymlicka, *Multicultural Citizenship: A Liberal Theory of Minority Rights* (New York: Oxford University Press, 1995), 105.
5. Alfred, *Peace, Power, Righteousness*, 53.
6. H. W. Brands, *The First American: The Life and Times of Benjamin Franklin* (New York: Anchor Books, 2002), 232–33.
7. Donald A. Grinde, Jr., "Iroquois Political Theory and the Roots of American Democracy," in *Exiled in the Land of the Free*, Lyons and Mohwak, eds., 263.
8. See Robert A. Williams, Jr., *Linking Arms Together: American Indian Treaty Visions of Law and Peace, 1600–1800* (New York: Oxford University Press, 1997), 171, n. 5
9. Ibid., 171–72, n. 5.
10. Ibid., 44.
11. Ibid., 112.
12. *Worcester* v. *Georgia,* 31 U.S. 515 (1832).
13. *Johnson* v. *McIntosh*, 21 U.S. 543 (1823).
14. *Worcester* v. *Georgia,* 31 U.S. 515, 559–60 (1832).
15. *Worcester* v. *Georgia,* 31 U.S. 515, 552 (1832).
16. *Worcester* v. *Georgia,* 31 U.S. 515, 560–61 (1832).
17. Robert A. Williams, Jr., *Like a Loaded Weapon: The Rehnquist Court, Indian Rights, and the Legal History of Racism in America* (Minneapolis: University of Minnesota Press, 2005), 191.
18. *Talton* v. *Mayes,* 163 U.S. 376 (1896).
19. S. James Anaya, *Indigenous Peoples in International Law,* 2nd ed. (New York: Oxford University Press, 2004), 22.

20. Ibid., 53.
21. Ibid., 114 quoting Erica-Irene A. Daes, "Some Considerations on the Right of Indigenous Peoples to Self-Determination," 3 *Transnational L. & Contemp. Probs.* 1, 9 (1993).
22. See, e.g., *Roper* v. *Simmons,* 543 U.S. 551 (2005) (striking down the death penalty for persons who were minors when they committed their offenses); *Lawrence* v. *Texas,* 539 U.S. 558 (2003) (striking down state sodomy law); *Atkins* v. *Virginia,* 536 U.S. 304 (2002) (striking down death penalty for mentally ill defendants).
23. Remarks of Associate Justice Sandra Day O'Connor at the Southern Center for International Studies, Atlanta, Georgia, Oct. 28, 2003, available at www .southerncenter.org/OConnor_transcript.

CHAPTER TEN: CONVENTIONS ON TRIBAL SOVEREIGNTY

1. *Hamdan* v. *Rumsfeld,* 126 S. Ct. 2749 (2006).
2. *Worcester* v. *Georgia,* 31 U.S. 515, 557 (1832).
3. Steven W. Perry, American Indians and Crime, A BJS Statistical Profile, 1992–2002 (U.S. Department of Justice, Office of Justice Programs, Bureau of Justice Statistics, NCJ 203097) (Dec. 2004).
4. The legislatures of Arkansas, Montana, Nevada, North Dakota, Oregon and Texas meet every other year. See the National Conference of State Legislatures, available at www.ncsl.org.
5. See L. Scott Gould, "Tough Love for Tribes; Rethinking Sovereignty After Atkinson and Hicks," 37 *New England L. Rev.* 669 (2003). ("Reconsidering *Martinez* from an individual point of view, that in some respect involves the federal judiciary, will entail a loss of tribal sovereignty. Yet the loss will only be superficial if, in exchange, tribal courts receive broader jurisdiction. The NCAI hopes to initiate legislation emphasizing such an exchange in the 108th Congress. A draft version would provide for federal appellate court review of tribal court decisions, while empowering tribes to assume both civil and criminal jurisdiction over all persons in their territory. Surely, proposals such as these, that protect the rights of individuals, are the surest way to regain sovereignty lost in the decades from *Montana* through *Atkinson* and *Hicks*" [685]).

BIBLIOGRAPHY

BOOKS

Aleinikoff, T. Alexander. *Semblances of Sovereignty: The Constitution, the State, and American Citizenship*. Cambridge, Mass.: Harvard University Press, 2002.

Alfred, Taiaiake. *Peace, Power, Righteousness: An Indigenous Manifesto*. Oxford, England: Oxford University Press, 1999.

Anaya, S. James. *Indigenous Peoples in International Law*. New York: Oxford University Press, 1996, 15, 42, 87.

Anderson, Terry L. *Sovereign Nations or Reservations? An Economic History of American Indians*. San Francisco: Pacific Research Institute, 1995.

Berkhofer, Robert F., Jr. *The White Man's Indian: Images of the American Indian from Columbus to the Present*. New York: Vintage Books, 1978, 29.

Blackstone, William. *Commentaries on the Laws of England, 1765,* Book 1. Oxford, England: Clarendon Press, 1976, 104–5.

Bordewich, Fergus M. *Killing the White Man's Indian: Reinventing Native Americans at the End of the Twentieth Century*. New York: Doubleday, 1996.

Bradley, John, and Kathryn Seton. "Self-Determination or 'Deep Colonising': Land Claims, Colonial Authority and Indigenous Representation." In *Unfinished Constitutional Business: Rethinking Indigenous Self-Determination*, Barbara A. Hocking, ed. Canberra, Australia: Aboriginal Studies Press, 2005, 32–36.

Brands, H. W. *Andrew Jackson: His Life and Times*. New York: Doubleday, 2005.

———. *The First American: The Life and Times of Benjamin Franklin*. New York: Anchor Books, 2002, 232–35

Brown, Michael F. *Who Owns Native Culture?* Cambridge, Mass.: Harvard University Press, 2003, 91.

Burton, Lloyd. *American Indian Water Rights and the Limits of Law*. Lawrence: University of Kansas Press, 1989.

Buti, Antonio D. *Separated: Aboriginal Childhood Separations and Guardianship*. Sydney, Australia: Institute of Criminology, 2004.

Clark, Blue. *Lone Wolf v. Hitchcock: Treaty Rights & Indian Law at the End of the Nineteenth Century*. Lincoln: University of Nebraska Press, 1994.

Cohen, Fay G. *Treaties on Trial: The Continuing Controversy Over Northwest Indian Fishing Rights*. Seattle: University of Washington Press, 1986, 54.

Colby, Bonnie G., John E. Thorson, and Sarah Britton. *Negotiating Tribal Water Rights: Fulfilling Promises in the Arid West*. Tucson: University of Arizona Press, 2005, xiii.

Cornell, Stephen. *The Return of the Native: American Indian Political Resurgence*. New York: Oxford University Press, 1988, 50.

Cramer, Renee Ann. *Cash, Color, and Colonialism: The Politics of Tribal Acknowledgment*. Norman: University of Oklahoma Press, 2005.

Curry, Steven. *Indigenous Sovereignty and the Democratic Project*. Hants, England: Ashgate Publishing, Ltd., 2004.

Darian-Smith, Eve. *New Capitalists: Law, Politics, and Identity Surrounding Casino Gaming on Native American Land*. Toronto: Thomson-Wadsworth, 2004, 52–53.

Dombrink, John, and William N. Thompson. *The Last Resort: Success and Failure in Campaigns for Casinos*. Reno: University of Nevada Press, 1990, 1–2.

Dorris, Michael. *The Broken Cord: A Family's Ongoing Struggle with Fetal Alcohol Syndrome*. New York: Harper and Row, 1989, 176.

———. "Indians on the Shelf." In *The American Indian and the Problem of History*. New York: Oxford University Press, 1987, 102.

Feraca, Stephen E. "Inside BIA: Or, "We're Getting Rid of All These Honkies." In *The Invented Indian: Cultural Fictions and Government Policies,* James A. Clifton, ed. New Brunswick, N.J.: Transaction Publishers, 1990, 278.

Fryd, Vivien Green. "Imaging the Indians in the United States Capitol During the Early Republic." In *Native Americans and the Early Republic,* Frederick E. Hoxie et al. eds. Charlottesville: University Press of Virginia, 1999, 297.

Garroutte, Eva Marie. *Real Indians: Identity and the Survival of Native America*. University of California Press, 2003.

Getches, David H., Charles F. Wilkinson, and Robert A. Williams, Jr. *Cases and Materials on Federal Indian Law*, 5th edit. St. Paul, Minn.: West, 2005, 714–15.

Gidley, Mick. *Edward S. Curtis and the North American Indian, Incorporated*. Cambridge, England: Cambridge University Press, 1998, 279.

Gilley, Brian J. *Becoming Two-Spirit: The Search for Self and Social Acceptance in Indian Country*. Lincoln: University of Nebraska Press, 2006.

Goldberg-Ambrose, Carole. *Planting Tail Feathers: Tribal Survival and Public Law*. Los Angeles: UCLA American Indian Studies Center Publications, 1997.

Green, Michael D. *The Politics of Indian Removal: Creek Government and Society in Crisis*. Lincoln: University of Nebraska Press, 1982.

Grinde, Donald A., Jr. "Iroquois Political Theory and the Roots of American Democracy." In *Exiled in the Land of the Free: Democracy, Indian Nations, and the U.S. Constitution,* Oren R. Lyons and John C. Mohwak, eds. Santa Fe, N.M.: Clear Light Publishers, 1992, 263.

Hauptman, Laurence M., and James D. Wherry, eds. *The Pequots in Southern New England: The Fall and Rise of an American Indian Nation.* Norman: University of Oklahoma Press, 1993.

Hobson, Charles F., ed. *The Papers of John Marshall, Vol. XI, April 1827–December 1830.* Chapel Hill: University of North Carolina Press, 1990, 179 n. 2.

Holm, Tom. *The Great Confusion in Indian Affairs: Native Americans & Whites in the Progressive Era.* Austin: University of Texas Press, 2005, 35–38.

Hoxie, Frederick E. *A Final Promise: The Campaign to Assimilate the Indians, 1880–1920.* Cambridge, England: Cambridge University Press, 1989.

Indian Self-Rule: First-hand Accounts of Indian-White Relations from Roosevelt to Reagan. Kenneth R. Philip, ed. Salt Lake City: Howe Brothers, 1986, 321.

Johnston, Basil H. *Indian School Days.* Norman: University of Oklahoma Press, 1989.

Jones, B. J. *The Indian Child Welfare Act Handbook: A Legal Guide to the Custody and Adoption of Native American Children.* Chicago: American Bar Association, 1995, 306.

Josephy, Alvin M., Jr. *The Nez Perce Indians and the Opening of the Northwest.* New Haven, Conn.: Yale University Press, 1965, 319.

Kalt, Joseph P., and Joseph William Singer. *Myths and Realities of Tribal Sovereignty: The Law and Economics of Indian Self-Rule.* Cambridge, Mass.: John F. Kennedy School of Government, 2004, 40.

Kymlicka, Will. *Multicultural Citizenship: A Liberal Theory of Minority Rights.* New York: Oxford University Press, 1995, 105.

LaDuke, Winona. "Foreword." In *The New Resource Wars: Native Struggles Against Multinational Corporations,* Al Gedicks, ed. Boston: South End Press, 1993, xi.

Lane, Ambrose I., Sr. *Return of the Buffalo: The Story Behind America's Indian Gaming Explosion.* Westport, Conn.: Bergin and Garvey Paperback, 1995, 127.

Light, Steven Andrew, and Kathryn R. L. Rand. *Indian Gaming and Tribal Sovereignty: The Casino Compromise.* Lawrence: University of Kansas Press, 2005, 87, 91–92.

Limerick, Patricia Nelson. *The Legacy of Conquest: The Unbroken Past of the American West.* New York: W. W. Norton, 1987, 215.

Lyons, Oren R. "The American Indian in the Past." In *Exiled in the Land of the Free: Democracy, Indian Nations, and the U.S. Constitution,* Oren R. Lyons and John C. Mohwak, eds. Santa Fe, N.M.: Clear Light Publishers, 1992, 33.

Maddox, Lucy. *Citizen Indians: Native American Intellectuals, Race, and Reform.* Ithaca, N.Y.: Cornell University Press, 2005, 39.

Mason, W. Dale. *Indian Gaming: Tribal Sovereignty and American Politics.* Norman: University of Oklahoma Press, 2000, 257.

Mathiessen, Peter. *In the Spirit of Crazy Horse.* New York: Viking Penguin, 1983, 65–80.

McLoughlin, William G. *After the Trail of Tears: The Cherokees' Struggle for Sovereignty, 1839–1880.* Chapel Hill: University of North Carolina Press, 1993, 266.

McRae, Heather, et al, eds. *Indigenous Legal Issues: Commentary and Materials,* 3d edit. Sydney, Australia: Thomson Law Book, 2003.

Miller, Bruce Granville. *Invisible Indigenes: The Politics of Nonrecognition.* Lincoln: University of Nebraska Press, 2003, 145.

Momaday, N. Scott. *The Man Made of Words: Essays, Stories, Passages.* New York: St. Martin's Press, 1997.

Newton, Nell Jessup, et al. *Cohen's Handbook of Federal Indian Law.* Newark, N.J.: Matthew Bender, Lexis Nexis, 2005.

O'Connell, Barry, ed. *On Our Own Ground: The Complete Writings of William Apess, A Pequot.* Amherst: University of Massachusetts Press, 1992, xx–xxi, 157.

Ortiz, Simon J. "The Historical Matrix Towards a National Indian Literature: Cultural Authenticity in Nationalism." In *Critical Perspectives on Native American Fiction,* Richard F. Fleck, ed. Pueblo, Colo.: Passeggiata Press, 1993, 68.

Perdue, Theda and Michael D. Green. *The Cherokee Removal: A Brief History with Documents.* Boston and New York: Bedford Books of St. Martin's Press, 1995.

Plato, *The Republic,* Book VII, Stephanus, ed., 514–21.

Pommersheim, Frank. *Braid of Feathers: American Indian Law and Contemporary Tribal Life.* Berkeley: University of California Press, 1995.

Prayer to the Great Mystery: Edward S. Curtis. Bob Hausman and Bob Kapoun, eds. New York: St. Martin's Press, 1995, xviii–xix.

Price, H. Marcus III. *Disputing the Dead: U.S. Law on Aboriginal Remains and Grave Goods.* Columbia: University of Missouri Press, 1991.

Pritzker, Barry. *Edward S. Curtis.* Avenel, N.J.: Crescent Books, 1993, 13.

Prucha, Francis Paul. *The Great Father: The United States Government and the American Indians.* Abridged. Lincoln: University of Nebraska Press, 1984, 164.

———. *The Great Father: The United States Government and the American Indians.* Lincoln: University of Nebraska, 1986.

———. *Documents of United States Indian Policy,* 2nd edit. Lincoln: University of Nebraska Press, 1990, 2.

Rehnquist, William H. *The Supreme Court.* New York: Alfred A. Knopf, 2001, 363.

———. *The Supreme Court: How It Was, How It Is.* New York: William Morrow, 1987, 116.

Richter, Daniel K. *Facing East from Indian Country: A Native History of Early America.* Cambridge, Mass.: Harvard University Press, 2001, 243, 251.

Robertson, Lindsay G. *Conquest by Law: How the Discovery of America Dispossessed Indigenous Peoples of Their Lands.* New York: Oxford University Press, 2005.

Rowan, Carl T. *Dream Makers, Dream Breakers: The World of Justice Thurgood Marshall.* Boston: Back Bay Books, 1993.

Stratton, Kathleen, et al., eds. *Fetal Alcohol Syndrome: Diagnosis, Epidemiology, Prevention and Treatment.* Washington, D.C.: National Academy Press, 1996, 176.

Strickland, Rennard. *Tonto's Revenge: Reflections On American Indian Culture and Policy.* Albuquerque: University of New Mexico Press, 1997.

Thornton, Russell. *American Indian Holocaust and Survival: A Population History Since 1492*. Norman: University of Oklahoma Press, 1987, 91.

Tribe, Laurence H. *American Constitutional Law*, Vol. One, 3rd edit. New York: Foundation Press, 2000, 802.

Vizenor, Gerald. "Socioacupuncture: Mythic Reversals and the Striptease in Four Scenes." In *The American Indian and the Problem of History*, Calvin Martin, ed. New York: Oxford University Press, 1987, 182.

Watson, Harry L. *Liberty and Power: The Politics of Jacksonian America*. New York: Hill and Wang, 1990, 111.

Wilkins, David E. *American Indian Sovereignty and the U.S. Supreme Court: The Masking of Justice*. Austin: University of Texas Press, 1997, 215.

Wilkinson, Charles F. *American Indians, Time, and the Law*. New Haven, Conn: Yale University Press, 1987, 115.

———. *Blood Struggle: The Rise of Modern Indian Nations*. New York: W.W. Norton & Co., 2005, 139–43.

———. *Messages from Frank's Landing: A Story of Salmon, Treaties, and the Indian Way*. Seattle: University of Washington Press, 2000, 101.

Williams, Robert A., Jr. *Like a Loaded Weapon: The Rehnquist Court, Indian Rights, and the Legal History of Racism in America*. Minneapolis: University of Minnesota Press, 2005.

———. *Linking Arms Together: American Indian Treaty Visions of Law & Peace, 1600–1800*. New York: Oxford University Press, 1997, 171 n. 5.

Wilson, Edward O. *The Creation: An Appeal to Save Life on Earth*. New York: W.W. Norton & Co., 2006, 5.

Zinn, Howard. *A People's History of the United States 1492–Present*. Revised. New York: Harper Perennial, 1995, 10–11.

MAGAZINES, JOURNALS, NEWSPAPER AND INTERNET ARTICLES

Aguilar, Rose. "The Power of Thunder." *AlterNet*. www.alternet.org/story/34314/.

"American Gaming Association, Gaming Revenue: 10-Year Trends," Aug. 2004. www.americangaming.org/industry/factsheets/statistics.

Archibold, Randal C. "Commerce and Religion Collide on a Mountainside." *New York Times*, 23 Oct. 2005.

Associated Press. "Philip Morris to Stop Sales to Online Smoke Shops." *Indian Country Today*, 7 Feb. 2006.

Atwood, Barbara Ann. "Flashpoints Under the Indian Child Welfare Act: Toward a New Understanding of State Court Resistance." *Emory L.J.* 51 (2002): 587.

Ball, Milner S. "Stories of Origin and Constitutional Possibilities." *Mich. L. Rev.* 87 (1989): 2280, 2310.

Bringing Them Home. National Inquiry Into the Separation of Aboriginal and Torres Strait Islander Children from Their Families, Human Rights and Equal Opportunity Commission, Sydney, Australia, 1997.

Broader, John M. "Forces Clash on Tribal Lands." *New York Times*, 1 Jan. 2006.

Chin, Gabriel J. "Segregation's Last Stronghold: Race Discrimination and the Constitutional Law of Immigration." *UCLA Law Review* 46 (1998): 1, 30, quoting 13 Cong. Rec. 1584, 2031 (1882).

"City of Albuquerque Annual Information Statement," Jan. 23, 2004. cabq.gov/investor/annualstatement.html.

Clinton, Robert N. "Comity & Colonialism: The Federal Courts' Frustration of Tribal-Federal Cooperation." *Arizona St. L.J.* 367 (2004): 1.

Cover, Robert M. "Violence and the Word." *Yale Law Journal* 95 (1986): 1601.

Dussias, Allison. "Ghost Dance and Holy Ghost: The Echoes of 19th Century Christianization Policy in 20th Century Native American Free Exercise Cases." *Stan. L. Rev.* 49 (1997): 773.

———. "Kennewick Man, Kinship, and the 'Dying Race': The Ninth Circuit's Assimilationist Assault on the Native American Graves Protection and Repatriation Act." *Nebraska L. Rev.* 84 (2005): 55, 110–11.

Duthu, N. Bruce. "Crow Dog and Oliphant Fistfight at the Tribal Casino: Political Power, Storytelling, and Games of Chance." *Ariz. St. L.J.* 29 (1997): 171.

———. "The Thurgood Marshall Papers and the Quest for a Principled Theory of Tribal Sovereignty: Fueling the Fires of Tribal/State Conflict." Quoting from Memorandum of Justice Marshall, 6/25/81. *Vermont L. Rev.* 21 (1996): 47, 82.

"Feds Reject State's Call for Casino Payment." *Indian Country Today*, 3 Jan. 2006.

Fetal Alcohol Syndrome: Diagnosis, Epidemiology, Prevention and Treatment. Substance Abuse & Mental Health Services Administration, Fetal Alcohol Spectrum Disorders Center for Excellence, March 2004.

Field, Martha A. "Sources of Law: The Scope of Federal Common Law." *Harv. L. Rev.* 99 (1986): 881, 899.

Fleder, Anna, and Darren J. Rando. "Tribal Environmental Sovereignty: Culturally Appropriate Protection or Paternalism." *J. Nat. Resources & Envtl. L.* 19 (2004–5): 35.

Fleischman, John. "Out of the Ashes . . . The Rebirth of the Pequots." John Mason's account of this war is recorded in *The History of the Pequot War*, first published in 1677. *Yankee*, September 1998, 530.

Frickey, Philip P. "(Native) American Exceptionalism in Federal Public Law." *Harv. L. Rev.* 119 (2005): 431, 434.

———. "A Common Law for Our Age of Colonialism: The Judicial Divestiture of Indian Tribal Authority Over Nonmembers." *Yale L.J.* 109, no. 1 (1999): 36 n.178.

Getches, David H. "Conquering the Cultural Frontier: The New Subjectivism of the Supreme Court in Indian Law." *California L. Rev.* 84 (1996): 1573.

Gould, L. Scott. "Tough Love for Tribes; Rethinking Sovereignty After Atkinson and Hicks." *New England L. Rev.* 37 (2003): 669.

Grijalva, James M. "Where Are the Tribal Water Quality Standards and TMDLs?" *Natural Resources & Environment Journal* 18 (2003): 63, 68.

Holusha, John. "South Dakota Governor Signs Abortion Ban." *New York Times*, 6 March 2006.

Hutt, Sherry, and C. Timothy McKeown. "Control of Cultural Property as Human Rights Law." *Arizona St. L.J.* 31 (1999): 363.

"Intertribal Council on Utility Policy." www.intertribalcoup.org.

Kemper, Steve. "This Land Is Whose Land? A Territorial Dispute Between Indians and 'Settlers' in Connecticut." *Yankee*, September 1998, 46–54, 120–23.

Kymlicka, Will. "Theorizing Indigenous Rights." *U. Toronto L.J.* 49 (1999): 281, 289.

Lassila, Kathrin Day, and Mark Alden Branch. "Whose Skull and Bones?" *Yale Alumni Magazine*, May/June 2006, 20–22 at 20.

LaVelle, John P. "Rescuing Paha Sapa: Achieving Environmental Justice by Restoring the Great Grasslands and Returning the Sacred Black Hills to the Great Sioux Nation." *Great Plains Natural Resource Journal* 5 (2001): 42–101.

Monsivais, Jose J. "The Return of the White Buffalo: Taxation Issues Facing American Indian Tribes Conducting Gambling Enterprises on Tribal Lands." *Amer. Indian L. Rev.* 20 (1996–96): 399.

"National Gambling Impact Study Commission Final Report," June 1999. govinfo .library.unt.edu/ngisc.

"National Indian Gaming Association Media Release, National Indian Gaming Association (NIGA) Opens to Reflect $20 Billion Industry," April 4, 2006. www.indiangaming.org.

Newton, Nell Jessup. "Permanent Legislation to Correct *Duro v. Reina*." *American Indian L. Rev.* 17 (1992): 109.

Nordhaus, Robert J., G. Emlen Hall, and Anne Alise Rudio. "Revisiting *Merrion v. Jicarilla Apache Tribe*: Robert Nordhaus and Sovereign Indian Control Over Natural Resources on Reservations." *Natural Resources Journal* 43 (2003): 223, 265.

Ogunwole, Stella U. "We the People: American Indians & Alaska Natives in the United States." *Census 2000 Special Reports* 28 (February 2006). www.census.gov/population/www/socdemo/race/indian.html.

"Pataki Sued to Enforce New Law on Taxation of Native American Sales to Non-Native Americans," May 2, 2006. www.nyacs.org.

Perry, Steven W. *U.S. Department of Justice, American Indians and Crime: A BJS Statistical Profile, 1992–2002* (2004), available at www.ojp.usdoj.gov/bjs/abstract/aic02.htm.

Pommersheim, Frank. "Democracy, Citizenship, and Indian Law Literacy: Some Initial Thoughts." *T.M. Cooley L. Rev.* 14 (1997): 457, 465–66.

———. " 'Our Federalism' in the Context of Federal Courts and Tribal Courts: An Open Letter to the Federal Courts' Teaching and Scholarly Community." *Colorado L. Rev.* 71 (2000): 123, 128.

———. "Stewards of the Land: Indian Tribes, the Environment, and the Law." Statements at the VLR Symposium, Vermont Law School, South Royalton, fall 1996.

Resnik, Judith. "Dependent Sovereigns: Indian Tribes, States, and the Federal Courts." *University of Chicago L. Rev.* 56 (1989): 671, 712–21.

Royster, Judith V. "The Legacy of Allotment." *Ariz. St. L.J.* 27 (1995): 1.

———. "Of Surplus Lands and Landfills: The Case of the Yankton Sioux." *South Dakota Law Review* 43 (1998): 283.

Spilde, Katherine A. "Rich Indian Racism: The Uses of Indian Imagery in the Political Process." Presented at the 11th International Conference on Gambling and Risk-Taking, June 20, 2000. www.indiangaming.org/library/articles/rich-indian-racism.shtml.

Taylor, Jonathan B., and Joseph P. Kalt. "American Indians on Reservations: A Databook of Socioeconomic Change Between the 1990 and 2000 Censuses" (Cambridge: Harvard Project on American Indian Economic Development, January 2005), iv, available at www.ksg.harvard.edu/hpaied.

Urbina, Ian. "Trying to Keep Child Care in the Family." *New York Times,* 23 July 2006.

Washburn, Kevin K. "American Indians, Crime, and the Law," *Mich. L. Rev.* 104 (2006): 709, 711 n. 4.

Welch, John R., and Ramon Riley. "Reclaiming Land and Spirit in the Western Apache Homeland." *American Indian Quarterly* 25.1 (2001): 5–12.

Wirth, Rex, and Stefanie Wickstrom. "Competing Views: Indian Nations and Sovereignty in the Intergovernmental System of the United States." *American Indian Quarterly* 26.4 (2002): 509–25.

LEGAL CASES AND DOCUMENTS

Alvarado v. *Warner-Lambert Company,* 309 *Indian L. Rep.* (Lummi Nation Tribal Court 22 May, 2003) (Judge Pouley, Judge Pro Tem): 6174.

Alvarado v. *Warner-Lambert Company (& Pfizer, Inc.),* 30 *Indian L. Rep.* (Lummi Nation Tribal Court 2003): 6174.

Amoco Production Co. v. *Southern Ute Indian Tribe,* 526 U.S. (1999): 865.

Antoine v. *Washington,* 420 U.S. (1975): 194.

Arizona v. *California,* 373 U.S. (1963): 546.

Atkins v. *Virginia,* 536 U.S. (2002): 304.

Atkinson Trading Company v. *Shirley,* 532 U.S. (2001) (concurring opinion of Justice Souter, joined by Justices Kennedy and Thomas): 645.

Baker et al v. *McKinley et al,* 2006 Cherokee Nation Supreme Court 05–11 (affidavit of Brian J. Gilley, assistant professor of anthropology, University of Vermont).

Bonnichsen v. *United States,* 367 F.3d (9th Cir. 2004): 864.

Brendale v. *Confederated Tribes and Bands of the Yakima Indian Nation,* 492 U.S. (1989): 408.

Brown v. *Board of Education,* 347 U.S. (1954): 483.

Bryan v. *Itasca County,* 426 U.S. (1976): 373.

California v. *Cabazon Band of Mission Indians,* 480 U.S. (1987): 202, 219–20.

Carcieri v. *Norton,* 398 F.3d (1st Cir. 2005): 2280, 2310.

Cayuga Indian Nation of New York v. *Pataki,* 413 F.3d (2nd Cir. 2005): 266.

Chae Chan Ping v. *United States,* 130 U.S. (1888): 581, 595.

Cherokee Nation v. *Georgia,* 30 U.S. (1831): 1, 17.

City of Albuquerque v. *Browner,* 97 F.3d (10th Cir. 1996): 415.

City of Sherrill, New York v. *Oneida Indian Nation of New York,* 544 U.S. (2005), 125 S.Ct. 1478, 1483 n.1: 197.

Cobell v. *Norton,* 334 F.3d (D.C. Cir. 2003): 1128.

Confederated Salish & Kootenai Tribes of the Flathead Reservation v. *Namen*, 665 F.2d
        (9th Cir. 1982), Cert. denied, 459 U.S. 977 (1982): 963.

Cong.Indian Self-Determination and Education Assistance Act of 1975, Pub. L. 93–638,
        88 (1975).

Cotton Petroleum Corporation v. *New Mexico*, 490 U.S. (1989): 163.

Department of Taxation and Finance of New York v. *Milhelm Attea & Bros., Inc.*, 512
        U.S. (1994): 61.

Dickerson v. *United States*, 530 U.S. (2000): 428.

Doe v. *Mann*, 415 F.3d (9th Cir. 2005): 1038.

Duro v. *Reina*, 495 U.S. (1990): 676.

Ex Parte Crow Dog, 109 U.S. (1883): 556, 571, 43 Fed. Reg., at 39, 361 (1978).

El Paso Natural Gas Co. v. *Neztsosie*, 523 U.S. (1999): 473.

Ford Motor Company v. *Todecheene*, 394 F.3d (9th Cir. 2005): 1170.

Gideon v. *Wainwright*, 372 U.S. (1963): 335.

Grutter v. *Bollinger*, 539 U.S. (2003): 306.

Guerin v. *The Queen*, 1984 Supreme Court of Canada, 2 S.C.R. 335.

Hamdan v. *Rumsfeld*, S.Ct. 126 (2006): 2749.

Hoopa Valley Tribe v. *Bugenig*, 25 *Indian Law* (9th Cir. 1996): 6137, 6138.

In Re C.H., 997 P.2d (Montana 2000): 776.

In Re General Adjudication of All Rights to Use Water in the Big Horn River System, 753
        P.2d (Wyoming 1988): 76.

*In Re General Adjudication of All Rights to Use Water in the Gila River System and
        Source*, 35 P.3d (Arizona 2001): 68.

Iowa Mutual Ins. Co. v. *LaPlante*, 480 U.S. (1987): 951.

Johnson v. *McIntosh*, 21 U.S. (1823): 543.

Judy v. *White*, 2004 Navajo Supreme Court SC-CV-35-02 (Dine Life Way).

Kiowa Tribe of Oklahoma v. *Manufacturing Technologies, Inc.*, 523 U.S. (1998): 751.

Lawrence v. *Texas*, 539 U.S. (2003): 558.

Lewis v. *Norton*, 424 F.3d (9th Cir. 2005): 959.

Lone Wolf v. *Hitchcock*, 187 U.S. (1903): 553.

Lucy Allen v. *Cherokee Nation Tribal Council*, 2006 Judicial Appeals Tribunal of the
        Cherokee Nation.

Lyng v. *Northwest Indian Cemetery Protective Association*, 485 U.S. (1988): 439.

Mabo v. *Queensland*, 1992 Australian High Court, 107 A.L.R. 109.

MacArthur v. *San Juan County*, 391 F. Supp. 2d (United States District Court, Utah
        2005): 895, 937–38, 940, 953, n.90.

McBratney v. *United States*, 104 U.S. (1882): 621.

McClanahan v. *State Tax Commission of Arizona*, 411 U.S. (1973): 164, 179.

McDonald v. *Means*, 309 F.3d (9th Cir. 2002): 530.

Marbury v. *Madison*, 532 U.S. (1803): 137.

Means v. *Navajo Nation*, 432 F.3d (9th Cir. 2005): 924.

Merrion v. *Jicarilla Apache Tribe*, 455 U.S. (1982): 130.

Miranda v. *Arizona*, 384 U.S. (1963): 335.

Mississippi Band of Choctaw Indians v. *Holyfield*, 490 U.S. (1989): 30.

Montana v. *United States*, 450 U.S. (1981): 544.

Morton v. *Mancari,* 417 U.S. (1974): 535.

Narragansett Indian Tribe v. *State of Rhode Island,* 449 F.3d (1st Cir. 2006): 164, 179.

National Farmers Union Ins. Cos. v. *Crow Tribe,* 471 U.S. (1985): 845.

Native American Arts, Inc. v. *Waldron Corporation,* 399 F.3d (7th Cir. 2005): 871.

Navajo Nation Department of Justice, Brief for Respondents, *Atkinson Trading Company, Inc.* v. *Shirley,* 2001 WL (2001): 175274.

Navajo Nation v. *United States Forest Service,* 408 F.Supp. (District of Arizona 2006): 866.

Nelson v. *Pfizer,* 2003 Navajo Supreme Court SC-CV-01-02 (available at www.tribal institute.org/opinions/2003.nann.0000002.htm).

Nevada v. *Hicks,* 533 U.S. (2001): 353.

New Mexico v. *Mescalero Apache Tribe,* 462 U.S. (1983): 324.

Northern States Power Co. v. *Prairie Island Mdewakanton Sioux Indian Community,* 991 F.2d (8th Cir. 1993): 458.

Oklahoma Tax Commission v. *Chickasaw Nation,* 515 U.S. (1995): 450.

Oklahoma Tax Commission v. *Citizen Band Potawatomi Indian Tribe of Oklahoma,* 498 U.S. (1991): 505.

Oliphant v. *Schlie,* 544 F.2d (1976): 1007, 1014.

Oliphant v. *Suquamish Indian Tribe,* 435 U.S. (1978): 191.

Oregon Department of Fish & Wildlife v. *Klamath Indian Tribe,* Second Draft (White, J., Dissenting from Denial of Cert.) (1984): 5.

Oregon Department of Fish & Wildlife v. *Klamath Indian Tribe,* 473 U.S. (1985): 753.

Rice v. *Cayetano,* 528 U.S. (2000): 495.

Roberta Bugenig v. *Hoopa Valley Tribe,* 266 F.3d (9th Cir. 2001): 1201.

Roe v. *Wade,* 410 U.S. (1973): 113.

Roper v. *Simmons,* 543 U.S. (2005): 551.

Santa Clara Pueblo, Brief on Behalf of, WL 189105 (1977).

Santa Clara Pueblo v. *Martinez,* 436 U.S. (1978): 49, 62–63.

Seminole Tribe of Florida v. *Florida,* 517 U.S. (1996): 44.

Seminole Tribe v. *Butterworth,* 658 F.2d (5th Cir. 1981): 310.

Shenandoah v. *Halbritter,* 366 F.3d (2nd Cir. 2004): 89.

Skokomish Indian Tribe v. *United States,* 410 F.3d (9th Cir. 2005): 506.

South Dakota v. *Yankton Sioux Tribe,* 522 U.S. (1998): 329.

South Dakota, City of Oacoma v. *United States Department of Interior,* 423 F.3d (8th Cir. 2005): 790.

Strate v. *A-1 Contractors,* 532 U.S. (1997): 645.

Talton v. *Mayes,* 163 U.S. (1896): 376.

Tee-Hit-Ton v. *United States,* 348 U.S. (1995): 272.

United States v. Dion, 476 U.S. (1986): 734, 740.

United States v. Kagama, 118 U.S (1886): 375, 379.

United States v. Lara, 541 U.S. (2004): 193.

United States v. Mitchell, 463 U.S. (1983) (Mitchell II): 206.

United States v. Navajo Nation, 537 U.S. (2003): 488, 506.

United States v. Nice, 241 U.S. (1916): 591, 598.

United States v. Roberts, 185 F.3d (10th Cir. 1999): 1125.

United States v. Sandoval, 231 U.S. (1913): 28.

United States v. Sioux Nation of Indians, 448 U.S. (1980): 371.

United States v. State of Washington, 157 F.3d (9th Cir. 1998): 630.

United States v. Wheeler, 435 U.S. (1978): 313, 322–23.

United States v. Winans, 198 U.S. (1905): 371, 381.

Wagnon v. Prairie Band Potawatomi Nation, 126 S.CT. (2005): 676.

Washington v. Confederated Tribes of the Colville Indian Reservation, 447 U.S. (1980): 134, 152–153.

Washington v. Washington State Commercial Passenger Fishing Vessel Association, 443, U.S. (1979): 658.

White Mountain Apache Tribe v. Bracker, 448 U.S. (1980): 136, 141.

Williams v. Lee, 358 U.S. (1959): 217, 220.

Wilson v. Ake, 354 F.Supp.2d (M.D.Fla. 2005): 1298.

Winters v. United States, 207 U.S. (1908): 564.

Wi Parata v. Bishop of Wellington, 3 JUR. (N.S.) 72 (1877).

Worcester v. Georgia, 31 U.S. (1832): 515, 560–561.

ARCHIVES, PAPERS, TRANSCRIPTS

25 C.F.R., at 83.

42 C.F.R.: 136.54.

426 C.F.R.: 50.306.

Constitution of the Cherokee Nation of 1999, III, § 1.

8 U.S.C. § 1401(b).

18 U.S.C. § 1153.

25 U.S.C. § 177 (Non-Intercourse Act).

25 U.S.C. § 1301 et seq. (1991) (amended by Act of Oct. 28, 1991, 105 Stat. 646).

25 U.S.C. § 2701–21.

25.1 U.S.C. § 2501(f) (Memorandum of John G. Roberts, Jr., to Fred F. Fielding 1/18/83) (on file with author).

U.S.C. § 25 (1901–23).

U.S.C. § 42 (1996).

Associate Justice Antonin Scalia, to Associate Justice William Brennan. "No. 88-6546 – Duro v. Reina," 4 April 1990.

"Government to Government: Understanding State and Tribal Governments." Presented at the National Conference of State Legislatures, 2000.

Indian Self-Determination and Education Assistance Act, *Stat.,* No. 2203, Pub. L. 93–638 (1975).

Julia Martinez, Brief on Behalf of, WL 189106 (1977).

Justice Byron R. White, to Justice Harry Blackmun. "No. 79–639 United States v. Sioux Nation of Indians," 16 June, 1980. Papers of Justice Thurgood Marshall, Library of Congress, Washington, D.C.

Justice Sandra Day O'Connor, Remarks. Southern Center for International Studies, Atlanta, 28 Oct. 2003.

National Conference of State Legislatures, www.ncsl.org.

Trade and Intercourse Act, codified at 25 U.S.C. 177.

"Transcript: Day Four of Roberts Confirmation Hearings." Before the U.S. Senate Judiciary Committee. *Washington Post,* Sept. 15, 2005.

Treaty with the Makah. 4. Stat. 12 (1855): 939.

Treaty with the Yakima, 1855. Stat. 12 (9 June 1855): 951.

U.S. Constitution, Article 1, no. 8: 3.

U.S. Constitution, Amendment V.

Washington State Historical Society, www.treatytrail.org.

INDEX